CULTURAL AND HERITAGE TOURISM
An Overview

CULTURAL AND HERITAGE TOURISM

An Overview

Prem Nath Dhar

KANISHKA PUBLISHERS, DISTRIBUTORS
NEW DELHI-110 002

KANISHKA PUBLISHERS, DISTRIBUTORS
4697/5-21A, Ansari Road, Daryaganj
New Delhi -110 002
Phones : 2327 0497, 2328 8285
Fax : 011-2328 8285
E-mail : kanishka_publishing@yahoo.co.in
kanishkabooks@gmail.com

Cultural and Heritage Tourism: An Overview
First Published-2008
Edition-2022

ISBN: 978-81-8457-080-9

PRINTED IN INDIA

Published by Madan Sachdeva for Kanishka Publishers, Distributors, 4697/5-21A, Ansari Road, Daryaganj, New Delhi-110002, Typeset by Sunshine Graphics, Delhi, and Printed at G.S. Printers, Delhi.

Preface

Cultural and Heritage Tourism: An Overview provides readers with a holistic perspective of the theme under consideration. The book describes cultural tourism briefly and establishes its relationship with indigenous people and ecotourism. The culture tourism scenario prevailing in India is dealt in detail. Similarly, the relationship between heritage tourism and rural tourism has been analyzed. The heritage tourism scenario of India is reflected upon briefly and the economic impact of such initiatives have been critically evaluated. In this regard a case study has also been presented highlighting the challenges of estimating and using economic impacts of cultural tourism. The book also analyses major principles and guidelines, related to cultural and heritage tourism. It also provides readers with much required toolkit and resource manual for handling Cultural and heritage tourism in India and abroad. Supportive Case studies are also given, along with select success stories from around the world. Besides this publication gives full account of cultural heritage tourism in India and its various ramifications vis-à-vis railway tourism; yoga and meditation; festivals; temples; fairs; and states' initiatives. Very many examples from the aforementioned list have been illustrated. This book also provides readers with global charters developed for promoting cultural tourism and for preserving heritage sites. Focus lies on ICOSM and WHC. World heritage sites, identified and conserved around the world, have been listed and the initiatives to preserve cultural sites and conserve heritage sites are dealt in detail. The list of related acronyms glossary of important terms, websites, links and bibliography have been given so as to facilitate further insight into the subject.

Prem Nath Dhar

Contents

1

Introduction to Cultural Tourism

The cultural and social characteristics of all destinations are varied and unique, but are composed of the same basic elements:

- local history, including visible reminders,
- language or dialects spoken by the residents,
- traditions and folklore,
- methods of work and products or technology,
- art or music,
- styles of dress,
- distinctive architecture,
- educational systems,
- religion, including visible manifestations,
- leisure activities,
- handicrafts,
- gastronomy or food preparation,
- festivals or celebrations.

Cultural tourism can be seen as a dynamic tourist activity, one closely tied to physical experiences. Cultural tourism is a search for and a celebration of that which is unique and beautiful, representing our most valued inheritance: attributes we will want to keep and pass on to our descendants, attributes our communities may be proud of.

UNDERSTANDING CULTURAL TOURISM

Cultural tourism (or *culture tourism*) is the subset of tourism concerned with a country or region's , especially its arts. It generally focuses on traditional communities who have diverse customs, unique form of art and distinct social practices, which basically distinguishes it from other types/forms of culture. Cultural tourism includes tourism in urban areas, particularly historic or large cities and their cultural facilities such as museums and theatres. It can also include tourism in rural areas showcasing the traditions of indigenous cultural communities (i.e. festivals, rituals), and their values and lifestyle. It is generally agreed that cultural tourists spend substantially more than standard tourists do. This form of tourism is also becoming generally more popular throughout Europe.

Destination

By definition, the term *destination* refers broadly to any given area where tourism is a relatively important activity, like for instance having an economy significantly influenced by tourism revenues. However, it is complicated by the fact that a single, recognizable destination may include several cities, towns or municipalities, provinces, or other government entities—in island archipelago it may be the entire country.

Types

Living Cultural Areas

Due to globalization, technology and the onset of cultural tourism and ecotourism, the number of living cultural areas is continually declining. For an indigenous culture that has stayed largely separated from the surrounding majority, tourism can present both advantages and problems. On the positive side are the unique cultural practices and arts that attract the curiosity of tourists and provide opportunities for tourism and economic development. On the negative side is the issue of how to control tourism so that those same cultural amenities are not destroyed and the people do not feel violated.

Chiloé, Chile: A Case Study

Chiloé is Chile's largest island, located at the midway point between the capital, Santiago, and the country's extreme south at Tierra del Fuego. Chiloé is the site of the Chiloé Model Forest, member of the same network as the Calakmul and Eastern Ontario

Model Forests. Having evolved for centuries isolated from mainland Chile, the "Chilotes" developed a strong, self-reliant culture, rich in folklore, mythology and tradition. This very identity is what constitutes the island's major attraction for domestic tourists in Chile and increasingly, for international tourists. As in the Calakmul case above, tourism to Chiloé is very strongly based on the island's cultural heritage, predominantly consisting of crafts markets, appreciation of cultural landscapes, museum exhibitions, seafood cuisine and architectural heritage (Chiloé's old churches). However, the average tourist to the island will have little opportunity to see Chilotes involved in their living cultural activities, such as the elaborate preparation of the islands famous "curanto" meal, rich in shellfish, meat and potatoes, the management practices of their farm and forest lands, boat building and more. In order to overcome the cultural and organizational barriers that keep suppliers of living cultural heritage and tour operators apart, the Chiloé diocese of Ancud established a private foundation called "Fundación con Todos" (One for All Foundation). Among other activities, the Foundation has played a key role in helping a number of Chilote households organize themselves into an "agrotourism" network. The Foundation helped Chilote households make the preparation required to accommodate tourists (including training in sanitation and maintenance of facilities, the provision of basic infrastructure) and complemented this effort with a professional marketing campaign. These works were undertaken with the financial support of other agencies. Again, in cooperation with the EOMF and the Chiloé Model Forest, a cultural and natural heritage tour was organized to Argentina and Chile, including a three-day visit to Chiloé, permitting some of the Chilote households to host a group of cultural heritage tourists for the first time. The visits were very successful and should be the first of more to come, helping establish the credibility of Chiloé's agrotourism network among other tour operators.

Orissa Tribes: A Case Study

Nestling on the eastern coast of India, Orissa is one of the most exquisite regions dominated by exotic sandy beaches, plenteous wildlife, and holy temples famous for their architectural splendor and primitive lifestyle. The charm of the city is still well-nigh chaste and unrevealed by the visitors, up to its full extent. The other lure of the city lies in its tribal population dotted with more than 62 tribal communities. The tribal communities of Orissa constitute about 23 per cent of its total population. Orissa is inhabited by tribes like Saora or Sabar that had a respectable mentioning in the epic of Mahabharata. Mostly the Orissa tribes are high land habitats with opulent ethnic trait, cultures and customs dominated by varying languages. The culture conscious tribes are able to preserve their social customs and dignified values. The most primitive tribes are Bondas, Gadabas, Koyas, Kondhas and Sauras. The culture of tribal Orissa is affluent with their own folk songs and dances, their tattoos. Tribal culture of Orissa is well-depicted in its modern city in form of poems, art and craft or music. The tribes have adapted the Hindu traditions and culture from centuries, which is mixed with their own culture giving a distinct zest to the entire racial. Songs and dances are the essence of the tribal culture of Orissa. The traditions and the ceremonies for wedding, birth and death all are represented by singing songs, rural dances along with feasts. The Tribal Folk Orissan tribes are strong, assiduous and simple hospitable tribes, normally like to be reserved and maintain distance from the people of other communities, as they are too shy. The major occupation of these tribes is agriculture and fishing and hunting. Men usually wear loin attire and women rap long stretch of cloth around them. Women are adorned with ornaments like bangles, armlets, bracelets, necklaces, rings, hairpins etc., usually made of silvers, aluminium and brass. The practice of tattooing is prevalent among women folk. Girls above 5 years are found with tattoo mark on their faces and hands. Festival Celebration Numbers of deities are worshipped by the tribes for their happy life. Many festivals are also celebrated with much of enthusiasm and excitement. The ceremony rituals are observed throughout the year in order to appease their deities and ascendant. The most significant festival of the year are the *chaita parab* and *push parab*—this day all able men of the village go on a hunting expedition. The tribes with their cultural dance, song and music all distinguish custom of their artistic life, which demarcate them from the other non-tribal groups. Orissa acquire everything Orissa is a state, embellished with hilly terrain of the Eastern Ghats, where primitive tribes dwell and a beautiful stretch of the Indo-Aryans coast where modern life persists. A blend of 2 discrete civilization with contrast cultures, beautiful landscapes, beaches, rich wildlife, offers the best of India to its visitors.

- Historical Sites: All tourism engages interest in culture;
- Modern Urban District;
- Theme Parks and Country Clubs;
- Coastal or Island Ecosystems;
- Inland Natural Area.

Key Principles

Destination Planning

As the issue of globalization takes place to this modern time, the challenge of preserving the few remaining cultural community around the world is becoming hard. In a tribal based community, reaching economic advancement with minimal negative impacts is an essential objective to any destination planner. Since they are using the culture of the region as the main attraction, sustainable destination development of the area is vital for them to prevent the negative impacts (i.e. destroying the authentic identity of the tribal community) due to tourism.

Management Issues

Certainly, the principle of "one size fits all" doesn't apply to destination planning. The needs, expectations, and anticipated benefits from tourism vary greatly from one destination to another. This is clearly exemplified as local communities living in regions with tourism potential (destinations) develop a vision for what kind of tourism they want to facilitate, depending on issues and concerns they want to be settled or satisfied.

Destination Planning Resources

Planning Guides

Culture: The Heart of Development Policy: It is important that the destination planner takes into account the diverse definition of culture as the term is subjective. Satisfying tourists' interests such as landscapes, seascapes, art, nature, traditions, ways of life and other products associated to them—which may be categorized cultural in the broadest sense of the word, is a prime consideration as it marks the initial phase of the development of a cultural destination. The quality of service and destination, which doesn't solely depend on the cultural heritage but more importantly to the cultural environment, can further be developed by setting controls and policies which shall govern the community and its stakeholders. It is therefore safe to say that the planner should be on the ball with the varying meaning of culture itself as this fuels the formulation of development policies that shall entail efficient planning and monitored growth *(e.g. strict policy on the protection and preservation of the community)*.

Local Community, Tourists, the Destination and Sustainable Tourism: While satisfying tourists' interests and demands may be a top priority, it is also imperative to ruminate the subsystems of the destination's *(residents)*. Development pressures should be anticipated and set to their minimum level so as to conserve the area's resources and prevent a saturation of the destination as to not abuse the product and the residents correspondingly. The plan should incorporate the locals to its gain by training and employing them and in the process encourage them to participate to the travel business. Keep in mind that the plan should make travellers not only aware about the destination but also concern on how to help it sustain its character while broadening their travelling experience.

Planning Tools

Sources of Data: The core of a planner's job is to design an appropriate planning process and facilitate community decision. Ample information which is a crucial requirement is contributed through various technical researches and analyzes. Here are some of the helpful tools commonly used by planners to aid them:

1. Key Informant Interviews;
2. Libraries, Internet and Survey Research;
3. Census and Statistical Analysis;
4. Spatial Analysis with Geographical Information System (GIS) and Global Positioning System (GPS) technologies.

Key Institutions: Participating structures are primarily led by the government's local authorities and the official tourism board or council, with the involvement of various NGOs, community and indigenous representatives, development organizations, and the academe.

Case Studies

Cultural and Ecotourism in the Mountainous Regions of Central Asia and in the Himalayas

Tourism is coming to the previously isolated but spectacular mountainous regions of Central Asia, the Hindu Kush and the Himalayas. Closed for so many years to visitors from abroad, it now attracts a growing number of foreign tourists by its unique culture and splendid natural beauty. However, while this influx of tourists is bringing economic opportunities and employment to local populations, helping to promote these little-known regions of the world, it has also brought challenges along with it: to ensure that it is well-managed and that its benefits are shared by all. As a response to this concern, the Norwegian Government, as well as the UNESCO, organized an interdisciplinary project called the Development of Cultural and Eco-tourism in the Mountainous Regions of Central Asia and the Himalayas Project. It aims to establish links and promote cooperation between local communities, national and international NGOs, and tour agencies in order to heighten the role of the local community and involve them fully in the employment opportunities and income-generating activities that tourism can bring. Project activities include training local tour guides, producing high-quality craft items and promoting home-stays and bed-and-breakfast type accommodation.

As of now, the project is drawing on the expertise of international NGOs and tourism professionals in the seven participating countries, making a practical and positive contribution to alleviating poverty by helping local communities to draw the maximum benefit from their region's tourism potential, while protecting the environmental and cultural heritage of the region concerned.

ROLE OF INDIGENOUS PEOPLES

The term *indigenous peoples* has no universal, standard or fixed definition, but can be used about any ethnic group who inhabit the geographic region with which they have the earliest historical connection. However, several widely-accepted formulations, which define the term *indigenous peoples* in stricter terms, have been put forward by prominent and internationally-recognised organizations, such as the United Nations, the International Labour Organization and the World Bank. Indigenous peoples in this article is used in such a narrower sense.

Drawing on these, a contemporary working definition of "indigenous peoples" for certain purposes has criteria which would seek to include cultural groups (and their descendants) who have an historical continuity or association with a given region, or parts of a region, and who formerly or currently inhabit the region either:

- before its subsequent colonization or annexation; or
- alongside other cultural groups during the formation of a nation-state; or
- independently or largely isolated from the influence of the claimed governance by a nation-state.

[linguistic], cultural and social/organizational characteristics, and in doing so remain differentiated in some degree from the surrounding populations and dominant culture of the nation-state.

To the above, a criterion is usually added to also include:

- peoples who are self-identified as indigenous, and/or those recognised as such by other groups.

Note that even if all the above criteria are fulfilled, some people may either not consider themselves as indigenous or may not be considered as indigenous by governments, organizations or scholars.

Other related terms for indigenous peoples include *aborigines, aboriginal peoples, native peoples, first peoples, first nations* and *autochthonous* (this last term having a derivation from Greek, meaning "sprung from the earth"). *Indigenous peoples* may often be used in preference to these or other terms, as a neutral replacement where these terms may have taken on negative or positive connotations by their prior association and use. It is the preferred term in use by the United Nations and its subsidiary organizations.

Definitions

The adjective *indigenous* has the common meaning of "having originated in and being produced, growing, living, or occurring naturally in a particular region or environment." Therefore, in a purely adjectival sense any given people, ethnic group or community may be described as being *indigenous* in reference to some particular region or location. Key to a contemporary understanding of 'indigenousness' is the political role an ethnic group plays, for all other criteria usually taken to denote indigenous groups (territory, poverty, race, history, dependency on natural resources, etc.) can to a greater or lesser extent also be applied to majority cultures. Therefore, the distinction applied to indigenous ethnic groups can be formulated as: *A politically underprivileged group, who share a similar ethnic identity different to the nation in power, and who have been an ethnic entity in the locality before the present ruling nation took over power.* (Greller, 1997).

However, the specific term *indigenous peoples* has a much more restrictive interpretation when it used in more formalised, legalistic and academic settings, associated with the collective rights of human populations. In these contexts, the term is used to denote particular peoples and groups around the world who, as well as being native to or associated with some given territory, meet certain other criteria (such as those expressed in the definitions detailed in definitions and identity of indigenous peoples). This article is concerned with the latter, and not the former, sense of the term.

Characteristics of Indigenous Peoples: Overview

Population and Distribution

Indigenous societies range from those who have been significantly exposed to the colonizing or expansionary activities of other societies (such as the Maya peoples of Mexico and Central America) through to those who as yet remain in comparative isolation from any external influence (such as the Sentinelese and Jarawa of the Andaman Islands). Precise estimates for the total population of the world's indigenous peoples are very difficult to compile, given the difficulties in identification and the variances and inadequacies of available census data. Recent source estimates range from 300 million to 350 million as of the start of the 21st century. This would equate to just under 6 per cent of the total world population. This includes at least 5000 distinct peoples in over 72 countries. Contemporary distinct indigenous groups survive in populations ranging from only a few dozen to hundreds of thousands or more. Many indigenous populations have undergone a dramatic decline and even extinction, and remain threatened in many parts of the world. Some have also been assimilated by other populations. In other cases, indigenous populations are undergoing a recovery or expansion in numbers. Certain indigenous societies persist even though they may no longer inhabit their "traditional" lands, owing to migration, relocation, forced resettlement or having been supplanted by other cultural groups.

Common Characteristics

Characteristics common across many indigenous groups include present or historical reliance upon subsistence-based production (based on pastoral, horticultural and/or hunting and gathering techniques), and a predominantly non-urbanized society. Indigenous societies may be either settled in a given locale/region or exhibit a nomadic lifestyle across a large territory. Indigenous societies are found in every inhabited climate zone and continent of the world.

Common Concerns

Indigenous peoples confront a diverse range of concerns associated with their status and interaction with other cultural groups, as well as changes in their inhabited environment. Some challenges are specific to particular groups; however, other challenges are commonly experienced. Bartholomew Dean and Jerome Levi (2003) explore why and how the circumstances of indigenous peoples are improving in some places of the world, while their human rights continue to be abused in others. These issues include cultural and linguistic preservation, land rights, ownership and exploitation of natural resources, political determination and autonomy, environmental degradation and incursion, poverty, health and discrimination. The interaction between indigenous and non-indigenous societies throughout history has been complex, ranging from outright conflict and subjugation to some degree of mutual benefit and cultural transfer. A particular aspect of anthropological study involves investigation into the ramifications of what is termed *first contact*, the study of what occurs when two cultures first encounter one another. The situation can be further confused when there is a complicated or contested history of migration and population of a given region, which can give rise to disputes about primacy and ownership of the land and resources.

Historical Indigenous Cultures

The migration, expansion and settlement of societies throughout different territories is a universal, almost defining thread which runs through the entire course of human history. Many of the cross-cultural interactions which arose as a result of these historical encounters involved societies which might properly be considered as indigenous, either from their own viewpoint or that of external societies. Most often, these past encounters between indigenous and "non-indigenous" groups lack contemporary account or description. Any assessment or understanding of impact, result and relation can at best only be surmised, using archaeological, linguistic or other reconstructive means. Where accounts do exist, they frequently originate from the viewpoint of the colonizing, expansionary or nascent state.

Classical Antiquity

Greek sources of the Classical period acknowledge the prior existence of indigenous people(s), whom they referred to as "Pelasgians." These peoples inhabited lands surrounding the Aegean Sea before the subsequent migrations of the Hellenic ancestors claimed by these authors. The disposition and precise identity of this former group is elusive, and sources such as Homer, Hesiod and Herodotus give varying, partially mythological accounts. However, it is clear that cultures existed whose indigenous characteristics were distinguished by the subsequent Hellenic cultures (and distinct from non-Greek speaking "foreigners", termed "barbarians" by the historical Greeks).

European Expansion and Colonialism

The rapid and extensive spread of the various European powers from the early 18th century onwards had a profound impact upon many of the indigenous cultures with whom they came into contact. The exploratory and colonial ventures in the Americas, Africa, Asia and the Pacific often resulted in territorial and cultural conflict, and the intentional or unintentional displacement and devastation of the indigenous populations.

Europe

The Canary Islands had an indigenous population called the Guanches whose origin is still the subject of discussion among historians and linguists.

Contemporary Distribution and Survey

Indigenous populations are distributed in regions throughout the globe. The numbers, condition and experience of indigenous groups may vary widely within a given region. A comprehensive survey is further complicated by sometimes contentious membership and identification.

Africa

In the post-colonial period, the concept of specific indigenous peoples within the African continent has gained wider acceptance, although not without controversy. The highly-diverse and numerous ethnic groups which comprise most modern, independent African states contain within them various peoples whose situation, cultures and pastoralist or hunter-gatherer lifestyles are generally marginalised and set apart from the dominant political and economic structures of the nation. Since the late 20th century these peoples have increasingly sought recognition of their rights as distinct indigenous peoples, in both national and international contexts.

Although the vast majority of African peoples can be considered to be indigenous in the sense that they have originated from that continent and nowhere else, in practice identity as an "indigenous people" as per the term's modern application is more restrictive, and certainly not every African ethnic group claims identification under these terms. Groups and communities who do claim this recognition are those who by a variety of historical and environmental circumstances have been placed outside of the dominant state systems, and whose traditional practices and land claims often come into conflict with the objectives and policies promulgated by governments, companies and surrounding dominant societies. Given the extensive and complicated history of human migration within Africa, being the "first peoples in a land" is not a necessary pre-condition for acceptance as an indigenous people. Rather, indigenous identity relates more to a set of characteristics and practices than priority of arrival. For example, several populations of nomadic peoples such as the Tuareg of the Sahara and Sahel regions now inhabit areas in which they arrived comparatively recently; their claim to indigenous status (endorsed by the African Commission on Human and Peoples' Rights) is based on their marginalisation as nomadic peoples in states and territories dominated by sedentary agricultural peoples. The Indigenous Peoples of Africa Co-ordinating Committee (IPACC) is one of the main transnational network organizations recognised as a representative of African indigenous peoples in dialogues with governments and bodies such as the UN. IPACC identifies several key characteristics associated with indigenous claims in Africa:

- political and economic marginalisation rooted in colonialism;
- de facto discrimination based often on the dominance of agricultural peoples in the State system (e.g. lack of access to education and health care by hunters and herders);
- the particularities of culture, identity, economy and territoriality that link hunting and herding peoples to their home environments in deserts and forests (e.g. nomadism, diet, knowledge systems);

- some indigenous peoples, such as the San and Pygmy peoples are physically distinct, which makes them subject to specific forms of discrimination.

With respect to concerns expressed that identifying some groups and not others as indigenous is in itself discriminatory, IPACC states that it:

> "...recognises that all Africans should enjoy equal rights and respect. All of Africa's diversity is to be valued. Particular communities, due to historical and environmental circumstances, have found themselves outside the state-system and underrepresented in governance... This is not to deny other Africans their status; it is to emphasise that affirmative recognition is necessary for hunter-gatherers and herding peoples to ensure their survival."

At an African inter-governmental level, the examination of indigenous rights and concerns is pursued by a sub-commission established under the African Commission on Human and Peoples' Rights (ACHPR), sponsored by the African Union (AU), (successor body to the Organisation of African Unity (OAU)). In late 2003 the 53 signatory states of the ACHPR adopted the *Report of the African Commission's Working Group on Indigenous Populations/ Communities* and its recommendations. This report says in part (p. 62):

> ...certain marginalized groups are discriminated in particular ways because of their particular culture, mode of production and marginalized position within the state; [a] form of discrimination that other groups within the state do not suffer from. The call of these marginalized groups to protection of their rights is a legitimate call to alleviate this particular form of discrimination.

The adoption of this report at least notionally subscribed the signatories to the concepts and aims of furthering the identity and rights of African indigenous peoples. The extent to which individual states are mobilising to put these recommendations into practice varies enormously, however, and most indigenous groups continue to agitate for improvements in the areas of land rights, use of natural resources, protection of environment and culture, political recognition and freedom from discrimination.

The Americas

Indigenous peoples of the American continents are broadly recognised as being those groups and their descendants who inhabited the region before the arrival of European colonizers and settlers (i.e., Pre-Columbian). Indigenous peoples who maintain, or seek to maintain, traditional ways of life are found from the high Arctic north to the southern extremities of Tierra del Fuego. The impact of European colonization of the Americas on the indigenous communities was in general quite severe, with many authorities estimating ranges of significant population decline due to the ravages of various epidemic diseases (smallpox, measles, etc.), displacement, conflict and exploitation. The extent of this impact is the subject of much continuing debate. Several peoples shortly thereafter became extinct, or very nearly so. All nations in North and South America have *populations* of indigenous peoples within their borders. In some countries (particularly Latin American), indigenous peoples form a sizeable component of the overall national population—in Bolivia they account for an estimated 56 per cent, 70 per cent of the total nation, and at least half of the *population* in Guatemala and the Andean and Amazonian *nations* of Peru. In English, indigenous peoples are collectively referred to by several different terms which vary by region and include such ethnoynms as Native Americans, Amerindians, Indians. In Spanish or Portuguese speaking countries one finds the use of terms such as *pueblos indígenas, povos, nativos, indígenas,* and in Peru, *Comunidades Nativas,* particularly among Amazonian societies like the Urarina and Matsés. The Aboriginal peoples in Canada include the Inuit, Métis and other peoples designated as members of First Nations. The combined indigenous population is an estimated in almost a million (976,305). This means they represented 3.3 per cent of the Canadian population. Their status is recognized by Canada's Constitution Act, 1982. The Inuit have achieved a degree of administrative autonomy with the creation in 1999 of the territory of Nunavut. The self-administering Danish territory of Greenland is also home to a majority population of indigenous Inuit (about 85 per cent). In the United States, the combined populations of Native Americans, Inuit and other indigenous designations totalled 2,786,652 (constituting about 1.5 per cent of 2003 US census figures). Some 563 scheduled tribes are recognized at the Federal level, and a number of others recognized at the State level.

In Mexico, approximately 6,011,202 (constituting about 6.7 per cent of 2005 Mexican census figures) identify as *indígenas* (Spanish for natives or indigenous peoples). In the southern states of Chiapas, Yucatan and Oaxaca they constitute 26.1 per cent, 33.5 per cent and 35.3 per cent, respectively, of the population. In these states several conflicts and episodes of civil war have been conducted, in which the situation and participation of indigenous societies were notable factors (see for example EZLN). The Amerindians make up 0.4 per cent of Brazil's population, or about 700,000 people. Indigenous peoples are found in the entire territory of Brazil, although the majority of them live in Indian reservations in the North and Centre-Western part of the country. On 18 January 2007, FUNAI reported that it had confirmed the presence of 67 different uncontacted tribes in Brazil, up from 40 in 2005. With this addition Brazil has now overtaken the island of New Guinea as the country having the largest number of uncontacted tribes.

Asia

The vast regions of Asia contain the majority of the world's present-day indigenous populations, about 70 per cent according to IWGIA figures. The most substantial populations are in India, which constitutionally recognises a range of "Scheduled Tribes" within its borders. These various peoples (collectively referred to as Adivasis, or tribal peoples) number about 68 million (1991 census figures, approximately 8 per cent of the total national population). The languages of Taiwanese aborigines have significance in historical linguistics, since in all likelihood Taiwan was the place of origin of the entire Austronesian language family, which is spread across the whole of Oceania.

Indigenous peoples of Iran include the Bakhtiari, Laks, Lurs, and Qashqai. The Assyrians and Marsh Arabs are also indigenous to areas of the geocultural region of Mesopotamia which includes parts of Iraq, Syria and Turkey. The Lurs also inhabit parts of Iraq close to the Iranian border with the provinces of Lorestan and Ilam. Ainu people are an ethnic group indigenous to Hokkaidô, northern Honshû, the Kuril Islands, much of Sakhalin, and the southern most third of the Kamchatka peninsula. As Japanese settlement expanded, the Ainu were pushed northward, until by the Meiji period they were confined by the government to a small area in Hokkaidô, in a manner similar to the placing of Native Americans on reservations.

Europe

In Europe, present-day recognized indigenous populations are relatively few, mainly confined to northern and far-eastern reaches of this Eurasian peninsula. Whilst there are various ethnic minorities distributed within European countries, few of these still maintain traditional subsistence cultures and are recognized as indigenous peoples, *per se*. Notable indigenous populations include the Sami people of northern Scandinavia, the Nenets and other Samoyedic peoples of the northern Russian Federation, and the Komi peoples of the western Urals.

Caucasus is unique in its ethnic diversity, with a greater variety of languages spoken there than in any region of similar size in the world. Caucasus region is the home of over 50 indigenous ethnic groups.

Oceania

Many of the present-day Pacific Island nations in the Oceania region were originally populated by Polynesian, Melanesian and Micronesian peoples over the course of thousands of years. European colonial expansion in the Pacific brought many of these under non-indigenous administration. During the 20th century several of these former colonies gained independence and nation-states were formed under local control. However, various peoples have put forward claims for indigenous recognition where their islands are still under external administration; examples include the Chamorros of Guam and the Northern Marianas, and the Marshallese of the Marshall Islands. In New Zealand, the indigenous Mâori (see also Iwi) constitute nearly 15 per cent of the total population.

Indigenous Australians, including Aboriginal Australians and Torres Strait Islanders, account for 2.4 per cent of the total population of Australia (2001 census figures). The independent state of Papua New Guinea (PNG) has a majority population of indigenous societies, with some 700+ different tribal groups recognised out of a total population of just over 5 million. The PNG Constitution and other Acts identify traditional or custom-based practices and land tenure, and explicitly sets out to promote the viability of these traditional societies within the modern state. However, several conflicts and disputes concerning land use and resource rights continue to be observed between indigenous groups, the government and corporate entities.

Indigenous Rights, Issues and Concerns

Wherever indigenous cultural identity is asserted, some particular set of societal issues and concerns may be voiced which either arise from (at least in part), or have a particular dimension associated with, their indigenous status. These concerns will often be commonly held or affect other societies also, and are not necessarily experienced uniquely by indigenous groups. Despite the diversity of indigenous peoples, it may be noted that they share common problems and issues in dealing with the prevailing, or invading, society. They are generally concerned that the cultures of indigenous peoples are being lost and that indigenous peoples suffer both discrimination and pressure to assimilate into their surrounding societies. This is borne out by the fact that the lands and cultures of nearly all of the peoples listed at the end of this article are under threat. Notable exceptions are the Sakha and Komi peoples (two of the Northern Indigenous Peoples of Siberia), who now control their own autonomous republics within the Russian state. It is also sometimes argued that it is important for the human species as a whole to preserve a wide range of cultural diversity as possible, and that the protection of indigenous cultures is vital to this enterprise. An example of this occurred in 2002 when the Government of Botswana expelled all the Kalahari Bushmen known as the San from their lands on which they had lived they had lived off for at least twenty thousand years. President Festus Mogai has described the Bushmen as "stone age creatures" and a minister for local government, Margaret Nasha, likened public criticism of their eviction to criticism of the culling of elephants. In 2006, the Botswanan High Court ruled that the Bushmen had a right to return to their land in the Central Kalahari Game Reserve. In response, many have pointed out that in many cases the indigenous peoples often haven't been living self-sufficiently in an area for centuries, and that economic development was not an issue before because it was not an option.

Representation

The rights, claims and even identity of indigenous peoples are apprehended, acknowledged and observed quite differently from government to government. Various organizations exist with charters to in one way or another promote (or at least acknowledge) indigenous aspirations, and indigenous societies have often banded together to form bodies which jointly seek to further their communal interests. In cooperation, representatives of indigenous peoples have met in the World Council of Indigenous Peoples (WCIP), which held its first conference in British Columbia in 1975. Cooperation has continued in the research and education organization The Centre for World Indigenous Studies (CWIS), founded in 1984, in Olympia, Washington, USA.

United Nations

Indigenous peoples and their interests are represented in the United Nations primarily through the mechanisms of the Working Group on Indigenous Populations (WGIP). In April 2000, the United Nations Commission on Human Rights adopted a resolution to establish the United Nations Permanent Forum on Indigenous Issues (PFII) as an advisory body to the Economic and Social Council with a mandate to review indigenous issues. In late December 2004, the United Nations General Assembly proclaimed 2005-2014 to be the Second International Decade of the World's Indigenous People. The main goal of the new decade will be to strengthen international cooperation around resolving the problems faced by indigenous people in areas such as culture, education, health, human rights, the environment, and social and economic development. In September 2007, after a process of preparations, discussions and negotiations stretching back to 1982, the General Assembly adopted the Declaration on the Rights of Indigenous Peoples. The non-binding declaration outlines the individual and collective rights of indigenous peoples, as well as their rights to identity, culture, language, employment, health, education and other issues. Four nations with significant indigenous populations voted against the declaration: the United States, Canada, New Zealand and Australia. Eleven nations abstained: Azerbaijan, Bangladesh, Bhutan, Burundi, Colombia, Georgia, Kenya, Nigeria, Russia, Samoa and Ukraine. Thirty-four nations did not vote, while the remaining 143 nations voted for it.

Other Accredited Organizations

Various organizations are devoted to the preservation or study of indigenous peoples. Of these, several have widely-recognized credentials to act as an intermediary or representative on behalf of indigenous peoples' groups, in negotiations on indigenous issues with governments and international organizations. These include:

- African Commission on Human and Peoples' Rights (ACHPR);
- Society for Threatened Peoples International (STP);
- International Work Group for Indigenous Affairs (IWGIA);
- Indigenous Peoples of Africa Co-ordinating Committee (IPACC);
- Movement in the Amazon for Tribal Subsistence and Economic Sustainability;
- Survival International;
- Indigenous Dialogues;
- Cultural Survival;
- Asia Pacific Indigenous Youth Network.

International Day of the World's Indigenous People

The International Day of the World's Indigenous People falls on August 9 as this was the date of the first meeting in 1982 of the United Nations Working Group of Indigenous Populations of the Subcommission on Prevention of Discrimination and Protection of Minorities of the Commission on Human Rights. The UN General Assembly decided on 23 December, 1994, that the International Day of the World's Indigenous People should be observed on August 9 every year during the International Decade of the World's Indigenous People (resolution 49/214). Later on 20 December, 2004 the assembly decided to continue observing the International Day of Indigenous People every year during the Second International Decade of the World's Indigenous People (2005-2014) (resolution 59/174).

Indigenous Knowledge and Culture

Indigenous societies possess an often unique body of cultural and environmental knowledge. The preservation and investigation of specialised indigenous knowledge, particularly in relation to the resources of the natural environment with which the society is associated, is an increasingly sought-after goal of both the indigenous and the societies who thereby seek to identify new resources and benefits (example: partnerships established to research useful biological extracts from vegetation in the Amazon rainforests). For some people (e.g. indigenous communities from India, Brazil, and Malaysia and some NGOs such as GRAIN and Third World Network), indigenous peoples may be victims of biopiracy when they are subjected to unauthorised use of their biological resources, of their traditional knowledge on these biological resources, of unequal share of benefits between them and a patent holder. A controversial case of biopiracy was reported on human genes of a tribal community reported to be resistant to malaria and leprosy.

Viewpoints on Indigenous Societies

A range of differing viewpoints and attitudes have arisen from the experience and history of contact between indigenous and "non-indigenous" communities. The cultural, regional and historical contexts in which these viewpoints have developed are complex, and many competing viewpoints exist simultaneously in any given society, albeit promulgated with greater or lesser force depending on the extent of cross-cultural exposure and internal societal change. These views may be noted from both sides of the relationship.

Indigenous Viewpoints

"Non-indigenous" Viewpoints

Indigenous peoples have variously been identified as *primitives, savages* or *uncivilized.* These terms were common during the heyday of European colonial expansion. By the 17th century, indigenous peoples were commonly labelled "uncivilized". Proponents of civilization, like Thomas Hobbes, considered them merely savages; Enlightenment philosophers such as Jean Jacques Rousseau, considered them to be "noble savages". Those who were close to the Hobbesian view tended to believe themselves to have a duty to civilize and modernize indigenes. Although anthropologists, especially from Europe, used to apply these terms to all tribal cultures, it has fallen into disfavour as demeaning and, according to anthropologists, inaccurate (see tribe, cultural evolution). Survival International runs a campaign to stamp out media portrayal of indigenous peoples as 'primitive' or 'savages'. After World War I, however, many Europeans came to doubt the value of civilization. At the same time, the anti-colonial movement, and advocates of indigenous peoples, argued that words such as "civilized" and "savage" were products and tools of colonialism, and argued that colonialism itself was savagely destructive. In the mid-20th century, European attitudes began to shift to the view that indigenous and tribal peoples should have the right to decide for themselves what should happen to their ancient cultures and their ancestral lands. Several criticisms of the concept of indigenous peoples are:

- In many cases, such as with some Native American tribes, some people claim that the people termed indigenous arrived in an area *after* the people termed non-indigenous;
- Peoples have invaded or colonised each other's lands since before recorded history and so the division into indigenous and non-indigenous is a matter of judgement. Even in recent centuries there are difficulties: for example, are the Zulu people indigenous to South Africa?
- Lumping indigenous peoples into one group ignores the vast amounts of diversity among them and at the same time imposes a uniform identity on them, which may not be historically accurate.

RELATIONSHIP WITH ECOTOURISM

Ecotourism, also known as *ecological tourism,* is a form of tourism that appeals to the ecologically and socially conscious individuals. Generally speaking, ecotourism focuses on volunteering, personal growth, and learning new ways to live on the planet; typically involving travel to destinations where flora, fauna, and cultural heritage are the primary attractions. Responsible ecotourism includes programmes that minimize the negative aspects of conventional tourism on the environment, and enhance the cultural integrity of local people. Therefore, in addition to evaluating environmental and cultural factors, an integral part of ecotourism is in the promotion of recycling, energy efficiency, water conservation, and creation of economic opportunities for the local communities.

Criteria

Ideally, ecotourism should satisfy several criteria, such as:

- conservation of biological diversity and cultural diversity, through ecosystem protection.
- promotion of sustainable use of biodiversity, by providing jobs to local populations.
- sharing of socio-economic benefits with local communities and indigenous people by having their informed consent and participation in the management of ecotourism enterprises.
- tourism to unspoiled natural resources, with minimal impact on the environment being a primary concern.
- minimization of tourism's own environmental impact.
- affordability and lack of waste in the form of luxury.
- local culture, flora and fauna being the main attractions.

For many countries, ecotourism is not simply a marginal activity to finance protection of the environment but as a major industry of the national economy. For example, in places such as Costa Rica, Ecuador, Nepal, Kenya, Madagascar, and Antarctica, ecotourism represents a significant portion of the gross domestic product and economic activity. The concept of ecotourism is widely misunderstood, and in practice is often used as a marketing tool to promote tourism that is related to nature. Critics claim that ecotourism as practiced and abused often consists of placing a hotel in a splendid landscape, to the detriment of the ecosystem. According to them, ecotourism must above all sensitive people with the beauty and the fragility of nature. They condemn some operators as "greenwashing" their operations; using the label of "green-friendly", while behaving in environmentally irresponsible ways. Although academics disagree about who can be classified as an ecotourist and there is precious little statistical data, some estimate that more than five million ecotourists—the majority of the ecotourist population—come from the United States, with others from Western Europe, Canada and Australia. Currently there are various moves to create national and international ecotourism accrediation programmes, although the process is also controversial. Ecotourism certificates have been put in place at Costa Rica, although some critics have dismissed these programmes as greenwashing.

History

Ecotourism, responsible tourism, and sustainable development have become prevalent concepts since the late 1980s, and ecotourism has experienced arguably the fastest growth of all sub-sectors in the tourism industry. The popularity represents a change in tourist perceptions, increased environmental awareness, and a desire to explore natural environments. Such changes have become a statement affirming one's social identity, educational sophistication, and disposable income as it has about preserving the Amazon rainforest or the Caribbean reef for posterity. With its great potential for environmental protection, the United Nations celebrated the "International Year of Ecotourism" in 2002.

Criticisms

Definitional Problems and Greenwashing

To approach an understanding of the problem, a clear definition must delineate what is, and is not, ecotourism. Ideally, ecotourism satisfies several general criteria, including the conservation of biological diversity and cultural diversity through ecosystem protection, promotion of sustainable use of biodiversity, share of socio-economic benefits with local communities through informed consent and participation, increase in environmental and cultural knowledge, affordability and reduced waste, and minimization of its own environmental impact. In such ways, it contributes to the long-term benefits to both the environment and local communities. However, in the continuum of tourism activities that stretch from conventional tourism to ecotourism proper, there has been a lot of contention to the limit at which biodiversity preservation, local socio-economic benefits, and environmental impact can be considered "ecotourism". For this reason, environmentalists, special interest groups, and governments define ecotourism differently. Environmental organizations have generally insisted that ecotourism is nature-based, sustainably managed, conservation supporting, and environmentally educated. The tourist industry and governments, however, focus more on the product aspect, treating ecotourism as equivalent to any sort of tourism based in nature. As a further complication, many terms are used under the rubric of ecotourism. Nature tourism, low impact tourism, green tourism, bio-tourism, ecologically responsible tourism, and others have been used in literature and marketing, although they are not necessary synonymous with ecotourism. The problems associated with defining ecotourism have led to confusion among tourists and academics alike. Definitional problems are also subject of considerable public controversy and concern because of greenwashing, a trend towards the commercialization of tourism schemes disguised as sustainable, nature based, and environmentally friendly ecotourism. According to McLaren, these schemes are environmentally destructive, economically exploitative, and culturally insensitive at its worst. They are also morally disconcerting because they mislead tourists and manipulate their concerns for the environment. Despite objections, greenwashing continues to grow unabated. The Nature's Sacred Paradise, a theme park in Quintana Roo, Mexico, is responsible for displacing local Mayan communities and illegally keeping endangered species in captivity to attract visitors. The development and success of such large scale, energy intensive, and ecologically unsustainable schemes are a testament to the tremendous profits associated with being labelled as ecotourism.

The Negative Psycho-Social Impact of Ecotourism

Ecotourism is the trend towards the commercialization of tourism throughout the nation. This trend has become one of the fastest growing sectors of the tourism industry growing annual 10-15 per cent worldwide (Kamuaro, 2007). Ecotourism was first introduced in Africa in the 1950's with the legalization of hunting (Kamuaro, 2007). This need for recreational hunting zones lead to the creation of protected areas, national parks and game reserves. Today these areas have become important revenue-earning venues with the establishment of lodges and tourist campsites. One definition of ecotourism is "the practice of low-impact, educational, ecologically and culturally sensitive travel that benefits local communities and host countries" (Honey, 1999). Many of the ecotourism projects are not meeting these standards. Even if some of the guidelines are being executed, the local communities are still facing other negative impacts. South Africa is one of the countries that are reaping significant economic benefits from ecotourism, but negative effects—including physical displacement of persons, gross violation of fundamental rights, and environmental hazards—far out weigh the medium-term economic benefits (Kamuaro, 2007). A tremendous amount of money is being spent and human resources continue to be used for ecotourism despite the lack of success stories, and even more money is put into public relation campaigns to dilute the effects of the criticism. Ecotourism channels resources away from other projects that could contribute more sustainable and realistic solutions to pressing social and environmental problems. "The money tourism can generate often ties parks and managements to eco-tourism" (Walpole *et al.*, 2001). But there is a tension in this relationship because ecotourism often causes conflict and changes in land-use rights, fails to deliver promises of community-level benefits, damages environments, and has plenty of other social impacts. Indeed many argue repeatedly that ecotourism is neither ecologically nor socially beneficial, yet it persists as a strategy for conservation and development (West, 2006). While several studies are being done on ways to improve the ecotourism structure, these examples provide reason that it should just stop all together.

The ecotourism system exercises tremendous financial and political influence. The evidence above shows that at the very least a strong case exists for restraining such activities. Funding could be used for field studies aimed at finding alternative solutions to tourism and the diverse problems Africa faces in result of urbanization, industrialization, and over exploitation of agriculture (Kamuaro, 2007). At the local level ecotourism has become a source of conflict over control of land, resources, and tourism profits. There are many problems with the idea of ecotourism. Environmental, the effects on the local people, and conflicts over profit distribution are only a few of the negative effects of ecotourism. In a perfect world more efforts would be made towards educating tourists of the environmental and social effects of their travels. Very few regulations or laws stand in place as boundaries for the investors in ecotourism. These should be implemented to prohibit the promotion of unsustainable ecotourism projects and materials which project false images of destinations, demeaning local and indigenous cultures.

Direct Environmental Impacts

Ecotourism operations typically fail to live up to conservation ideals. It is often overlooked that ecotourism is a highly consumer-centered activity, and that environmental conservation is only a means to further economic growth. Although ecotourism is intended for small groups, even a modest increase in population, however temporary, puts extra pressure on the local environment and necessitates the development of additional infrastructure and amenities. The construction of water treatment plants, sanitation facilities, and lodges come with the exploitation of non-renewable energy sources and the utilization of already limited local resources. The conversion of natural land to such tourist infrastructure is implicated in deforestation and habitat deterioration of butterflies in Mexico and squirrel monkeys in Costa Rica. In other cases, the environment suffers because local communities are unable to meet the infrastructure demands of ecotourism. The lack of adequate sanitation facilities in many East African parks results in the disposal of campsite sewage in rivers, contaminating the wildlife, livestock, and people who draw drinking water from it. Aside from environmental degradation with tourist infrastructure, population pressures from ecotourism also leaves behind garbage and pollution associated with the Western lifestyle. Although ecotourists claim to be educationally sophisticated and environmentally concerned, they rarely understand the ecological consequences of their visits and how their day-to-day activities append physical impacts on the environment. As one scientist observes, they "rarely acknowledge how the meals they eat, the toilets they flush, the water they drink, and so on, are all part of broader regional economic and ecological systems they are helping to reconfigure with their very activities." Not do ecotourists recognize the great consumption of non-renewable energy required to arrive at their destination, which is typically more remote than conventional tourism destinations. For instance, an exotic journey to a place 10,000 kilometers away consumes about 700 liters of fuel per person. Ecotourism activities are, in of itself, issues in environmental impact because they disturb fauna and flora. Ecotourists believe that because they are only taking pictures and leaving footprints, they keep ecotourism sites pristine, but even harmless sounding activities such as a nature hike can be ecologically destructive. In the Annapurna Circuit in Nepal, ecotourists have worn down the marked trails and created alternate routes, contributing to soil impaction, erosion, and plant damage. Where the ecotourism activity involves wildlife viewing, it can scare away animals, disrupt their feeding and nesting sites, or acclimate them to the presence of people. In Kenya, disruption of wildlife observers drive cheetahs off their reserves, increasing the risk of inbreeding and further endangering the species.

Environmental Hazards

We already understand that biodiversity and environmentally intact lands form the basis of ecological stability. Unfortunately, industrialization, urbanization, and unsustainable agriculture practices have all had serious effects on the environment. Ecotourism is now also playing a role in this depletion. While the term ecotourism may sound relatively benign, one of its most serious impacts is its consumption of virgin territories (Kamuaro, 2007). These invasions often include deforestation, disruption of ecological life systems and various forms of pollution, all of which contribute to environmental degradation. The number of motor vehicles crossing the park increases as tour drivers search for rare species. The number of roads has disrupted the grass cover which has serious effects on plant and animal species. These areas also have a higher rate of disturbances and invasive species because of all the traffic moving off the beaten path into new undiscovered areas (Kamuaro, 2007). Ecotourism also has an effect on species through the value placed on them. "Certain species have gone from being little known or valued by local people to being highly valued commodities. The commodification of plants may erase their social value and lead to overproduction within protected areas. Local people and their images can also be turned into commodities" (West, 2006). Kamuaro brings up a relatively obvious contradiction, any commercial venture into unspoiled, pristine land with or without the "eco" prefix as a contradiction in terms. To generate revenue you have to have a high number of traffic, tourists, which inevitably means a higher pressure on the environment.

Local People

Most forms of ecotourism are owned by foreign investors and corporations that provide few benefits to local communities. An overwhelming majority of profits are put into the pockets of investors instead of reinvestment into the local economy or environmental protection. The limited numbers of local people who are employed in the economy enter at its lowest level, and are unable to live in tourist areas because of meager wages and a two market system. In some cases, the resentment by local people results in environmental degradation. As a highly publicized case, the Maasai nomads in Kenya killed wildlife in national parks to show aversion to unfair compensation terms and displacement from traditional lands. The lack of economic opportunities for local people also constrains them to degrade the environment as a means of sustenance. The presence of affluent ecotourists encourage the development of destructive markets in wildlife souvenirs, such as the sale of coral trinkets on tropical islands and animal products in Asia, contributing to illegal harvesting and poaching from the environment. In Surinam, sea turtle reserves use a large portion of their budget to guard against these activities.

Displacement of People

One of the most powerful examples of communities being moved in order to create a park is the story of the Masai. About 70 per cent of national parks and game reserves in East Africa are on Masai land (Kamuaro, 2007). The first undesirable impact of tourism was that of the extent of land lost from the Masai culture. Local and national governments took advantage of the Masai's ignorance on the situation and robbed them of huge chunks of grazing land, putting to risk their only socio-economic livelihood. In Kenya the Masai also have not gained any economic benefits. Despite the loss of their land, employment favours better educated workers. Furthermore, the investors in this area are not local and have not put profits back into local economy. In some cases game reserves can be created without informing or consulting local people, who come to find out about the situation when an eviction notice is delivered (Kamuaro, 2007). Another source of resentment is the manipulation of the local people by their government. "Eco-tourism works to create simplistic images of local people and their uses and understandings of their surroundings. Through the lens of these simplified images, officials direct policies and projects towards the local people and the local people are blamed if the projects fail" (West, 2006). Clearly tourism as a trade is not empowering the local people who make it rich and satisfying. Instead ecotourism exploits and depletes, particularly in African Masai tribes. It has to be reoriented if it is to be useful to local communities and to become sustainable (Kamuaro, 2007).

Threats to Indigenous Cultures

Ecotourism often claims that it preserves and "enhances" local cultures. However, evidence shows that with the establishment of protected areas local people have illegally lost their homes, and most often with no compensation (Kamuaro, 2007). Pushing people onto marginal lands with harsh climates, poor soils, lack of water, and infested with livestock and disease does little to enhance livelihoods even when a proportion of ecotourism profits are directed back into the community. The establishment of parks can create harsh survival realities and deprive the people of their traditional use of land and natural resources. Ethnic groups are increasingly being seen as a "backdrop" to the scenery and wildlife. The local people struggle for cultural survival and freedom of cultural expression while being "observed" by tourists. Local indigenous people also have strong resentment towards the change, "Tourism has been allowed to develop with virtually no controls. Too many lodges have been built, too much firewood is being used and no limits are being placed on tourism vehicles. They regularly drive off-track and harass the wildlife. Their vehicle tracks criss-cross the entire Masai Mara. Inevitably the bush is becoming eroded and degraded" (Kamuaro, 2007).

Mismanagement of Ecotourism Sites

While governments are typically entrusted with the administration and enforcement of environmental protection, they often lack the commitment or capability to manage ecotourism sites effectively. The regulations for environmental protection may be vaguely defined, costly to implement, hard to enforce, and uncertain in effectiveness. Government regulatory agencies, as political bodies, are susceptible to making decisions that spend budget on politically beneficial but environmentally unproductive projects. Because of prestige and conspicuousness, the construction of an attractive visitor's centre at an ecotourism site may take precedence over more pressing environmental concerns like acquiring habitat, protecting endemic species, and removing invasive ones. Finally, influential groups can pressure and sway the interests of the government to their favour. The government and its regulators can become vested in the benefits of the ecotourism industry which they are supposed to regulate, causing restrictive environmental regulations and enforcement to become more lenient. Management of ecotourism sites by private ecotourism companies offers an alternative to the cost of regulation and deficiency of government agencies. It is believed that these companies have a self-interest in limited environmental degradation, because tourists will pay more for pristine environments, which translates to higher profit. However, theory indicates that this practice is not economically feasible and will fail to manage the environment. The model of monopolistic competition states that distinctiveness will entail profits, but profits will promote imitation. A company that protects its ecotourism sites is able to charge a premium for the novel experience and pristine environment. But when other companies view the success of this approach, they also enter the market with similar practices, increasing competition and reducing demand. Eventually, the demand will be reduced until the economic profit is zero. A cost-benefit analysis shows that the company bears the cost of environmental protection without receiving the gains. Without economic incentive, the whole premise of self-interest through environmental protection is quashed; instead, ecotourism companies will minimize environment related expenses and maximize tourism demand. The tragedy of the commons offers another model for economic unsustainability from environmental protection, in ecotourism sites utilized by many companies. Although there is a communal incentive to protect the environment, maximizing the benefits in the long run, a company will conclude that it is in their best interest to utilize the ecotourism site beyond its sustainable level. By increasing the number of ecotourists, for instance, a company gains all the economic benefit while paying only a part of the environmental cost. In the same way, a company recognizes that there is no incentive to actively protect the environment; they bear all the costs, while the benefits are shared by all other companies. The result, again, is mismanagement. Taken together, the mobility of foreign investment and lack of economic incentive for environmental protection means that ecotourism companies are disposed to establishing themselves in new sites once their existing one is sufficiently degraded.

Improving Sustainability

Regulation and Accreditation

Because the regulation of ecotourism is poorly implemented or non-existent, ecologically destructive greenwashed operations like underwater hotels, helicopter tours, and wildlife theme parks are categorized as ecotourism along with canoeing, camping, photography, and wildlife observation. The failure to acknowledge responsible, low impact ecotourism puts these companies at a competitive disadvantage. Many environmentalists have argued for a global standard of accreditation, differentiating ecotourism companies based on their level of environmental commitment. A national or international regulatory board would enforce accreditation procedures, with representation from various groups including governments, hotels, tour operators, travel agents, guides, airlines, local authorities, conservation organizations, and non-governmental organizations. The decisions of the board would be sanctioned by governments, so that non-compliant companies would be legally required to disassociate themselves from the use of the ecotourism brand. Crinion suggests a Green Stars System based on criteria including a management plan, benefit for the local community, small group interaction, education value and staff training. Ecotourists who consider their choices would be confident of a genuine ecotourism experience when they see the higher star rating. In addition, environmental impact assessments could be used as a form of accreditation. Feasibility is evaluated from a scientific basis, and recommendations could be made to optimally plan infrastructure, set tourist capacity, and manage the ecology. This form of accreditation is more sensitive to site specific conditions.

Guidelines and Education for Ecotourists

An environmental protection strategy must address the issue of ecotourists removed from the cause-and-effect of their actions on the environment. More initiatives should be carried out to improve their awareness, sensitize them to environmental issues, and care about the places they visit. Tour guides are an obvious and direct medium to communicate awareness. With the confidence of ecotourists and intimate knowledge of the environment, they can actively discuss conservation issues. A tour guide training programme in Costa Rica's Tortuguero National Park has helped mitigate negative environmental impacts by providing information and regulating tourists on the parks' beaches used by nesting endangered sea turtles.

Small Scale, Slow Growth, Locally Based Ecotourism

The underdevelopment theory of tourism describes a new form of imperialism by multinational corporations that control ecotourism resources. These corporations finance and profit from the development of large scale ecotourism that causes excessive environmental degradation, loss of traditional culture and way of life, and exploitation of local labour. In Zimbabwe and Nepal's Annapurna region, where underdevelopment is taking place, more than 90 per cent of ecotourism revenues are expatriated to the parent countries, and less than 5 per cent go into local communities. The lack of sustainability highlights the need for small scale, slow growth, and locally based ecotourism. Local peoples have a vested interest in the well-being of their community, and are therefore more accountable to environmental protection than multinational corporations. The lack of control, westernization, adverse impacts to the environment, loss of culture and traditions outweigh the benefits of establishing large scale ecotourism. The increased contributions of communities to locally managed ecotourism create viable economic opportunities, including high level management positions, and reduce environmental issues associated with poverty and unemployment. Because the ecotourism experience is marketed to a different lifestyle from large scale ecotourism, the development of facilities and infrastructure does not need to conform to corporate Western tourism standards, and can be much simpler and less expensive. There is a greater multiplier effect on the economy, because local products, materials, and labour are used. Profits accrue locally, and import leakages are reduced. However, even this form of tourism may require foreign investment for promotion or start up. When such investments are required, it is crucial for communities for find a company or non-governmental organization that reflects the philosophy of ecotourism; sensitive to their concerns and willing to cooperate at the expense of profit. The basic assumption of the multiplier effect is that the economy starts off with unused resources, for example, that many workers are cyclically unemployed and much of industrial capacity is sitting idle or incompletely utilized. By increasing demand in the economy it is then possible to boost production. If the economy was already at full employment, with only structural, frictional, or other supply-side types of unemployment, any attempt to boost demand would only lead to inflation. For various laissez-faire schools of economics which embrace Say's Law and deny the possibility of Keynesian inefficiency and under-employment of resources, therefore, the multiplier concept is irrelevant or wrong-headed. As an example, consider the government increasing its expenditure on roads by

$1 million, without a corresponding increase in taxation. This sum would go to the road builders, who would hire more workers and distribute the money as wages and profits. The households receiving these incomes will save part of the money and spend the rest on consumer goods. These expenditures in turn will generate more jobs, wages, and profits, and so on with the income and spending circulating around the economy. The multiplier effect arises because of the induced increases in consumer spending which occur due to the increased incomes—and because of the feedback into increasing business revenues, jobs and income again. This process does not lead to an economic explosion not only because of the supply-side barriers at potential output (full employment) but because at each "round", the increase in consumer spending is less than the increase in consumer incomes. That is, the Marginal Propensity to Consume (MPC) is less than one, so that each round some extra income goes into saving, leaking out of the cumulative process. Each increase in spending is thus smaller than that of the previous round, preventing an explosion. Ecotourism has to be implemented with care.

CULTURE TOURISM IN INDIA : AN OVERVIEW

Take a cultural tour to India to understand what makes the country so interesting and beautiful. The people of India belong to different religions, caste and faith as such inhabitants of every region, state, city and even within it have their own set of beliefs and practices that guide them in their lives. Each of these cultural practices has its own importance and charm. On a cultural trip to India, you will not only discover the intricacies of each of these cultures individually but will also understand how so many cultures co-exist peacefully. India finds its root extend to that time which don't even exist in the yellow books of history or in the researches of historians. As the time passed, different shades of traditions and rituals have been adding to the Indian culture and heritage resulting in a multi hued culture which India proudly boasts of. People following different religions, caste and faith coming from various region and state have made a nice amalgamation of diverse culture enriching the Indian culture even more. India's culture is like a rainbow of multiple facets which accommodates music, dance, performing arts, paintings and literature in itself which have gained recognition and fame from every corner of the world. It is not a very easy task to uncover the multiple feathers of Indian culture co-existing with each other for centuries. You have to be prepared to spend some quality time in the country and travel a lot if you are really keen to get an in depth knowledge of the culture of India. For those who do not have much of a time, there is really nothing to worry about because even a brief glimpse of the culture of India is absolutely pleasurable. An extensive cultural trip into the vast land of India is sure to change your taste and sense of culture for the rest of your life while you will be amazed by the cultural diversity of the country.

2

Heritage Tourism and its Economic Impacts: An Introductory Overview

The National Trust defines cultural heritage tourism as travelling to experience the places, artifacts and activities that authentically represent the stories and people of the past and present. It includes cultural, historic and natural resources. The Heritage Tourism Programme provides assistance ranging from how-to cultural heritage tourism publications to consulting services tailored to meet the needs of individual clients. The National Trust's Heritage Tourism Programme's experienced staff provides fee-for-service assistance in heritage tourism development, management and marketing. The staff also works at the national level to track national trends, provide how to training tools and programmes and advocate for increased national support for heritage tourism. Through years of experience the National Trust's Heritage Tourism Programme has developed five guiding principles for successful and sustainable cultural heritage tourism development as well as four steps for getting started. These principles and steps have been adopted broadly across the United States and are also being used in Canada and several other international destinations. These principles and steps serve as the foundation of all of the work of the Heritage Tourism Programme. What are the benefits of cultural heritage tourism? Studies have consistently shown that cultural heritage travellers stay longer and spend more money than other kinds of travellers. A good cultural heritage tourism improves the quality of life for residents as well as serving visitors.

RELATIONSHIP WITH RURAL HERITAGE

Rural America, which includes some 55 million people and 80 per cent of the nation's landscape, contains a diverse array of historic resources. Rural historic places range from farmsteads and ranches to Main Streets, country stores, schools, churches, mill villages, bridges, scenic byways, fieldstone walls, archeological sites and much more. Increasingly, our rural heritage is threatened. Major economic, cultural and demographic shifts are bringing major changes to rural communities, not all of them welcome. In some rural regions, shrinking agricultural, forestry, mining and manufacturing employment is leading to population loss, neglect and abandonment of historic structures and sites. In high growth areas near cities and resorts, new development is literally consuming the historic rural landscape. The National Trust calls attention to threatened historic sites through its annual list of America's 11-Most Endangered Historic Places. More than 20 rural endangered places have been included on this list since 1988.

The Rural Heritage Collaborative

The National Trust is working with partners at the local, state and national levels to protect our rural heritage and foster "heritage-based" rural development and conservation approaches. The Rural Heritage Collaborative brings together the full range of National Trust resources and expertise, including existing programmes as well as several new initiatives, to help protect our rural heritage and revitalize rural communities.

Factory Farms and America's Rural Heritage

Factory farms are impacting the nation's historic rural landscape. Also known as Concentrated Animal Feeding Operations ("CAFOs"), factory farms use industrial production techniques to raise thousands of animals in one location. These farms affect rural historic places in several ways, the most obvious impact is a highly unpleasant odour. However, there are indirect impacts from factory farms to consider as well. The concentration of livestock operations into large facilities is one of the factors behind the decline in the number of farms nationally, particularly middle-sized family farms. As small and medium-sized producers are forced out of agriculture, historic farms are sold and consolidated and many historic farm structures are abandoned. Historic rural communities and Main Street businesses suffer because factory farms employ fewer people than small farms and typically purchase feed and supplies from sources outside of the community. Learn more about how factory farms are impacting America's rural heritage.

NATIONAL TRUST RESOURCES FOR RURAL HERITAGE PRESERVATION

Small communities must work hard to keep their commercial areas competitive in today's marketplace. The National Trust Main Street Centre is the nation's largest full-service commercial district revitalization organization. Established in 1980, the Centre developed the Main Street Four-Point Approach™, a comprehensive methodology that has been used by over 1,800 communities to revitalize their traditional commercial districts. These local Main Street programmes have created more than 67,000 new businesses and 300,000 new jobs nationwide. The approach, which has been tailored to assist communities with populations as small as 350, focuses the work of local staff and volunteers in four key areas: organization, design, promotion and economic restructuring. The Center offers fee-for-service technical assistance, conferences and workshops, and informational resources to individual Main Street communities as well as state, citywide, and regional coordinating programmes across the country.

Heritage tourism can help attract visitors, boost local pride and foster economic development in rural areas. With more than 15 years of experience working with communities across the country, the National Trust's Heritage Tourism Programme has developed principles for successful and sustainable heritage tourism development and steps for getting started. Additional information about developing, promoting, and managing cultural heritage tourism can be found at culturalheritagetourism.org, a website managed by the National Trust's Heritage Tourism Programme on behalf of Partners in Tourism. This site includes numerous heritage tourism success stories from around the country, including many examples of successful projects in rural communities and regions.

Community and Countryside Workshops

The National Trust's Community and Countryside workshops focus on community revitalization, historic preservation, land use and design issues in rural communities. These two-day workshops offer case studies, illustrated presentations and small group activities for local elected and appointed officials as well as business and community leaders.

- A grant from the W.K. Kellogg Foundation is supporting the National Trust's *Rural Heritage Development Initiative (RHDI)*, a four year demonstration project involving pilot projects in two rural regions: the Arkansas Delta and the Central Kentucky Heartland. Working with local and state partners, the National Trust is seeking to demonstrate the value of heritage-based rural development strategies through these four-year demonstration projects. Download the two videos below to see an overview of the heritage assets and the issues impacting the two pilot regions.
- Grants from the Harvest Foundation and the Public Welfare Foundation are supporting a National Trust rural heritage development effort in Martinsville and surrounding Henry County, Virginia. This work is being led by the National Trust's *Southern Field Office*.
- The National Trust is partnering with the Piedmont Environmental Council and other organizations on the *Journey Through Hallowed Ground* project, which is seeking to implement preservation strategies for the fast-growing Route 15 corridor through the historic landscape of northern Virginia, Maryland, and Pennsylvania, terminating at Gettysburg.

Other Regional Initiatives to save Rural Heritage

- The National Trust's Southern Office is leading the *Rosenwald Schools Initiative*. Between 1917 and 1932, some 5,300 mostly rural schools were built for African American children with funds provided by Julius Rosenwald. Many communities are now seeking ways to adapt these historic structures—no longer used for schools—to serve new needs. The Lowe's Charitable and Educational Foundation is partnering with the National Trust for Historic Preservation to support the rehabilitation and restoration of Rosenwald Schools. *Grant applications must be postmarked by November 30, 2007.*

- The Mountains/Plains Office worked with Preservation North Dakota and the State Historical Society of North Dakota to develop the *Prairie Churches of North Dakota* project, aimed at saving that state's ethnically and architecturally diverse collection of rural churches. With the help of a statewide small grants programme, these rural churches are being rehabilitated for continued use or adapted for new uses, such as performing arts centres and community centers.
- In Maryland, the Southern Field Office, Preservation Maryland, the Maryland Historical Trust and other groups are working to save endangered Tobacco Barns of Southern Maryland. A new grant programme is providing assistance to property owners seeking to repair their Tobacco Barns and adapt them to serve new uses.

Improving Rural Public Policy

Federal agriculture, conservation and rural development policies greatly affect the health and vitality of rural communities and landscapes. The impact of these policies on rural heritage is also significant. The National Trust is seeking greater support for rural heritage in the next Farm Bill, due to be written by Congress in 2007. The National Trust worked with former congressman Jim Leach of Iowa to establish the Main Street/Hope VI housing programme to help fund affordable housing rehabilitation projects in the historic downtowns of communities under 50,000 population.

National Trust Financial Assistance

The National Trust provides financial assistance to preservation projects through the National Preservation Endowment, which includes a range of state, regional and national grant and loan programmes. Information on funds that may be available for rural heritage projects in your area is available through the National Trust Regional Offices, which serve each state.

The National Trust Community Investment Corporation manages several programmes that provide equity investment to real estate projects involving federal and state tax credits. Among these programmes is the Small Deal Fund, which targets projects involving as little as $200,000 in federal tax credits.

Preservation Easements

Historic preservation easements offer one of the most effective legal tools for property owners seeking to permanently protect their historic properties, including those located in rural areas. Easements may also provide significant tax benefits to property owners. An introduction to easements prepared by the National Trust provides additional information about the benefits of preservation easements.

Rural Historic Sites

Among the National Trust's collection of 28 historic sites are several properties that are located in rural areas or have a strong connection to our nation's rural heritage, including:

- Belle Grove Plantation in the Shenendoah Valley near Middletown, Virginia.
- Chesterwood Estate and Museum in Stockbridge, Massachusetts.
- Cooper-Molera Adobe in Monterey, California.
- Drayton Hall outside of Charleston, South Carolina.
- Filoli in Woodside, California.
- The Gaylord Building in Lockport, Illinois.
- James Madison's Montpelier in Montpelier Station, Virginia.
- Lyndhurst in Tarrytown, New York.
- Oatlands in Leesburg, Virginia.
- Shadows-on-the-Teche in New Iberia, Louisiana.

HERITAGE TOURISM IN INDIA: A CASE STUDY

The glorious past of India has ensured that the present and subsequent generations have plenty of historical and cultural heritage to be proud of. The fascinating monuments and heritage sites in the country stand quietly today to retell their story of joy, sorrow, courage and sacrifice before you. Each of the story is so enchanting and singular that you will be left asking for more at the end of each narration. For centuries, people migrating into the rich country, India, with their respective culture and tradition and later mixing with the rituals of the Indians have given birth to a new colour of heritage and culture. This amalgamation of culture have slowly but gradually have enriched the values and faiths of the Indians even further with each sun rise and sun set in the sky. The host country welcomed this huge change with open arms as a result of which the flavour of Hinduism, Buddhism, Islam, Jainism and Christianity floats in the atmosphere of India making it one of the largest secular country of the world where Diwali, Christmas, Eid and Buddha Jayanti are celebrated with equal enthusiasm and exuberance. As one turns the pages of history, the rich heritage of India comes alive with all its fragrance and colour which are still breathing in the heritage forts, palaces, temples and monuments fringed in each and every corner of this multi facet country, India. The splendid architecture, minutely carved motifs, embellished facades of the heritage monuments narrate the immense skill of the craftsmen of the yore which have been fascinating the world for many centuries. If you start counting, you may fail to accommodate all the heritage sites of India in your fingers which have evolved with the passage of time. UNESCO has come up with the mission to protect these treasures which are the finest gifts to world from India so that generations to come feel them as fortunate as we consider ourselves after acquainting with these incredible Indian heritage sites. Be it the exquisite marble inlay work of the Taj Mahal or the titillating sculptures of the Khajuraho Temples or the excellent fusion of science and art in Konark Sun Temple, Indian heritage sites are the manifests to the extremely rich heritage of India. The number of important monuments and sites in India is so great that a single tour to discover the multifarious facets of its wonderful heritage is not enough. Nevertheless, it will give you an admirable glimpse into the Indian history and heritage. At the end of your trip, you will surely develop a huge respect for the Indian heritage while craving for more such tour in the near future.

ANALYSING ECONOMIC IMPACT OF CULTURAL TOURISM INITIATIVES

In the space available for this article, there is not the opportunity to explore all aspects of cultural tourism monitoring and evaluation. In order to focus the discussion, I have chosen to examine the job creation and economic development dimensions of the field given the central role these concerns play in public and private sector resource allocation decision-making. In fact, I have focused my discussion on the use of indicators in the process. Monitoring the impact of visitors on sites, the success of particular forms of conservation treatments, the quality of interpretive techniques, and the effect of cultural tourism initiatives on local communities will have to be explored in other ICOMOS publications or forums.

Many areas of planning and development activity have not had the resources or the interest (often the case) to assess whether plans and policies when implemented have met their goals and objectives. In addition, unintended results have rarely been identified and assessed. This lack of monitoring and assessment is also true of many specialist forms of planning and policy-making such as heritage resource management and cultural tourism. It is fair tc say that based on this lack of monitoring and evaluation, little is learned from plan implementation. The issue of monitoring and evaluation is becoming increasingly important in heritage conservation given the many ambitious claims made concerning the potential of cultural tourism to satisfy a range of cultural and societal goals:

- to provide the resources necessary to pay for the capital and operating expenditures associated with many areas of heritage development and activity;
- to increase public awareness and acceptance of heritage conservation;
- to provide employment and create economic development.

Often claims of the benefits of heritage tourism have been based on anecdotal information or hope and not evidence produced from a scientific assessment process. (Exceptions exist particularly in Alberta where the provincial government has developed sophisticated impact assessment tools). In better financial times it was possible to make claims and not have to back them up. There is no doubt that in these difficult economic times, cultural tourism benefits will have to be well-understood and documented if public and private sector funding is to be allocated for cultural preservation purposes. I would argue that it is essential for the ongoing health of the entire heritage conservation movement that it become more sophisticated in understanding and documenting the benefits and costs of using tourism as an important development tool in meeting the goals of the conservation movement, as well as the larger society. While monitoring in all aspects of conservation is complex, monitoring and evaluation in cultural tourism is especially difficult given the wide range of actors and activities which must be considered. Not only do we have the traditional conservation specialists but in addition, we have entire communities and regions as well as a new series of specialists such as tourism planners, hospitality and tourism management workers, town planners and economists. Each brings his/her particular concerns and methodologies to the exercise. The challenge here is to ensure that the form of assessment evolving is consistent with the needs of all affected by cultural tourism initiatives.

Cultural Tourism Impact Assessment

If we are to truly understand the impacts of cultural tourism we must develop and use tools which will allow the heritage conservation community to learn from its experience, using reliable methods and producing results which are comparable and produce lessons which can serve to influence future practice. The objective of any cultural tourism planning and development process must be to minimize negative impacts and ensure that the benefits are realized in an equitable manner. I recognize the problems associated with doing this but there are approaches which will assist in this impact assessment process.

Cultural Tourism Impacts: The first major issue in assessing cultural tourism has to be a recognition of the wide range of possible impacts which must be considered if a comprehensive understanding of effects are to be understood. These impacts are both direct as well as indirect and have to be seen in local as well as regional terms. Very often the direct economic impact of a development may not be significant but when viewed from an overall community economic perspective can be seen to have significant overall benefits. The nature of these dimensions can be illustrated by looking at both the positive as well as negative effects. There are a number of employment and economic development related potential benefits of cultural tourism. They include:

(*i*) increased resources for the protection and conservation of natural and cultural heritage resources.
(*ii*) increased income from tourism expenditures.
(*iii*) increased induced income from tourism expenditures.
(*iv*) new employment opportunities.
(*v*) new induced employment opportunities.
(*vi*) increased tax base.
(*vii*) increased civic pride leading to a better environment for.
(*viii*) economic development.
(*ix*) improved infrastructure.
(*x*) revival of local traditions and the associated income.
(*xi*) producing potential of local people.
(*xii*) development of local handicrafts.
(*xiii*) increased community visibility leading to other economic development opportunities.

There are also a number of potential costs/disadvantages:

(*i*) much of tourism employment is seasonal in nature.
(*ii*) employment in this field is often low paying.
(*iii*) tourism development can produce inflation.
(*iv*) if not properly planned for and managed, tourism.
(*v*) development can lead to increased costs (land, housing, food, services).
(*vi*) pollution, increased crime and increased.
(*vii*) traffic/congestion can lower the attractiveness of a community or region for investors.
(*viii*) increased taxes.

(*ix*) not authentic development which can reduce the attractiveness of an area as a tourism destination.

Measuring Cultural Tourism Impacts vs. Tourism in General: One of the difficulties in assessing the impacts of cultural tourism lies in the fact that it is but one form of tourism which many visitors participate in when they travel. Forms of tourism may include the following activity based on a series of demographic as well as motivational factors: aboriginal, ecotourism, sports related (skiing, swimming etc.), adventure, game/hunting, shopping, leisure, camping, and business associated travel activities conferences. Isolating the specific cultural dimensions of much of tourism is a challenge especially when one is considering local as well as regional economies and employment structures.

Job Creation vs. The Overall Local Economy: While job creation must be seen as an important objective, concern for the overall local economy must also be a major concern. This implies that jobs and economic benefits may be realized from a number of sources. It may also mean that jobs are created as the result of entrepreneurial activity as well as community initiative (i.e. cooperatives, development corporations, training opportunities as well as local support for tourism initiatives through the provision of infrastructure). Measuring the economic impact and job creation activities of cultural tourism must be carried out in an integrated fashion, taking into account direct and indirect job creation as well as the economic well-being of the community (taxes, infrastructure development and provision, resources for education, etc.). There are techniques for estimating the impact of tourism which include such factors as tourism multiplier models, employment multipliers, input-output analysis, and the measurement of direct, induced, and indirect impacts.

Accuracy of Assessing Job Creation: While it may be possible to calculate with a level of certainty, the job potential of some areas of economic activity, the calculation of possible employment levels related to cultural tourism is difficult, at least in conventional terms. As discussed earlier, many employment opportunities may be seasonal and adjuncts to other forms of income generation. This situation in no way diminishes the importance of the job and income generation, but rather calls for other measurement tools and techniques.

Employment and Business Development Opportunities

In order to understand the nature of possible impacts, it is important to acknowledge that employment and business development opportunities exist in a number of areas within the tourism sector. Since monitoring and evaluation are forward looking there will be a need to scan and understand the role of cultural tourism in all these areas. These employment opportunities include the following:

Public Sector: Opportunities exist in the public sector in tourism planning and management. Planning and management are critical areas for ensuring successful tourism initiatives. This is a sector of the tourism industry which often does not receive sufficient attention. Control, facilitation, and regulation of the environment are essential to the industry and trained professionals and officials (e.g. municipal officers, town managers, tourist information officers, economic development officers, main street coordinators, planners).

Hospitality Sector: This sector is the best understood within the industry. It requires a wide range of skills and knowledge including personnel for the accommodation sector (hotels, motels, B & Bs) as well as restaurants. The major challenge is to develop the managerial capacity within the community as opposed to importing skills and knowledge.

Service Sector: Guided tours, equipment rentals, and maintenance facilities offer significant opportunities. For many rural areas, little effort has been made to offer these services in a proactive manner. Guided tours, such as walking, cycling, hiking, back-country tripping, cross-country ski trips, and canoe and boat trips, offer a means for encouraging the tourist to spend a longer period of time in an area.

Attractions Management: Cultural experiences and activities are also important trends in tourism. The development of ventures which involve traditional activities, such as food, dance, music, festivals, plays, and re-enactments can be important attractions. Historic sites, museums, and museum villages require trained interpreters, site managers, designers and crafts people.

Arts and Handicrafts: The development of cottage industries for arts and handicrafts is an important source of full or part-time employment.

Working Holidays: Working holidays on farms and in fishing villages have great potential. Farm holidays have been developed and have achieved some success in Ontario, Quebec and the Prairie provinces. "Living on the Land" with an Aboriginal family—a cultural day or week long experience, such as attending a fishing camp in the Arctic—offers opportunities for unique experiences. A tour company in Inuvik handles the booking of tours for cultural day tours to be spent with a local family in Tuktoyatuk. The day includes a tour of Tuktoyatuk and stories of local experiences as well as a traditional meal. The company also provides links with other operators offering river tours, visits to a reindeer station, and nature tours. It is important to understand that there are a number of obstacles to creating employment related to cultural tourism. These include: the market and its receptivity to the heritage attractions; community acceptance of tourism and its treatment of tourists; the need to meet environmental standards and respect carrying capacities; the lack of integration within the industry in general, as well as in the heritage industry, in particular governmental and institutional roadblocks both in terms of regulation as well as facilitation, and the lack of trained personnel in a wide range of tourism areas.

Indicators in Cultural Tourism Monitoring

One of the important first steps in ensuring quality monitoring and evaluation in cultural tourism is to establish indicators which can be used to measure success and failures. Given the interdisciplinary and wide ranging impacts of cultural tourism, it is impossible to deal with all variables and therefore reliable indicators will help the assessment process. I would like to extract a few principles for the purpose of this article. Some of the factors to be considered in developing and using indicators include:

- (*i*) Given the large number of factors that exist, the challenge is to select a few indicators for development.
- (*ii*) It is important to carefully select indicators which will have an important impact on future resource allocations.
- (*iii*) The development and use of indicators can be costly and time consuming. A commitment must be made early on in the process "to stay the course". The process should

then be carefully assessed in order to ensure that the information being produced is accurate and useful in future decision-making.

(*iv*) Not all indicators are of equal weight. The use of a weighting system must be instituted.

(*v*) The process of assessing community economic impacts created by cultural tourism will produce conflicting assessment. The assessment process must recognize the need to both consider and balance these conflicts.

(*vi*) For the indicators process to be accepted by a range of actors within the conservation process, the data must be of use in several different situations. For example, data on the characteristics of visitors to a site may be used for assessing economic impact for refining an interpretive programme and to guide the development of a strategic planning process.

The development of indicators will have to be undertaken as a serious first step in being able to make the case for the role that cultural tourism plays in both heritage conservation, as well as community economic development.

This indicator design process must be followed by an agreement on the need to collect and share the data in order to allow collective experiences to guide practice and make the case for investment in cultural tourism. The use of indicator data and its dissemination will not always demonstrate the effectiveness of cultural tourism in economic development since situations will exist where investment cannot be seen to be justified on strictly job and wealth creation grounds. In these situations a full impact assessment might demonstrate other societal and heritage conservation benefits. For the assessment process to have any influence, it must be future oriented and tied into the plan making and policy process. It must include the skills and knowledge of other specialists not normally seen as crucial to the conservation world. The impact process will require the following:

(*a*) an improved planning and management development approach which looks at the past and requires that ongoing assessment be seen as essential to conservation;

(*b*) coordination and cooperation among a wide range of specialists;

(*c*) the training of existing and future conservation personnel in monitoring techniques.

The ICOMOS Canada Cultural Tourism Committee, in concert with other committees, must begin to assist the conservation community in developing a full range of indicators and monitoring techniques which are of immediate use as well as capable of producing comparable data sets which can be used in heritage development and planning exercises in other parts of the country as an important first step.

CULTURAL TOURISM: A CASE STUDY

Sound bytes and simplicity. These concepts pervade our "modern" cognitive processing and decision-making. Society seems to demand quick answers and simple solutions to almost everything. Often the media reinforces these expectations. Environmental, social and political issues are presented in brief snippets through "headline news" formats; promotions for upcoming news stories are almost as long as the news stories themselves. A long, in-depth news story is presented in a 20-minute segment that, when time is removed for commercial advertising, is only about 13 minutes. Actions and solutions are considered "right or wrong", "good or bad", "black or white"... with little room for shades of gray or complexity. Even complex issues around which political decisions are made are reduced to "simple" issues as portrayed in political advertising. When time is brief and attention superficial, it is impossible to rely on processing of thoughtful, analytical arguments and weighing of multiple, interacting variables. Thus, political pundits use image association and value-based arguments, relying on the strength of strongly held values rather than thoughtful analysis. The same is true for commercial advertising. Ads rely on pulling at heart strings to get people to untie their purse strings.

So what does this have to do with economic impact assessment for cultural tourism? Investment, development and policy decisions frequently are driven by their potential for economic benefit. No matter how socially or educationally positive the benefits of an effort, they may receive little support unless they also can be justified financially. In recent years, educational facilities, arts organizations, and other cultural institutions have realized that they no longer will be supported automatically for their "good works" unless they also show positive economic benefits. Consequently, performing arts, museums, historic sites and other cultural institutions have commissioned numerous economic impact studies to demonstrate their value in terms understandable by legislators, community and economic development authorities, and other entities responsible for allocating increasingly limited resources. (America for the Arts 2002; Clarion Associates 2002; Lane 2001; National Governors Association 2001; Stronge 2000; TIA 2001, 2003). Having limited or no training in business or economics, many are interested in a high dollar value "outcome" yet are unaware of or unconcerned with how the number is derived.

Numerous studies link economic benefits with tourism revenues that, often viewed as "new money" to a community or state, provide additional justification to support investment in arts and culture. Recent literature is full of reports indicating that cultural tourism is growing and that cultural tourists spend more, stay longer, and tend to stay at hotels rather than campgrounds or with friends/family more than do "general" tourists. Consequently, these tourists would be deemed "desirable" in terms of the economic contribution to the state or a region. However, calculating impacts is dependent on several assumptions—about the accuracy of visitation data, about which museum visitors/users to include in analysis, about which expenditures during a tourist trip are attributed to cultural institutions and the heritage experience (beyond direct expenditures at a cultural site), about inclusion of a site's operational expenses, multiplier effects, and numerous other factors. Using different assumptions results in substantially different outcomes. Also, results and models based on data aggregated at a state-wide level cannot be applied directly to individual communities or institutions. Further complicating the impact scenario are the differences between individual museums, including factors such as differences in physical size, annual budget, "mission mix", annual visitation, and nature of the site (mix of land, infrastructure, historic structure/fabric, artifacts/ archives, etc.). Using Michigan's museum-based visits as a context, this paper explores the challenges of reporting and using economic impact data, specifically as related to heritage tourism. While a brief summary of the study is presented, the focus of this paper is on the challenges of estimating, interpreting and using economic impact data. Definitional and contextual challenges are incorporated throughout. The original impetus for the study was to measure the importance and impact of cultural/heritage tourism (hereafter labelled "heritage tourism") to the state of Michigan, in part to justify investment in and support for Michigan's involvement in heritage tourism, a travel market segment recognized nationally and internationally as significant (TIA 2003). Despite a long-held perception of Michigan as primarily a woods-and-water-based outdoor recreation mecca, the state also contains many sites of national, state and local historic and cultural significance. Heritage attractions include facilities and special events celebrating the state's maritime, mining, agricultural, environmental, automotive, Native American, ethnic and other heritages. Most historic sites and events associated with these heritages are tourist attractions. In fact, one can argue that heritage and culture are part of most tourism activity in Michigan and elsewhere. Additionally, tourism itself and tourist destinations are integral parts of the State's history and culture. Thus, it is difficult to establish boundaries around the broad notion of heritage/ cultural tourism. This presents the first major challenge in identifying and isolating economic impacts associated specifically with heritage tourism. Because economic impact analysis requires a reasonably clear definition of the activity generating the impacts, the complex and intertwining nature of tourism experiences and sites make it challenging to isolate what is "heritage or culture" from other types or components of trips. Thus, for this study, it was necessary to narrow the context and operationalize a definition and component of the travel experience for conducting a study. Museums and their associated programmes constitute a tangible set of facilities and activities. Museums represent many of the state's major heritage themes and, in many cases, are focal points for tourism activity related to these themes. Museums, therefore, provide a logical starting point for better documenting the size and economic importance of heritage tourism in the state. Most importantly for this study, museums provide a concrete sampling frame to identify organizations and visitors/trips that clearly fall within the scope of heritage tourism. One caveat: in choosing to focus on museums, only one portion of heritage tourism is documented. This study does not cover impacts associated with special events and community festivals, performing arts, or a host of historical sites and attractions that are not formally associated with a "museum." To the extent that visits to such sites are included in trips that include at least one museum visit, trip spending associated with these other sites is partially captured.

Methods

To gather both visitor spending data and operational expenditures contributing to local and state economies, two separate surveys, targeting different audiences, were used in this study. The first was a census of museum administrators (providers). The second was a visitor survey conducted of a sample of museum visitors at 35 selected museums across Michigan during June through September 2002. Museums, for this study, were identified based on the American Association of Museum's (AAM) broad definition that includes any facility having at least one physical site and offering programmes and services to visitors. Facility types included: general interest museums, history museums, natural history museums, science museums, children's museums, art museums, historic sites and buildings, nature centres, botanical gardens, zoos, aquariums, planetariums and special interest museums such as maritime museums, lighthouses, historic ships, automobile and railroad museums.

Administrator Survey

The survey of museum administrators, sent to 470 museums, was designed to gather visitation and budget data to be used in estimating the overall volume of museum visits, and to profile annual operating budgets, levels of employment, and revenue sources of Michigan museums. A six-page instrument was developed to be consistent with the 1996 MMA administrator survey. Additional items about tourism (tourism season[s], tourist visitation patterns, and museum's relationship with tourists/ tourism) and budget/economic issues were added to this instrument. Using a modified Dillman approach, museums received the original survey letter and instrument, a reminder postcard, reminder letter and duplicate survey, as needed. Administrators could complete the hard copy survey or respond on line, using a provided code number.

Visitor Survey

The survey of museum visitors gathered demographic and travel party information, trip characteristics and spending data. Specific information needed for the economic analysis included primary trip purpose, zip code origin of visitors (to classify as local or not, based on travel more or less than 50 miles one way), whether a day or overnight trip, lodging type for overnight trips, and spending by the travel party within 30 miles of the museum. Museum visitors were contacted at museums where they completed a short on-site survey, and were invited to complete a more comprehensive post-trip survey by mail or on the web. This survey gathered detailed spending and other information after visitors completed their trips. Ultimately, the museum visitor sample was taken from 35 "large" and "medium" museums across Michigan, representing a range of geographic locations and museum types. Based on a planned sampling strategy unique to each site, visitors were contacted on dates selected to represent weekend and weekday visitors and different times of day. To serve as a contact site, the museum had to be willing to participate, have staff to conduct surveys, offer an incentive for study participation, and serve enough visitors to obtain an on-site sample efficiently. "Small" museums were not included because (1) they are assumed to have minimal economic impact, and (2) it was unlikely that they would have the staff or resources to conduct the on-site surveys. Visitors not responding to the initial "long" survey were sent reminders, via mail or email, based on their chosen response mode.

Economic Impact Analysis

Economic estimates for visitor spending are produced using the Michigan Tourism Economic Impact Model (MITEIM). Three major inputs to the model are (Stynes, 2000):

1. Number of visits divided into trip type segments (day or overnight; local or tourist; type of lodging if overnight).

Trip type segments are defined from the museum visitor survey based on (1) whether or not the visitor lives within 50 miles of the museum (local visitors), (2) if they are staying overnight away from home on the trip, and (3) the type of lodging. These segments help define distinct markets and also explain differences in spending. Formally, the four museum trip type segments are defined as follows:

(a) *Local Day Trips*: Trips for which visitors travelled less than 50 miles and did not stay overnight away from home on the trip.

(b) *Non-local Day Trips*: Trips for which visitors travelled more than 50 miles from home but did not stay overnight in the local area (within 30 miles of the museum). This segment includes those whose primary destination was the museum as well as some visitors stopping en route to other destinations or as a side trip.

(c) *Overnight Hotel Trips*: Trips for which visitors stayed in hotels, motels, cabins or B&B's within 30 miles of the museum.

(d) *Other Overnight Trips*: Trips for which overnight visitors stayed in campgrounds, with friends and relatives, at owned seasonal homes or other types of lodging within 30 miles of the museum.

Visitors in the non-local day trip and the two overnight trip segments are considered "tourists".

2. Trip spending averages for each segment.
3. Economic multipliers for the state and local region.

These inputs were estimated from data gathered in the visitor and museum administrator surveys. The visitor survey identifies the mix of trip types/segments and provides the data to estimate spending averages. The administrator survey was used to estimate total museum visits in 2001 (used to extrapolate spending to all visitors) and also to estimate museum employment, revenues and operating expenses (used to estimate impacts of museum operations). Multipliers were taken from the MITEIM model, which was updated to 2000 using recent IMPLAN data for Michigan. Economic ratios (jobs to sales, income to sales) specific to Michigan museums were estimated from the administrator survey and substituted for more generic ones typically used in the MITEIM model. Spending profiles for each segment were created by estimating the average spending within 13 spending categories for visitors falling into each trip type segment. Spending was first estimated on a party trip basis and then converted to a party day/night basis by dividing by the length of stay in the area.

Results

Response Rates, Demographics and Trip Characteristics: Forty-six per cent of the museum administrators responded to the survey (182 museums). A total of 6,417 museum visitors were contacted at cooperating museums. Sixty per cent of these visitors agreed to participate in the post-trip survey and 34 per cent of those agreeing actually completed the post-trip survey. Potential non-response bias in the visitor survey was assessed by comparing the on-site sample with those completing the post-trip survey. No significant differences were observed between the two groups in terms of trip purposes, but there were some differences in trip types. Local visitors were somewhat less likely to respond to the post-trip survey while visitors on overnight trips are over-represented in the post-trip sample. Because visitors on overnight trips spend considerably more than local visitors, spending estimates would be biased upward, if not adjusted for. Museum visitors were fairly evenly distributed across age groups, sixty per cent had household incomes between $25,000 and $75,000, three quarters had some college education or higher, and ninety per cent were White/ Caucasian. Almost one-fourth of museum visitors were retired. Only general admission adult visitors (age 18 or older) were sampled, so these statistics exclude visitors who were part of organized school or adult groups and visitors to most special events. Museum visitors were similar to the Michigan population as a whole with respect to age, but included fewer minorities. However, they had higher levels of education and income. About two-thirds of the sample were women. There were no significant differences in demographic characteristics across trip types. About half of the museum visitors came from within 50 miles of the museum. Forty-one per cent of the trips involved an overnight stay in the local area. Two-thirds of the trips were made primarily to visit the museum where the visitor was sampled, nineteen per cent of respondents were visiting the community more generally, 8 per cent were visiting friends and relatives, and 6 per cent of trips were for other reasons. Day trips were more likely to be primarily to visit the museum; 81 per cent of local day trips and 77 per cent of non-local day trips were made primarily to visit the museum. Thirty-eight per cent of overnight trips were made principally to visit the museum. The average party size for museum visitors was about three persons across all regions and segments. The average length of stay in the community was 2.4 nights for hotel visitors and 3.4 nights for visitors staying in other types of lodging.

Economic Impacts: Spending within 30 miles of the museum was itemized in 13 categories, grouped by expenditures inside the museum and those in the community. Spending averages were first computed on a party trip basis for each segment and then converted to a per day/night basis. Local day visitors and non-local day visitors spent $49 and $70 per party per trip, respectively, in the local community (Table 2.1). Non-local day visitors spent more on shopping, restaurant meals, and gas and oil than day visitors. Overnight visitors staying in hotels spent $569 per party per trip, $215 more than overnight visitors staying in other types of lodging. Almost half of the expenses of visitors in hotels was for lodging. Overnight visitors spent about $32 per party inside the museum compared to about $21 per party for day visitors. Spending averages were converted to a party day basis by dividing party trip spending by the average length of stay. Hotel visitors spent $237 per party per day in the local community, mainly lodging expenses $108, restaurants $49, and shopping (including gift shop in the museum) $33. Other overnight visitors spent $104 per party per day in the community, mainly on shopping, camping fees and restaurants. Interestingly, spending averages based on visitor data differ from those based on spending reported by museum administrators. The original in-museum spending averages (visitor reports) when applied to visitation numbers yield total museum revenues from both general admissions and gift shop sales that are higher than corresponding revenue figures reported by museum administrators. This is probably due in part to the selection of "large" and "medium" museums for contacting visitors when about 3/4 of all Michigan museums are "small." Thus, we assume that the museums where visitors were sampled over-represent those having higher admission fees, more extensive gift shops and other spending opportunities inside the museum. Another possible contributing factor is the widespread use of inaccurate methods for determining annual visitation, especially by small museums (e.g., voluntary sign-in, clicker-counts, guesstimates). The in-museum spending averages were adjusted to 71 per cent of the sample average to balance the state-wide estimates with reported museum revenues.

Table 2.1: Visitor Spending within 30 Miles of the Museum by Lodging Segment ($ Per Party Per Trip, Except as Noted)

Spending Category	*Day Trips*		*Overnight Trips*	
	Local	*Non-local*	*Hotel*	*Others*
Inside the Museum:				
Museum or exhibit admission	9.31	10.22	14.31	16.77
Gift shop or snack bar	8.36	13.01	14.70	15.22
All other expenses	1.24	1.79	2.19	2.29
Total in Museum	**18.90**	**25.01**	**31.20**	**34.26**
In the Community:				
Lodging	0.00	0.00	259.47	79.01
Restaurants and bars	12.51	15.31	118.04	75.66
Grocery and take-out food	1.72	3.14	12.30	32.41
Gas and oil	4.68	9.51	34.41	40.09
Other transportation	0.70	1.52	18.32	15.99
Admissions to other museums	1.08	1.28	7.66	9.38
Other admissions	1.18	1.18	8.62	6.27
Shopping	7.81	11.37	64.14	50.58
Casino gaming	0.00	1.57	8.99	5.83
All other expenses	0.23	0.09	5.37	3.88
Total in Community	**29.91**	**44.94**	**537.31**	**319.10**
Grand Total within 30 Miles (per party per trip)	48.81	69.95	568.51	353.36
Per cent of spending inside the museum	39%	36%	5%	10%
Number of cases	406.00	198.00	281.00	197.00
Grand Total within 30 Miles (per party per day/night)	48.81	69.95	236.88	103.93

As indicated in the "introduction," economic impact estimates can vary based on the assumptions used. To illustrate, three different scenarios—based on differing sets of assumptions—were calculated using study data and extrapolating to all museums in Michigan, based on reported 2001 annual visitation by admissions-paying general visitors. The three scenarios use different components of visitor spending and are based on different assumptions about which visitors to include and about how much of the spending outside the museums is attributable to the "heritage" portion of the trip:

Scenario A : All trip spending for all trips (local and non-local, day and overnight) that included a museum visit.

Scenario B : All spending for trips for which visiting the museum was indicated as the "primary purpose" + all in-museum spending for "non-primary purpose" trips + 25 per cent of non-museum spending for "non-primary" trips.

Scenario C : Scenario B—local visitor spending outside museum.

Based on these scenarios, the impacts ranged from $219 million to $733 million. Assuming the basic equation for calculating economic impact is [Economic Impact = # Visits * Spending * Multipliers], the proportional difference for spending at Michigan museums would be: Scenario A: $100; Scenario B: $50; Scenario C: $46. An additional $625 million is contributed statewide to local economies by the museums' operations (in salaries, direct spending, and value added). This additional contribution was estimated using financial and employment data from the survey of museum administrators. Museum revenue, operating budget and employment profiles were estimated from 182 museums responding, though not all museums completed the financial information. Operating budget data was completed by 128 museums, 90 museums reported revenue information, and 122 reported the number of paid employees. Because museum sizes, annual budgets and staff wages range widely (representing varying mixes of paid/unpaid and full-time/part-time/seasonal staff), six museum size categories were used to extrapolate economic impact figures to all state museums. Additionally, revenue sources are variable across, as well as within, museum size categories. Smaller museums rely more on membership fees, gifts, and grants while larger museums generate more revenue from one or more of admissions, endowments or government sources, further confounding the "impact" picture. Across all museums in Michigan, about one third (32 per cent) of museum operations are supported by visitor spending in the form of general admissions, special tickets, and gift shop and food sales. In estimating economic impacts of museums, we therefore count 68 per cent of museum operating expenses as being in addition to the impacts of visitor spending presented in Scenarios A-C above.

Discussion: Complexities in Estimating Economic Impacts

Even in the simplified presentation of results above, some of the complexities and challenges of estimating economic impacts of heritage tourism begin to appear. Complexities arise out of (1) definitional challenges, (2) variability in museum size, visitation, structure, budget and income sources, (3) uncertainties about visitor counts, (4) assumptions and estimates for extrapolating to all museums, (5) assumptions about what portions of trip spending to attribute to heritage tourism, (6) complexities and assumptions used in calculating economic impacts, (7) differences between economic impact and economic significance, and (8) differences in multiplier effects statewide versus in different parts of the state and individual communities.

Definitions: Simply defining what is heritage and what is culture provides fodder for an entire discussion paper. Culture to some is restricted to "high" culture—the arts, both performing and visual. Heritage, to some, is restricted either to "history" or to people of different ethnicities. Broader definitions include anything that influences lifeways and lifestyles of humans in any community, historically and in the present, which can include the arts, food, labour, sports, recreation and natural resources. Regardless of the operational or scholarly definition selected by researchers, people being surveyed typically have a wide range of personal definitions that influence their responses if the terms "culture" or "heritage" are used in the survey instrument to solicit responses.

Museum Differences: So many factors about museum structure, mission and function influence the heritage/cultural tourism-based contributions to the local or state economy. Some museums have missions focussed primarily on serving the local community; others are developed as attractions to serve national and global visitors. Some museums focus on research and archival collections; others focus on education and visitor services. Some protect resources and tell stories of local significance, others of national or global significance. Some museums are individual sites; others are systems that might have multiple sites of different kinds throughout the state. Depending on the type and number of structures, historic buildings and artifacts, financial demands for resource management vary widely. Some museums charge admission fees, others charge only for special exhibits or events, others charge no fees; still others are open only by appointment. Some target the general public, others service primarily school and other youth groups. Some promote programmes and services broadly; others do not advertise at all. These and other factors greatly influence the economic impacts that can, and should, be attributed to heritage tourism.

Visitor Count Methods and Extrapolating: As determined in a 1996 study (Michigan Museums Association, 1998) and reconfirmed in this study, very few museums have reliable and consistent methods for determining visitor counts; these are primarily the large museums that charge admission, have a clear fee structure and registration procedures for facility use, and target tourists as part of their mission. The vast majority (three quarters) are small, have relatively low visitation, and have limited personnel (often only or mostly unpaid). Accurately counting visitors is a low priority. Visitor count strategies include reliance on automated systems (footpads or traffic counters that count people and vehicles [that do not distinguish between staff, service visitors, tourists, local visitors], voluntary visitor sign-in, clicker counts, and "guesstimates"). When spending data from surveys is extrapolated to all museums, and the visitor counts upon which these extrapolated results are based are faulty, those inaccuracies are reflected in the estimates of economic impacts. Further, many museums that do have accurate visitor counts do not differentiate between local visitors and tourists.

Attributions to Heritage Tourism: Some of the challenges associated with attributing visitor spending and economic impacts specifically to heritage tourism are affected by the problems discussed in the "definitions" section. Other challenges are illustrated by the discussion of the three scenarios presented in the results section. The kinds of spending intended to be captured in the 25 per cent of non-museum spending for "non-primary" trips (an expert opinion-based estimated percentage itself) include spending for heritage-based transportation (e.g., trolleys, horse-drawn carriages, sleighs, tandem bicycles), local heritage crafts sold outside of museums, and food and lodging at adaptively re-used historic structures. In addition to the "estimated" nature of this calculation, other spending related to heritage may not be captured. This includes (1) tourism influenced by the general attractiveness of the community or region due to preservation of historic districts, redevelopment of historic waterfronts, protection of heritage landscapes; (2) spending associated with longer stays induced by non-fee-based experiences such as heritage walking tours (e.g., architecture, history theme-based), linear parks and trails, and outdoor interpretive exhibits; (3) spending at museums other than where survey respondents were contacted; (4) "shopping" and other spending occurring at adaptively re-used historic structures (e.g., factories, warehouses) converted to mixed use structures that include shopping/lodging/restaurants; (5) spending related to agricultural or natural resource-based heritage experiences. One alternative to the researcher making assumptions about what spending to attribute to heritage tourism is to ask the visitor what portion of their trip spending they attribute to the cultural/heritage portion of the travel experience. In fact, this question was asked in this study. However, the estimates based on visitor assessments of their heritage-based spending differed from those calculated in Scenarios A, B and C. This is assumed to result from the widely variable personal interpretations of what visitors consider to be cultural or heritage. Thus, for this study, we relied more on visitor indications of "primary trip purpose." However, it is expected that there is also variability among visitors about how their trip motive may impact spending related to heritage or cultural components of their trip. Finally, most individuals and travel parties participate in a variety of activities and experiences during any trip. Determining which portion of total trip spending to attribute to various "tourism types" will be influenced by the number of different activities as well as the intensity or duration of engagement in each. To illustrate the problems of not apportioning the attributions, assume a single vacationing family golfs on one day, charters a fishing trip the next day, goes on a dinner cruise one evening, spends the next day shopping at heritage as well as modern stores, and visits a museum. Additionally, they take lodging one night at a historic B&B, one night aboard a historic ship, and one night at a chain motel. Another evening is spent at the local outdoor theatre production, followed by a walk along the waterfront boardwalk. On two days, the parents let the children spend their time at the beach and a nearby water fun park. If that family were surveyed for several different tourism studies – golfing, boating, fishing, water-based recreation, heritage/culture – and all trip spending was used to calculate their economic impact on the community for each trip type, those expenditures could be counted as many as five times... exaggerating the impact. Furthermore, some travel experiences may be blended to such an extent that activities cannot be separated. For example, a golf resort may be developed on a historic tourism site, extensively using historic structures and facilities (perhaps even the golf course itself). Historic tourism experiences may be the basis for the modern experience. How would such a trip's economic impacts be attributed? Attribution challenges exist also in economic contributions other than direct spending and associated multipliers based on tourist spending. Development of historic districts, restoration or redevelopment of waterfronts, renovation and expansion of museums provide benefits to both the community and to tourists. Future programmes and facilities may serve both locals and tourists. Spending (for example, by museums) for water, electricity, janitorial services and other maintenance, as well as for purchase of supplies and wages for staff, supports provision of programmes and services for both residents and tourists. Various methods could be used for deciding how to attribute portions of the expenditures to tourism, but regardless of what method is used, the assumptions and guidelines are rarely questioned by those interested in "the big economic impact number."

Economic Impact vs. Economic Significance: Another source of potential confusion for users of study results is the difference between economic impacts and economic significance. Economic *significance* usually reflects *all* spending by people engaged in an activity (in this case, visits to museums), both local residents and tourists. In this study, estimates are first derived from all museum visitor spending (Scenario A) and then just the impacts directly attributed to museums plus a portion of other spending attributed to the heritage experience (Scenario B). Impacts are reported in terms of sales, personal income, jobs and value added, with direct effects itemized by sector and secondary effects reported in the aggregate. Direct effects include the sales, jobs and income in those businesses directly selling to museum visitors. Secondary effects cover sales, jobs and income from so-called "multiplier effects" resulting from economic activity in backward linked industries and household spending induced by the income received from employees in directly or indirectly affected businesses. Economic *impacts*, on the other hand, measure only the changes in spending as a result of a particular activity being available or not (in this case, a community with or without a museum), specifically as a result of new dollars coming into a region from non-local visitors attracted to the facility (e.g., museum). Scenario C more closely reflects this condition, as spending by local visitors is removed. If an existing museum were to leave a community, all spending associated with that facility would be gone, not just the impacts from tourist spending. Another consideration is that some spending— by both residents and tourists, assuming other attractions are available to tourists in the community—could simply be redirected to other places and experiences. It is difficult to determine how much of this would be spent in the community or redirected outside the region/community.

Multiplier Effects and Scope of Application: Multiplier effects will be larger when assessing impacts on the state economy than when assessing impacts on local areas. Thus, a standard multiplier for a specific sector based on statewide data cannot be applied to a smaller region, an individual community, or a single museum or cultural/heritage site. Further, an increase in tourism spending in "community A"—for example, as a result of creation of a new cultural or heritage attraction—may be a result of attracting tourists who might previously have gone to "community B". Thus, economic benefits to "community A" would increase, but the impact or contribution to the state's economy might go unchanged. Therefore, it is important to recognize and acknowledge the scale of analysis (site, local, regional, state) desired. If economic impact or significance information is to be used in planning (statewide cultural tourism, community development, or site planning), the purpose and use should be identified at the outset. The first consideration is the scale to which the analysis will be applied. Second, a decision should be made about whether the economic impact analysis will be used to estimate changes in economic activity (sales, jobs, income) or to identify impacts as a result of some action (development, policy, marketing and management). Finally, monitoring and follow-up research should be conducted to determine if the estimates (and assumptions upon which they were made) are valid.

Beyond Economic Impacts: Finally, it should be remembered that heritage, culture, the arts, museums and related facilities and services contribute in many ways in addition to economic. While economic benefits do accrue from presence of cultural and heritage sites available to tourists, they should not be the only ones valued. Preservation of history and heritage, education, facilitating discussion about social and environmental issues, and enhancement of quality of life all are legitimate benefits of heritage institutions and experiences. Not all museums and other heritage institutions will contribute in the same ways and to the same economic extent. Some may contribute more effectively to the economic portion of the contribution equation when clustered or packaged or partnered with other organizations and experiences (for both locals and tourists). Recommendations for proper use of economic impact analyses include: (1) use as part of the planning process; (2) identify the region, scope and purpose of the analysis before collecting data; and (3) balance the economic benefits with other benefits and contributions. Finally, remember that both residents and tourists accrue benefits from tourism-based development, and that enhanced economic impacts usually are associated with other types of impacts — to community social structure, the environment, the infrastructure, tax base and structure, traffic, etc. — which should be balanced with potential economic benefits.

3

Cultural and Heritage Tourism: Principles, Guidelines, Toolkit and Resource Manual

CULTURAL AND HERITAGE TOURISM

History and culture provide a key opportunity for travel promoters and planners. The educational experience from heritage tourism can be partnered with other tourist attractions. The National Trust for Historic Preservation identified five principles to guide the combining heritage and tourism: Collaborate; find the fit between a community or region and tourism; make sites and programmes come alive; focus on authenticity and quality of experience; and preserve and protect resource.

Cultural heritage tourism means travelling to experience the places and activities that authentically represent the stories and people of the past and present. It includes irreplaceable historic, cultural and natural resources.

Tourism is big business. In 2004, travel and tourism directly contributed $600 billion to the U.S. economy. Travel and tourism directly employs more than 7.3 million people and creates a payroll income of $162 billion and tax revenues of $100 billion for federal, state and local governments.

In addition to creating new jobs, new business and higher property values, well-managed tourism improves the quality of life and builds community pride. According to a 2003 national research study (*The Historic/Cultural Traveller* by the Travel Industry Association and *Smithsonian Magazine*) 81 per cent (118 million) U.S. adults who travelled in 2002 were considered cultural heritage travellers. These travellers included historical or cultural activities on almost 217 million person trips last year, up 13 per cent from 192 million in 1996. Visitors to historic sites and cultural attractions stay longer and spend more money than other kinds of tourists. Cultural and heritage visitors spend, on average, $623 per trip compared to $457 for all U.S. travellers excluding the cost of transportation. 30 per cent of cultural heritage travellers report that their destination choice was influenced by a specific historic or cultural event or activity. (*Source:* 2003 *The Historic/Cultural Traveller, TIA*). Perhaps the biggest benefits of cultural heritage tourism, though, are diversification of local economies and preservation of a community's unique character.

One challenge is ensuring that tourism does not destroy the very heritage that attracts visitors in the first place. Furthermore, tourism is a competitive, sophisticated, fast-changing industry that presents its own challenges. It is generally a clean industry: no smokestacks or dangerous chemicals. But it does put demands on the infrastructure — on roads, airport, water supplies and public services like police and fire protection.

By working in local communities across the country over the past decade, the National Trust has developed five guiding principles to create a sustainable cultural heritage tourism programme.

1. Collaborate.
2. Find the fit between a community and tourism.
3. Make sites and programmes come alive.
4. Focus on quality and authenticity.
5. Preserve and protect resources.

The Heritage Tourism Programme provides technical assistance in strategic planning, preservation, tourism development, interpretation and marketing on a fee-for-service basis. The Heritage Tourism Programme has also developed a series of "how-to" publications and programmes to help individuals and organizations developing cultural heritage tourism programmes.

To help communities, regions, and states develop or enhance cultural heritage tourism activities, the National Trust has developed a series of publications and products.

Make the most of your opportunities for cultural heritage tourism by following the National Trust for Historic Preservation's five basic principles. Follow these principles and you'll avoid many difficulties that could otherwise arise when culture, heritage and tourism become partners. Much more can be accomplished by working together than by working alone. Successful cultural heritage tourism programmes bring together partners who may not have worked together in the past. Balancing the needs of residents and visitors is important to ensure that cultural heritage tourism benefits everyone. It is important to understand the kind and amount of tourism that your community can handle.

Competition for time is fierce. To attract visitors, you must be sure that the destination is worth the drive.

Quality is an essential ingredient for all cultural heritage tourism, and authenticity is critical whenever heritage or history is involved.

A community's cultural, historic, and natural resources are valuable an often irreplaceable.

Much more can be accomplished by working together than by working alone. Successful cultural heritage tourism programmes bring together partners who may not have worked together in the past.

Building partnerships is essential, not just because they help develop local support, but also because tourism demands resources that no single organization can supply. Its success depends on the active participation of political leaders, business leaders, operators of tourist sites, artists and craftspeople, hotel/motel operators, and many other people and groups. Regional partnerships are also useful to cultural heritage tourism efforts. Cooperating in a regional arrangement lets you develop regional themes, pool resources, save money and expand your marketing potential. Those resources include not only money for marketing campaigns, for example, but also facilities (accommodations for travellers, say) or expertise in tourism, preservation, the arts or another area.

Local priorities vary. So do local capabilities. In other words, local circumstances determine what your area needs to do and can do in cultural heritage tourism. Programmes that succeed have widespread local acceptance and meet recognized local needs. They are also realistic, based on the talents of specific people as well as on specific attractions, accommodations, and sources of support and enthusiasm. One of the reasons cultural heritage tourism is on the rise in the United States is that travellers are seeking out experiences that are distinctive, not homogenized. They want to get the feel of a very particular place or time. You can supply that experience, and benefit in the process—but only if your cultural heritage tourism programme is firmly grounded in local circumstances. Base your cultural heritage tourism programme on what is appropriate and sustainable for your area.

(*a*) Do the residents of your area want tourism?
(*b*) Why do they want it?
(*c*) Are there certain times of year or certain places they do NOT want to share?
(*d*) How will tourism revenues improve life in your area and affect services such as fire and police protection?
(*e*) What is the maximum number of cars or buses your area can handle? On roads? In parking lots?
(*f*) Can you accommodate group tours? Do sites accommodate at least forty people at once with amenities such as restrooms, snacks, and a seating area?
(*g*) Can you accommodate visitors with disabilities or special needs?

The human drama of history is what visitors want to discover, not just names and dates. Interpreting sites is important, and so is making the message creative and exciting. Find ways to engage as many of the visitor's five senses as you can, as the more visitors are involved, the more they will retain.

On average, visitors will remember:

10 per cent of what they HEAR
30 per cent of what they READ
50 per cent of what they SEE
90 per cent of what they DO

The true story of your area is the one worth telling. The story of the authentic contributions previous generations have made to the history and culture of where you live is the one that will interest visitors, because that is what distinguishes your area from every other place on earth. It's authenticity that adds real value and appeal. Your area is unique, and its special charm is what will draw visitors. By doing the job right—by focusing on authenticity and quality—you give your area the edge.

As a good look around almost any city or town will show, people are often tempted to provide a quick fix of "band-aid" solution—to cover up an old storefront inexpensively, for example, rather than to restore it. But when your historic and cultural assets are at the heart of your plans to develop tourism, it's essential to protect them for the long-term. Hearts break when irreplaceable structures are destroyed or damaged beyond repair, instead of preserved and protected as they deserve. A plaque pointing out "on this site a great building once stood" can't tell that story. Equally tragic is the loss of traditions: a way of crafting wood or farming, of celebrating holidays or feasting on "old world" cuisine. The preservation and perpetuation of traditions is important to telling the story of the people who settled the land. By protecting the buildings, landscape or special places and qualities that attract visitors, you safeguard the future.

CASE STUDY: PRESERVING THE PAST

The Setting

Nestled in Northeast Tennessee's scenic mountains is a town with so many firsts that it can be a challenge to name them all. Jonesborough was the first town founded in the region (1779), the first capital of the "Lost State of Franklin" (1784), the first town in the new state of Tennessee (1796), site of the first regularly published abolitionist periodical (1820), the first Tennessee town listed on the National Register of Historic Places (1969), site of the first National Storytelling Festival (1973)...and the list goes on.

What Happened Next ?

Lifelong resident Jimmy Neil Smith (who served as Mayor from 1978-84 and today is President of the International Storytelling Centre) recalls that as residents searched for ways to save their community, assistance arrived in an unexpected way—through a grant application for sewer line repairs.

Smith explains that in working with the nearby Johnson City Office of the Tennessee State Planning Commission, Jonesborough's leaders learned:

- They had to have their own Planning Commission in order to receive the grant.
- The Commission's formation propelled Jonesborough to begin a planning process that focused on restoration and preservation.
- Continued support from the State Planning Commission helped Jonesborough to build its capacity and find the necessary financial resources.

As Jonesborough's reputation has grown among travellers:

- Local residents have benefited with the creation of jobs including owning or working in a bed and breakfast, retail store or restaurant.
- Jonesborough is the nation's mecca for storytelling began growing more than 30 years ago, and today the town has a unique attribute as home of the National Storytelling Festival and the International Storytelling Centre.

Results

- About 100 acres, with the heart in the downtown district, is listed on the National Register of Historic Places, the first community to receive this designation in Tennessee.
- Jonesborough was awarded the designation of *Dozen Distinctive Destinations* by the National Trust for Historic Preservation in 2005.
- The National Storytelling Festival began in 1973 with an audience of 60 people. Today, the festival draws a crowd of 10,000 to this small town each year.
- The International Storytelling Centre opened in 2002, creating a year-round destination for visitors who enjoyed storytelling. An ongoing state of programmes, including the Teller-in-Residence programme, attracts visitors to Jonesborough throughout the year.

- Jonesborough's cultural heritage tourism programme has generated jobs for residents including more than two dozen shops, six bed and breakfasts (all in historic buildings) and several tour companies.

Timeline

- 1960s—Planning Commission and Jonesborough Civic Trust established.
- 1969—National Register of Historic Places designation.
- 1973—First National Storytelling Festival.
- Late 1970s—Northeast Tennessee Tourism Association Forms.
- 1982—Jonesborough Visitors Centre and History Museum constructed.
- 1990-1992—Jonesborough participates in National Trust for Historic Preservation's Heritage Tourism Initiative.
- 2001—Jonesborough Civic Trust, Historic Jonesborough Foundation and Jonesborough/Washington County History Museum merge to become the Heritage Alliance of Northeast Tennessee and Southwest Virginia.
- 2002—International Storytelling Centre opens.
- 2005—National Trust for Historic Preservation awards *Dozen Distinctive Destinations*.
- 2006—*Preserve America* awards grant.

CULTURAL HERITAGE TOOLKITS

1. Bureau of Land Management (BLM) Heritage Tourism Toolkit

The toolkit includes how-to reference materials and information about other BLM heritage tourism programmes.

2. Colorado's Heritage Tourism Toolkit

Resources for cultural heritage tourism practitioners. Examples of best practices in the field, funding opportunities, helpful organizations and research pointing out the benefits of cultural heritage tourism.

3. National Trust for Historic Preservation *Dozen Distinctive Destinations* Toolkit

The toolkit includes ideas from communities that have been chosen as *Dozen Distinctive Destinations.*

4. Texas Cultural Tourism Basics

The Texas Commission on the Arts has devoted a section of the Texas Cultural and Arts Network website to cultural tourism basics: ideas on how to tell your community's story for tourism purposes; guidelines for developing different types of tours; sample letters and agendas for your tourism committee; a tourism assessment survey; sample tourism messages; community surveys; funding and information resources; and more.

5. Texas Heritage Trails

The Texas Heritage Trails programme received a $147,000 Preserve America Grant to the State Historic Preservation Office. Those funds were to help provide in-depth training for community representatives on the successful development of heritage tourism plans and to develop a new Heritage Tourism Guidebook and a workshop series.

6. Tribal Tourism Toolkit

The National Association of Tribal Historic Preservation Officers has developed a Tribal Tourism Toolkit for the Lewis and Clark Bicentennial and other Tribal Opportunities.

7. Utah's Heritage Tourism Toolkit

The Utah State Historical Society's Office of Preservation has developed a Heritage Tourism Toolkit with practical tools that communities or groups can use to develop, manage or protect their resources.

8. Virginia's Tourism Handbook

The Virginia Department of Historic Resources has developed a

Tourism Handbook. A print version can be ordered and the introduction to the latest version is available online.

9. Vermont's Cultural Heritage Tourism Toolkit

The Vermont Arts Council has developed a toolkit booklet as "a comprehensive and practical guide to developing and promoting cultural heritage tourism in your community." The booklet can be downloaded in a PDF format or ordered from the Vermont Arts Council for a nominal shipping and handling fee.

Cultural heritage tourism site has been developed as a resource for organizations and individuals who are developing, marketing or managing cultural heritage tourism attractions or programmes. These cultural heritage tourism "practitioners" can come from a variety of fields—tourism, historic preservation, the arts, humanities, museums, economic development, main street, heritage areas, and many other fields. Practitioners can include non-profit organizations, government entities, federal agencies and coalitions formed to bring these and other partners together. While the variety of different partners contribute to the richness of cultural heritage tourism, it can also make it more difficult to track down resources and how-to information. This electronic clearinghouse includes information provided by many different members of *Partners in Tourism,* a coalition of the national organizations and agencies with an interest in cultural heritage tourism. For those just getting started, there are guiding principles and how-to steps for launching a new effort. The success stories featured here will both inspire and inform, and the resources section includes key contacts in virtually every state as well as national resources for funding, technical assistance and other programmes.

THE PARTNERS: ANALYSING THE RELATIONSHIP

1. Washington State Arts Commission

Olympia, WA.

2. Jack Straw Foundation

Seattle, WA—Dedicated to the production and presentation of all forms of audio art, the foundation focusses on arts and heritage partnerships. Jack Straw also runs a full-service recording studio.

3. National Endowment for the Arts

Washington, D.C.

4. Northwest Heritage Resources

Olympia, WA—A non-profit organization that administers heritage grant projects.

5. USDA Forest Service Olympic National Forest

The Forest Service manages six national forests in Washington State.

6. Washington State Department of Transportation

Olympia, WA.

FIVE PRINCIPLES OF CULTURAL HERITAGE TOURISM

Principle 1

Collaborate: The partners helped shape the rural auto tours in Washington. WSAC's goal was refined by WSDOT's interest in focussing the tours along specific corridors versus broad regions. The DOT provided a level of expertise with the mapping of resources that would have been difficult to achieve by the Folk Arts Programme. On the Olympic Peninsula, the U.S. Forest Service's participation through Rural Community Assistance funding ensured that the tour focusses on the significance of wood and timber-dependent lifestyles. Ongoing support from the National Endowment for the Arts has also played a critical role.

Principle 2

Find the Fit between the Community and Tourism: Lund literally took to the streets, visiting museums, radio stations, parks, bars and workplaces to find his subjects for the tours. In one community after another, he talked to the locals, asked who had folkways to share, or songs to sing, stories to tell. It was an organic process that relied heavily on the willingness of people to participate, and the information found in one locale often led him to the next. Thus, the shape of the tour route at times was determined by his subjects, while keeping within a predetermined framework for the overall tour.

Principle 3

Make Sites and Programmes Come Alive: The tape tours include oral histories and interviews with local folk artists and often feature obscure art forms and cultural traditions. For visitors who don't have the time to seek out locals, the tapes help them gain a better understanding of unique cultural heritage traditions. "In Soap Lake, in the centre of the state, I heard an astonishingly beautiful Russian choir at the Slavic Brethren Church," says Lund. "They are an economically stressed community, yet the voices of the people are filled with hope and wonder. It was a fantastic surprise and one I was delighted to find and share with travellers."

Principle 4

Focus on Quality and Authenticity: In sifting through a vast amount of information that can be included in each tour, a folklorist selects information that provides an accurate representation of the diverse folk traditions along each route. Quality is essential, and only clear recordings and high quality photographs are included in the final product.

Principle 5

Preserve and Protect Resources: Not only do the tape/booklet tours capture and acknowledge significant Washington state folk art traditions, the research preceding the production of the tours results in thousands of documents, photographs and a wealth of audio-taped information. What can't be included in the tours due to space constraints becomes a valuable resource, managed by

WSAC, for teachers, researchers, and others who wish to trace the history and heritage of the state.

Whether you are just starting or taking your programme to the next level, always follow the National Trust for Historic Preservation's four basic steps for success in cultural heritage tourism:

TOWARDS ASSESSING THE POTENTIAL

Assessing your area's potential for heritage tourism is an essential first step. Evaluate your assets in these five areas:

(*i*) Attractions.
(*ii*) Visitor Services.
(*iii*) Organizational Capabilities.
(*iv*) Protection.
(*v*) Marketing.

Start by listing resources. But don't stop there. Your goal is not just to enumerate assets but also to evaluate potential, quality, and level of service. Your initial assessment also gives you baseline data, benchmark information you can use to measure progress and help you make key decisions as your cultural heritage tourism programme develops. Begin by assessing your *attractions*, current and potential. What historic, cultural, and natural resources does your area have to offer? To assess *historic or archaeological resources*, find our which of your area's historic sites are already listed on the National Register of Historic Places. List the sites that are currently open to the public or that add to the story of your area. Also, look at sites that are eligible for the National Register—normally at least 50 years old and significant for their architecture or archaeology, or association with an event or person. State and local designations also exist so consider listing these sites as well. All states have standard recording forms to use for surveying historic resources and many states also supply survey guidelines, so you'll probably want to contact your State Historic Preservation Office. You may find that your community or region has already been surveyed. Don't underestimate the drawing power of other *cultural resources* such as museums, theatres, or local cuisine, crafts, songs and dances.

Every state has a state arts agency and many states have state museum associations, so if you aren't sure who your cultural partners are locally, that's a good place to start. If you need help identifying the cultural resources in your community, consider working with a folklorist with experience in cultural heritage tourism. The culture and heritage of an area are often shaped by *natural resources*. Keep in mind that natural resources like local, state, national parks need not be right next door to serve as a resource for your community. If a major natural resource is within a day's drive, it can bring tourists your way. Another suggestion: check out parks, sports facilities, and recreational facilities that already attract visitors. You can partner heritage sites and events with attractions like these to keep visitors in your area longer. If they are linked by a visually appealing drive, even better. Scenic by-ways make the journey as rewarding as the destination. Do you have *untapped resources* that could play an important part in heritage tourism? What could become a resource if it were rehabilitated, developed, trained or interpreted? Use your imagination. Now, prioritize your resources. Not all sites will draw visitors. A site may be the actual reason why an individual or group will travel to a place—a *destination* in its own right. Tourists will add sites or events as *part of the itinerary* when they plan trips to a particular destination. Visitors will learn about some sites once they are in the region and *tour while there*. Finally, there are sites that are important to *local residents only* but will not hold much appeal to visitors. Keep in mind the need for service and quality. Are museum collections designed to educate and engage visitors? Are exhibits visually appealing and interactive? Are sites accessible to the public? Are museums and other attractions open daily or only occasionally? If you have historic neighbourhoods, are there organized tours and printed maps easily available to tourists? Are cultural events well-organized, held at times that make sense for tourists, well-publicized? Are attractions easy to find? Can they accommodate visitors? Ask questions like these now, so you get an accurate sense of your area's tourism potential. When you have done a thorough job of site assessment, you'll know where you face challenges in site interpretation, staff training, hours of operation, and so forth—the components addressed in steps 2, 3 and 4. Next you need to assess other aspects of *visitor services*. Visitor services encompass the basic elements most travellers need: places to eat, park, sleep, go to the restroom, and get gasoline. It also includes services which make travelling more enjoyable: shopping and touring. Take a look at these areas: lodging, restaurants, shops and infrastructure. Keep your goal in mind—to record the variety of resources available and the levels of service they provide.

Basic Elements for Attracting Tourists

To lure cultural heritage visitors to your community or region, look at all the existing resources you have to offer—historic, cultural and natural.

Historical and Archaeological Resources

How many of these historic resources are in your area?

- Museums.
- Historic properties listed on the National Register of Historic Places—or otherwise designated as landmarks.
- Historic neighbourhoods, districts, or even entire towns or villages.
- Depots, county courthouses, or other buildings that have historic significance because of their architecture or engineering features, the people associated with them, their contribution to historic events.
- Bridges, barns, battlefields and parks.
- Fountains, sculptures and monuments.

Cultural Resources

Consider the cultural amenities of an area by exploring the traditions, indigenous and artistic products presented by:

- Artists
- Craftspeople
- Folklorists
- Other entertainers, like singers and storytellers
- Museums
- Galleries

- Theatres
- Ethnic restaurants
- Special events—like reenactments, festivals and craft fairs
- Farming, commercial fishing and other traditional lifestyles.

Natural Resources

Look beyond established local, state, and national parks to resources that could attract visitors if they were properly developed.

- Unique landscapes
- Rivers
- Gorges
- Scenic vistas
- Forests
- Hiking trails
- Scenic by-ways
- Heritage areas
- Roads, canals, abandoned railroad corridors or other transportation facilities with unique historic, scenic or recreational significance.

Visitor Services Checklist

Lodging

- Are hotels and motels available for visitors?
- What about country inns or bed and breakfast establishments?
- Are there public campgrounds within 50 miles?
- Are other overnight accommodations available?
- Are new lodging facilities architecturally compatible with the historic character of the communities where they are located?
- Is the décor in new lodging facilities compatible with the historic character of the communities where they are located?

Restaurants

- Is there a selection of places for visitors to eat?
- Do they offer some variety of cuisine and prices?
- In addition to national chains, are there local restaurants that serve local food?
- Are franchises designed to fit in with the existing buildings?

Shops

- Do local shops sell products that will interest visitors?
- Is there shopping downtown?
- Can visitors buy a wide variety of products?
- Are some products indigenous or locally made?

Infrastructure

- What interstates or other major highways connect your area to major population centres?
- Is there good access from airports, railroads, bus lines?
- Is there an information centre open everyday for visitors?
- Do signs direct visitors to the centre and to major attractions?
- What about public transportation?
- Is enough parking available, not just for cars but also for buses, RV's and vans?
- Are there enough public restrooms where they're needed?
- Are gas stations open when visitors need to buy gas? Are there ATMs or credit card machines for visitors to use?
- Do banks or other establishments offer currency exchange and other financial services for international visitors?

To assess your organizational capabilities, identify all the local organizations that are involved in tourism, preservation, the arts, museums, humanities, economic development and other related fields. Are these groups financially strong? Are some of them members of national organizations that provide additional resources? The purpose of your assessment is to scout the possibilities—and potential support—for identifying or establishing a "primary provider" organization that can focus local energies at a single group.

Some Other Key Questions to Answer during Your Assessment

- Have these organizations worked together in the past? If yes, do they have a good working relationship?
- While the missions of the organizations are (and should be) different, can everyone agree on the common ground for a working cultural heritage tourism partnership?
- Is there one organization or individual that stands out as a natural leader, or will it be necessary to create a new entity to manage the cultural heritage tourism efforts?
- What can each organization contribute to the effort? Consider human and financial resources as well as advice and political support.

Organizational Checklist

- Is your lead organization "mission driven?" That is, does it have a clear sense of what it aims to accomplish?
- Does the organization operate from a plan that lays out goals and sets up ways to meet them?
- Does it have a capable board of directors, people who have a track record of working together and getting things done?
- Are committees active, productive, drawn from a strong membership base?
- Is there a paid staff? If not, should there be?

The *protection* of your area's assets is a major concern. Protection in this context means the full array of measures needed to protect the value of historic, cultural and natural assets. At the assessment stage, find out what protection local zoning ordinances, preservation ordinances, and city, county or even regional land use plans already offer. Which measures need to be strengthened? Where are the gaps?

Marketing is such an integral part of successful cultural heritage tourism that it is a step in its own right. Your assessment should include an initial inventory of all marketing related activities which are currently in place.

- Assess all available demographic information about who comes to visit your area, why they come, how much they spend, and what they want. Talk with your state travel office, state divisions of economic development, local chambers of commerce, state and national parks, major tourist attractions and other entities to gather information that can help you learn more about your visitors.
- Assess promotional materials. Pull together copies of all of the brochures, maps, guides and so forth that are already available. What kind of image do they convey? Do they promote historic and cultural sites? If not, could they be adapted? Are the materials effective—informative, accurate, attractively presented? Have you uncovered possibilities for collaboration—for marketing attractions jointly or developing themed itineraries?
- What travel-related associations do local sites, agencies or organizations have memberships in? What information and resources do they provide? What organizational activities could enhance your marketing efforts?
- What trade shows, conferences, educational tours and sales missions have been organized to market travel to your area? What activities are annual? Are there ways for heritage sites to be included?

Compile all of these components—the list of attractions, visitor services and marketing materials, the organizational and protection profile—to get a good idea of where you are, where you want to go and what you have to do to develop and market your heritage for tourists.

Plan and Organize

Make good use of human and financial resources. They are the keys that open the doors to sustainable cultural heritage tourism.

Human Resources

A community united can accomplish a lot; a community divided is not ready for cultural heritage tourism. So, begin to organize by building a local consensus that supports cultural heritage tourism.

- Gain the support of local business people—of bankers, people in the travel industry, owners of restaurants and stores, operators of hotels and motels, for example. You need their expertise and enthusiasm. In fact, bring in all the movers and shakers you can—prominent families involved in the community, religious leaders, and other individuals who have influence and credibility.
- Unite local government behind your efforts. From local government can come leadership, the establishment of arts and entertainment districts, preservation ordinances, design review boards, landmarks commissions and so forth.
- Seek the backing of service organizations with strong membership bases and good track records on community projects.

Once you have solid community support, it's time to organize. There are nearly as many ways to organize as there are organizations. Also, as your cultural heritage tourism programme grows, you'll need to reorganize, may be more than once.

As you organize locally, reach out to organizations and people elsewhere who can supply additional expertise and resources. Make recruiting and developing leaders a key part of organizational management. Whether your heritage tourism programme has paid staff or depends on volunteers, you need to bring along leaders who can stimulate the growth of the programme and expand its opportunities.

When you reach out to tap new resources, consider:

- Various state and national organizations, some public and some private, are good general sources of information about organizational development, tourism, preservation, the arts and other specialized topics. Many offer technical expertise in these areas and possible funding.
- Regional sources offer different kinds of assistance. Regions can be as large as several states or as small as several counties within a state.

After you have established an organization—or committee of an existing organization— you can create a cultural heritage tourism mission, define goals and layout specific objectives. Be sure to set reasonable timelines. The tendency is to underestimate how long it takes to organize a cultural heritage tourism effort, develop and enhance tourist attractions, achieve financial viability and reach new markets. Be realistic about time—and funding.

Financial Resources

The question of how to finance a cultural heritage tourism initiative has no easy answer, alas, and no single answer. Your goal is long-term, stable funding. Your chances of reaching it improve if you have built a strong local consensus, for then the problem of funding becomes one many people help solve.

Before you look for funding, draw up a financial plan. You need to know just how much money you'll need for which projects, and when. Potential backers want to know exactly what they are supporting and how their contributions fit into your organization's overall effort.

A good financial plan takes both hard and soft costs into account.

- Hard costs, such as the cost of restoring a historic building, are the most obvious and easiest to estimate.
- Just as important are the soft—but real—costs of staffing your organization, of interpreting and maintaining local sites, and of marketing.

Where can you look for funding? Here are some possibilities to explore: public funds, both grants and loans, available from federal, state and local governments; private establishments including corporations, foundations and non-profit organizations, individuals for memberships, specific grants and endowments.

Local

Hold fundraising drives, assess membership dues, or arrange house tours, art fairs or other special activities.

State

Your state may have funds for tourism, the arts, preservation, or economic development for which your organization could qualify.

National

Foundations and corporations fund activities in their area of interest. Listings can be found on the Internet or in your local library.

Box: Ways to Build Support

- Hold a town meeting.
- Write guest editorials for local newspapers.
- Send out surveys asking residents their opinions about tourism, culture and heritage goals and report the results to community leaders.
- Set up focus groups or a task force with representatives from tourism, preservation, business, and other appropriate groups to study services needed and to brainstorm heritage tourism strategies.
- Bring national experts to speak to local organizers about trends in cultural heritage tourism and economic opportunities.
- Organize visits to OTHER towns or regions where local leaders can see first hand results.
- Bring speakers from other successful cultural heritage tourism efforts who can explain how to get results.
- Sit down one-on-one with community leaders to educate them and gain their support for cultural heritage tourism.
- Develop an audio-visual or PowerPoint presentation about your area's goals for cultural heritage tourism and set up a speakers' bureau.

Prepare, Protect and Manage

As you take this step, look to the future as well as the present. When you prepare for visitors, be sure that the choices you make also improve your community for the long-term. Plan to win the war, not just the battle.

Prepare

Preparing for visitors means readying your historic resources by preserving their historical integrity, constructing new museums, and generally cleaning up your community—but it is also the time to figure out how you are going to tell your story and make your community hospitable to visitors.

Remember that good *interpretation* is vital. What exactly does interpretation mean? It means making your community's history, culture, or scenery emotionally accessible to visitors. To engage visitors in experiences they understand, learn from and respond to emotionally use these materials to interpret your resources:

- Signs
- Brochures
- Maps
- Videotapes
- Guidebooks
- Guides
- Living history
- Exhibits.

As you make your heritage resources emotionally accessible, make them physically accessible, too.

- Keep attractions open at convenient times. Remember tourists travel seven days a week, not just on weekdays. Hours of operation need to reflect the times visitors are in your community.
- Use entryways, signs, maps and information centres to help visitors find their way around your region.
- Make sure sites meet the Americans with Disabilities Act (ADA) accessibility requirements.

Remember that visitors take home memories. Much of the pleasure of a trip comes from how well-visitors are treated. A short-tempered ticket agent, an uninformed guide, a rude bus driver—

most travellers have had an unfortunate experience with someone like this, and it can be the experience they remember longest. The travel industry depends on many different people doing different jobs, so the challenge is to build community pride and understanding of the visitor's needs.

To build a strong tourism employee base, try an approach that has produced good results elsewhere: hospitality training. The goal of *hospitality training* is to teach participants how to welcome visitors and to encourage a better understanding of the area and cultural heritage tourism. Visitors are likely to meet front line staff, and often these entry level positions turn over quickly—so it's important to schedule hospitality training on a regular basis.

Protect

To ensure that your cultural heritage tourism resources have a long and productive life, you need to protect them. How? Developing a comprehensive preservation plan can provide overall guidance to help protect your historic structures. Other regulatory and planning mechanisms include:

- Seeking the designation of historic resources (be sure to determine which designations bring restrictions and which do not).
- Using zoning to specify land uses and restrictions on the density of development near sensitive historic sites.
- Establishing design review ordinances that establish design guidelines so that renovations and new buildings will be compatible with neighbouring historic structures and a design review board to administer the guidelines.
- Providing design assistance to people interested in rehabilitating their property.
- Requiring demolition review so that property owners cannot abruptly tear down buildings that have historic significance.
- Developing a sign ordinance that regulates such matters as size, materials, illumination and placement of signs.

Be sure that your museum collections are stored or exhibited in protected environments. Remember that collection items can be fragile. Sunlight, temperature changes, humidity and even just handling the items can have a negative impact over time.

Some of your contemporary cultural resources can be protected as well. For example, if you are promoting an artists district, consider what you can to keep the district affordable and appealing for the artists you have—and artists who may become part of the district in the future.

Manage

Preparing, protecting and managing heritage resources is a big job, one that involves not only producing tangible improvements to places and structures but also coordinating multiple activities and maintaining momentum on numerous projects simultaneously. To keep the job reasonable and feasible, develop a management plan.

If your assessment of visitor services has revealed major omissions or difficulties, include remedies in the management plan. Plan to improve roads, public facilities, police and fire protection, and other aspects of the infrastructure that affect—and are affected by—tourism.

A well-managed cultural heritage tourism programme is one that balances competing considerations. Balancing the "carrying capacity" of your area—its ability to host visitors without compromising service or overstraining resources—with the demands visitors make on it is one particularly important consideration. Why? Runaway "success" can destroy the very resources on which heritage tourism depends.

Say a summer festival begins to draw so many visitors to your revitalized "Main Street" that the roads into town clog with traffic, overwhelmed vendors start importing mass-produced quilts from China, and the city council paves a huge new parking lot for 3,000 cars at the expense of green space or a historic building. Danger! You're on the verge of killing the goose that lays the golden egg.

Organizational management includes monitoring change and adjusting your programme—or your personnel—to meet your objectives. Incorporate ways to monitor and measure progress into your plan. Build in systems of measurement from the beginning—ways to count numbers of visitors, for example, or to measure the economic impact of the money they spend—so you'll know where you have made progress (and where problems may be brewing). You'll also be able to demonstrate accomplishments to hard-working committee members and interested donors.

Box: Ways to Improve Community Appearance

- Protect entryways and roads that have outstanding scenic or historic importance.
- Protect scenic vistas: bury utility wires, screen unsightly intrusions.
- Protect trees and landscape character: plant street trees, landscape parking lots.
- Prohibit billboards.
- Limit the size, height, and number of other outdoor signs.
- Encourage tourist support facilities—hotels, motels, restaurants and shops—to locate in historic buildings or to build new structures that are architecturally compatible with the community but not imitative of your town's authentic historic buildings.

(From *Community Appearance and Tourism: What's the Link* by Ed McMahon)

Market for Success

To draw new people and money into your community, develop a multi-year, many-tiered marketing plan. Your goal is to reach your target market and to seize opportunities to partner with local, regional, state, or national groups. Include these four components in your marketing plan:

1. Public Relations,
2. Advertising,
3. Graphic Materials,
4. Promotions.

Keep in mind that developing a new domestic market takes approximately three years and producing results from an international audience takes five years—even when you use every one of the techniques presented here.

Public Relations

Public relations is a cost-effective way to get your message out via the media. The third-party reporting often provides more credibility for your area and creates additional angles to "sell your story" with articles on people, events, buildings, food or new activities.

Prepare a *press kit* (a folder filled with useful background information) to introduce your area to journalists. Keep accurate, current records of media contacts—local and also of journalists in major markets (say, at magazines with a national readership) that are interested in your subject-matter. Keep separate lists for electronic (radio, television and Internet) and print (newspaper and magazine) media since their interests will vary.

When something newsworthy happens, or is about to happen—a Christmas tour, for example, a visit by a group of Dutch dignitaries, the award of a grant, the publication of a brochure for a new cultural tour—announce it in a *press release*.

Arrange *educational tours* for travel writers and other members of the media to acquaint them with your area's attractions. Arrange them for tour operators and travel agents, too.

You may not at first think of your own area when you think of marketing, since new visitors come from marketing to outside audiences. But building *community awareness* is both courteous and an essential investment.

- Organize an educational tour for local officials to help them understand and appreciate heritage tourism.
- Plan special events for the general public to build enthusiasm, and it might even produce more volunteers willing to help with the work. Put on a special slide show, for example, a free-to-the-public day at a museum, or a candle light tour of historic homes.
- Reach out to children, for example, organize cultural or heritage programmes in schools to tie in to the requirements to learn local history or art.
- Have a community open house, have residents show their driver's licenses for free admission to area attractions, museum or concerts.

Box: Tools of a Public Relations Practitioner

Media relations

- Press kits,
- Press releases,
- Public service announcements, and
- Educational tours.

Community Awareness/Special Events
Photo library (be sure to have electronic images!)
Speakers' bureau
Crisis management plan

Use public service announcements—short spots on radio and television that are free to non-profit organizations—to publicize special events.

Make sure you document successes with photographs, and be sure to include digital images, slides and prints in your *image library* so you can find what you need. A reminder: journalists appreciate high resolution digital images, good black and white photos, and original slides (or at least first generation duplicates). Audio-visual presentations, slide shows. PowerPoint presentations or video-tapes can give your story emotional and visual impact.

Set up a *speaker's bureau* so you are ready to respond to requests for information about your cultural heritage tourism programme with the names, addresses, and phone numbers of people who are willing to make public presentations.

What if you have a fire at the museum or your area is hit by an earthquake, a hurricane, or some other sort of natural disaster? How will you contact the media and your target audiences? Have a *crisis management plan* that specifies a key spokesperson and outlines a response to crises.

Advertising

An effective—though costly method—of marketing to targeted audiences, advertising requires creation of a compelling message and supporting visuals, appropriate media placement, fulfilling inquiries, and measuring effectiveness.

When you advertise, match the medium to your message—and your budget. Remember, advertising of any kind is effective only if it is frequent enough. Consumers are so barraged with messages from the media that YOUR message registers only if you repeat it.

Ads in newspapers and magazines, *print advertising*, are generally less expensive than ads in electronic media like radio and television, so cultural heritage tourism groups with limited budgets often begin with print ads. Good ads depend on good materials—on a simple message, crisp photos, and effective copy. Good placement is essential as well, so buy space carefully.

Use ads on radio, television or the Internet, *electronic advertising*, when your message is visual and you need immediate communication with a target audience. Production costs add to the expense of this sort of advertising for radio and television. Another limitation is time: you must put your message across in no more than 60 seconds, and often as few as 15 seconds. A tip: radio ads can be especially effective for promoting holiday activities and other special events.

Through *consumer advertising*, you reach tourists directly whereas *trade advertising* reaches travel-industry professionals. Use both.

"Co-op" *advertising* is a good way to share costs. Multiple partners cooperate to produce advertorials or special sections dedicated to their area or destination. Magazines and newspapers provide special rates for advertising participants which are usually matched with editorial information.

Use co-op ads when you are targeting a new market or entering an expensive venue like a national magazine. For partners, consider a regional or national travel organization, your state tourism office, a department store, or a public/private partnership. *Note*: you'll need a budget for the special or increased inquiries a successful cooperative venture produces.

Don't think in terms of buying a random ad or two; do think in terms of mounting a coherent advertising campaign. Plan to measure the results of the campaign. Did it produce inquiries? How many? How many of the inquiries turned into actual visitors? Find out how well this campaign worked so you can plan for the next one.

Graphic Materials

Every community or region should develop an image package that can be transferred to all graphic materials. A colour scheme or unique design element that appears throughout all the graphic materials created by the area helps define the image of the region and establishes an identification for the visitor.

Choose a *logo*, or graphic symbol, to fix the identity of your cultural heritage tourism programme. Use it widely and consistently so it becomes closely associated with your programme.

Developing a *website* has become an essential component of any cultural heritage tourism marketing campaign. Keep in mind that the website is just one tool, and you will need to find ways to drive users to your website and ensure that your website is in good working order.

Print brochures. Their primary purpose is to introduce visitors to your area's attractions, but you'll use them in other ways as well: include them in press kits, for example, send them off to travel writers, display them at trade shows. Most essential is a general destination brochure that you display on racks at key locations: at your visitors' centre, for example, and at historic, cultural, and natural sites. Develop specialized brochures for special sites, special events, or special tours—for a walking tour through a historic neighbourhood, for example, or a driving tour along a scenic by-way.

Before you print a brochure, run through a mental checklist. Who is the audience? Where will you distribute it—at a state welcome centre, or at a local visitors' centre, in hotel racks, at trade shows? Do you have a place to store extra materials? Do you have a website or 800 number, postage for mailing and follow-up materials, or some other way to respond to direct inquiries? To get the most for your money, don't print before you think about these matters.

Remember that visitors need directions and other specific information on where to stay, where to shop, what to tour and where to eat. Keep a *visitor services directory* on hand at the visitors' centre. Done well, a directory solves problems for visitors AND promotes local businesses.

To attract large groups of visitors to your area, prepare a *group services directory* that describes special arrangements and discounts for organized tours. Make it easy for tour operators to market your destination. Besides supplying specific contacts and price information, the directories can suggest themed or multi-day itineraries.

Promote special tours—tours organized around a special theme or aimed at a special group—by printing *special itineraries*. These itineraries can suggest a day, half-day, or multi-day itinerary that includes tour options not available to drop-in visitors.

Put *signs* in the places where visitors will see them. Make them legible—big enough to read, informative and interesting. International symbols help guide visitors to restrooms, information centres, museums, or cultural centres, gas stations, lodgings, and dining establishments. Signs with graphic symbols such as logos help designate sites and roadways which are part of a regional theme or identify a cultural heritage.

Sometimes the most effective sign is a *map* that highlights key attractions or major features of a single attraction. Design an accurate, attractive, easy-to-read map and you'll find many uses for it, in printed pieces as well as along a trail or scenic by-way.

Even when you have done your best to make all these graphic materials attractive and informative, you won't always get them right the first time. So assess how well your materials are working. Do you need more pieces? Different types of materials to reach different audiences? Take time to find out.

Promotions

When you take your area's message to *travel industry shows*, you face expenses for exhibit design and erection, registration, travel, staffing and entertainment. But exhibiting at trade shows delivers information straight to professionals who can send visitors your way. It also gives you useful contacts. To reduce expenses, find a partner.

To find out what shows are scheduled, check with your state's travel office. Also, contact local and regional tourism organizations to learn what promotions they're planning.

At *consumer trade shows*, you take your message directly to consumers. The benefit: you reach the people who actually travel, sometimes hundreds of thousands of them in the course of a large, multi-day show. The cost: promoting your area at these shows is expensive, since you need a vast supply of literature. After the show, gear up for a lot of written, phone and electronic inquiries.

Sales missions take you to a specific city or country to call on travel agents, tour operators, journalists, and other key people to share information on your cultural heritage tourism products. Airlines and regional, state, or national travel organizations make good partners for these missions. Typically, a sales mission includes not just meetings but also a special function that presents some aspect of America's heritage, like an exhibit of indigenous crafts.

Contests that connect soft drinks, foods or other products with travel destinations give you another opportunity to reach new markets through direct mail, grocery stores, or fast-food establishments.

Whew! There's a lot you can do to market for success. Jump in. Try things out. Learn as you go. Those tactics have helped many communities entice visitors, as they can help yours.

A word to the wise. Make sure the experience a glossy brochure leads visitors to expect is an experience your area can genuinely offer. That is, marketing only what you can realistically deliver. Marketing is effective only AFTER you are really ready for visitors. It's the last step for a reason.

Top Shows

International Market: The Discover America International POW WOW, held in early summer in a different city each year brings international buyers and journalists together with U.S. suppliers. The Travel Industry Association of America coordinates this show. *Group Tours*. The National Tour Association and the American Bus Association host conferences each fall to connect hotels, travel offices, visitor service companies and other suppliers with buyers who develop and market group tours.

Credits

Heritage Tourism Initiative Project Manager: Cheryl Hargrove, former Heritage Tourism Director, National Trust for Historic Preservation.

Editor for Electronic Version: Amy Jordan Webb, Heritage Tourism Director, National Trust for Historic Preservation.

16 Pilot Areas Participating in the National Trust Tourism Initiative

Indiana

- Columbus

- Gary
- Historic Southern Indiana
- Nappanee.

Tennessee

- America's First Frontier
- Tennessee's Natchez Trace Corridor
- Tennessee Overhill Experience
- Tennessee's Backroads Heritage.

Texas

- Galveston
- LBJ Heartland Area
- Mission Trail of El Paso
- Texas Cotton Republic.

Wisconsin

- Fox-Wisconsin Rivers Heritage Corridor
- Frank Lloyd Wright Heritage Tour
- Lac du Flambeau Chippewa Reservation
- Wisconsin's Ethnic Settlement Trail.

How were These Principles and Steps Developed?

The National Trust for Historic Preservation's Heritage Tourism Programme coordinated a three year "Heritage Tourism Initiative" with funding from the National Endowment for Arts between 1990 and 1993. During that time, the Heritage Tourism Programme worked with 16 pilot areas in four states (Indiana, Tennessee, Texas and Wisconsin) to see what it took to create heritage tourism programmes that were both successful and sustainable.

This initiative resulted in the development of the National Trust for Historic Preservation's five guiding principles and four basic steps for getting started in cultural heritage tourism. Over the years, these principles and steps have been successfully used in cultural heritage tourism programmes in rural and urban areas across America as well as abroad.

Developing cultural heritage tourism is an incremental process, and communities will repeat the four steps at each stage of development. Keep in mind that developing a strong cultural heritage programme will require an investment and a commitment—an investment of financial resources and a commitment of human resources including strong leadership.

Not every community can have a successful cultural heritage tourism programme. Communities that have lost too much of their heritage, or not nurtured their cultural potential may not have the historic, cultural and natural resources it takes to develop a programme that will attract cultural heritage visitors.

How have These Steps and Principles Worked for Others?

How have the National Trust for Historic Preservation's guiding principles and steps for successful and sustainable cultural heritage tourism worked for others?

The success stories featured on this website show the principles in action, and demonstrate the steps that different programmes have taken to reach their goals. Collaboration is essential in today's competitive tourism market, and with increasing pressures on local resources, it is critical to find the fit between the community and tourism to ensure that tourism efforts are sustainable for the long term. When done correctly, cultural heritage tourism helps to preserve the irreplaceable resources that a community treasures.

Today's cultural heritage travellers are more well-travelled and more well-educated than previous generations of travellers, and they expect more from their travel experiences—making quality and authenticity more important than every before. These same higher expectations and increasing competition for the visitors' time also mean that the visitor experience has to make the site or programme come alive.

All too often, local stakeholders think that getting involved in tourism means publishing a brochure or launching a new website. These four steps show that promotion is, in fact, the final step of "marketing for success." Before getting to that final step, it is important to know what it is that you have—and what you want—to share with visitors. Next it is time to match up what you have with what potential visitors are looking for—and then make the necessary changes to be sure that you are offering the best visitor experience possible. Once you are truly ready, it is finally time to look at marketing.

Cultural heritage tourism development is a gradual process that takes a long-term commitment. These four steps of assessing, planning, preparing and marketing are ones that successful programmes repeat time and time again as they continue to expand their offerings—and their audience.

The Pay Off

Hard work pays off. The list of areas that have succeeded in heritage tourism is long and growing. To encourage you to start your own programme, we'd like to share what a few of the participants in the National Trust's Heritage Tourism Initiative have said about their experience when the initiative ended as well as comments from others who have used the principles and steps.

> "The growth of tourism was inevitable for Nappanee, but tourism growth could easily mean the destruction of the values and qualities of our small town. The National Trust for Historic Preservation has helped us preserve our heritage and yet share it with our visitors."
>
> — Larry Andrews, Manager, Nappanee Main and Market Streets, Indiana

> "The Heritage Tourism Initiative has allowed us to develop an approach to tourism that is appropriate for our region. The programme has also helped us to develop the Texas Heartland Network of visitor centres, natural and cultural heritage corridors, informational materials, and an educational programme. Expanding this network of comprehensive services and products is the basis for our next three-year action plan."
>
> — Julia Jarrell, Pilot Area Manager, LBJ Heartland Council, Texas

> "The Heritage Tourism Initiative has meant that Wisconsin was able to bring into being the largest historic preservation project ever attempted in the state. A 12-county, 200-mile corridor containing hundreds of potential restoration sites is now being organized for public tourism access."
>
> — Alan C. Pape, Project Manager, Wisconsin's Ethic Settlement Trail

> "Lac du Flambeau has "been buzzing with visitors all

summer," reported Pat Hrabik, project manager of the community's heritage tourism pilot project in Wisconsin. Attendance is up at the Lac du Flambeau Museum/Cultural Centre. The Indian Bowl Pow-Wows were "extremely well-attended." Tribal employees have been trained in techniques of surveying and identifying archaeological sites. In these and many other activities, the town has continued "to encourage tourism without impacting in a negative way on the culture and sacred sites located on the reservation."

Historic Southern Indiana, says its director, Darrel E. Bigham, "has grown considerably in the quality as well as the quantity of its products and services." Of special value, he feels, has been the push "to sharpen our focus regarding all aspects of long-range planning, including marketing; to assess and to reshape our priorities; to develop a stronger structure...to improve the quality of promotional materials; and to establish projects...which lay the basis for long-term regional growth and improvement."

In the Tennessee Overhill area, as in many other places, the development of cultural tourism has spun off other activities; new attractions (a textile museum), new events (a rail excursion, a Native American festival), historic preservation (purchase of a theatre for use as an auditorium, studies of historic zoning, and much else), economic development, and new partnerships. In addition to local investments or private contributions, $70,000 from out-of-town sources has been infused into the area. Says Linda Caldwell, project director of the Tennessee Overhill Experience, "From the start we believed that a cultural tourism programme...could be successful and serve as a springboard for overall regional cooperation and development. Today, as our third project year begins in the Tennessee Overhill, I am astonished at the spin-off activities that have resulted from this programme. Has the Heritage Tourism Initiative been worth it? You bet!"

The National Trust for Historic Preservation's five principles and four steps have continued to guide cultural heritage tourism programmes beyond the Heritage Tourism Initiative. Here are what leaders in the cultural heritage tourism industry had to say more than a decade after the initiative ended:

> "As an original participant of the Heritage Tourism Initiative, I continue to marvel at the impact this programme has had on

the travel industry. Communities that felt they could not be a part of the travel industry because they didn't have traditional "tourist" attractions began to realize that they could draw upon their history and culture to bring visitors, and their economic impact, into their community."

— Rene Campbell, Executive Director,
Columbus Visitors Centre, Columbus, Indiana

"The Heritage Tourism Programme was the first to articulate the who, what, how and where of heritage tourism. Many of us were nurtured on their step-by-step guide, Getting Started: How to Succeed in Heritage Tourism."

— Mitch Bowman, Executive Director,
Virginia Civil War Trails, Inc.

"The National Trust's Heritage Tourism Programme has literally written the book on heritage tourism. Their five guiding principles and four steps are the definitive parameters for successful programmes."

— Ed McMahon, Vice-President, The Conservation Fund

Through their own efforts, and with a little help from their friends, these communities and regions have reclaimed their heritage and helped it belong to us all. In the process, they have discovered new ways to thrive. Can your area succeed in heritage tourism? You bet! Now is the time to get started.

SUCCESS STORIES: CASE STUDIES

Arizona

Beyond the Grand Canyon: Arizona's Statewide Heritage Tourism Programme.

Respecting Differences: Arizona Tribal Tourism.

Colorado

A Hands-on Colorado Vacation: Saving Puebloan Ruins in Sand Canyon.

Florida

Home-grown Festival Stops Highway Construction: Eatonville, Florida's Zora Neale Hurston Festival.

Illinois

A Cultural Mosaic: Chicago's Neighbourhood Tours.

Louisiana

Keeping Traditions Alive: Sweet Home Folk Life Days.

Maine

More Than Lobsters, Lighthouses, and L.L. Bean: Maine's Statewide Cultural Tourism Programme.

Massachusetts and Rhode Island

Renewing a Revolution: The Blackstone Valley National Heritage Corridor in Massachusetts and Rhode Island.

Michigan

A Niche in the Northwoods: Michigan's Great Outdoors Culture Tour.

Minnesota

A New Growth Industry: Agritourism in Minnesota.

Montana

Montana Reins in Wide Open Spaces: The Yellowstone Heritage Partnership.

New York

Building Bridges to Success: The Seaway Trail in New York.

North Carolina

Shaping Craft Heritage Trails in Western North Carolina: Hand-made in America.

Pennsylvania

Commerce and Canals: The Delaware and Lehigh National Heritage Corridor.

Tennessee

From Furs to Factories to Tourism: The Tennessee Overhill Heritage Association.

Historic Jonesborough: Preserving the Past—One Story and One Building at a Time.

Virginia

Travelling with the Ghosts of Conflict: Virginia Civil War Trails.

Washington

Culture, Corridors and Cars: Washington State's Heritage Tours.

Beyond the Grand Canyon

The Setting

Arizona evokes images of deserts and the Grand Canyon. But the Arizona Humanities Council (AHC) staff knew the state was much more—it offered distinct geographic regions, each with a unique culture and heritage. The AHC decided to find ways to help develop the "product"—sites, stories and traditions—that could tell Arizona's story to visitors. They approached the project from the perspective that cultural heritage tourism is not only preservation, it is economic development.

What Happened Next

Work began by documenting the economic development potential of cultural heritage tourism and then creating programmes to support its development:

- Produced a study documenting the potential for an improved economy.
- Recruited involvement from museums, cultural sites and economic development organizations.
- Created a workbook, Cultural Heritage Tourism, to guide local development.
- Revised the AHC's website, Arizona History Traveller.
- Produced a CD-ROM highlighting the economics of cultural heritage tourism.

Results

- Built strong collaborations in many communities.
- Created an "Arts and Culture Build Communities" fund to award grants to rural areas.
- Received support from Arizona Tourism Alliance in request for state funding.

Respecting Differences

The Setting

Recognizing the economic opportunities of tourism was only one part of the equation for American Indians living on reservations in Arizona. Other concerns loomed even larger—how to share unique cultural practices without destroying those resources and making residents feel violated. Assistance came from the Native Nations Institute for Leadership, Management and Policy at the Udall Centre for Studies in Public Policy in Tucson, the Centre for American Indiana Economic Development in Flagstaff and the Arizona American Indian Tourism Association.

What Happened Next

One Native American tribe, the Hualapai Nation, had embraced tourism since 1975 when they began offering Colorado River rafting services in the portion of the Grand Canyon that is part of their reservation. This decision led to economic success:

- Employing up the 45 people during the peak season.
- In 2000, escorting 4,000 people on river trips and generating $900,000.
- The Hualapais began offering guided tours along the rim of the canyon in 1988. By 2000, more than 100,000 visitors were taking these trips.
- The tribe built a lodge and hired a marketing director to promote the facility.

Another tribe, the Hopi Nation, moved cautiously into the tourism arena. Deciding they wanted to control the tourism they were already getting, the Hopi Nation took several steps:

- Organizing neighbourhood clean-up projects including landscaping and signage.
- Craftspeople put up signs noting the location of their shops.
- Tours were offered for a fee.
- Several villages began marketing campaigns.

Results

- In 2000, Hualapai Lodge reached 48 per cent occupancy and was moving toward profitability.
- The Hualapai Grand Canyon Resort Corporation has planned infrastructure improvements.
- The First Mesa villages are developing a Hopi cultural centre.

Saving Puebloan Ruins in Sand Canyon

The Setting

Sand Canyon's ancient Puebloan ruins were slowly destroyed by insensitive visitors and centuries of weathering. Could the area be preserved and still be accessible to visitors?

What Happened Next

The land, owned by the federal government and managed by the

Bureau of Land Management, attracted thousands of tourists each year, including those who were guests of Rodney and Kristie Carriker. The Carrikers owned Kelly Place and founded McElmo Canyon Research Institute and used the area as an attraction for their guests.

- The Carrikers proposed a partnership with BLM to complete an archaeological survey.
- Recruited Elderhostel participants for the project.
- Surveyed 1,600 acres and identified 136 cultural resources.

Results

- 313 people participated in a working vacation on the archaeological excavation.
- Volunteers and archaeologists helped keep the area open.
- Four archaeological sites have been stabilized.
- BLM reports that visitors have become more respectful of the site.
- BLM has contacted other commercial outfitters about becoming involved in Sand Canyon.

Homegrown Festival Stops Highway Construction: Eatonville, Florida's Zora Neale Hurston Festival

The Setting

Eatonville, Florida is a small town known as "the oldest incorporated municipality in the United States founded by people of African descent." In 1987, the community learned of plans to turn its main road, the two-lane Kennedy Boulevard, into a five-lane thoroughfare which would destroy the historic character of the community. Residents rallied to stop the plan and found the solution in the legacy of their most famous resident, noted author and folklorist Zora Neale Hurston. But how could they capitalize on this legacy?

What Happened Next

Concerned citizens formed The Association to Preserve the Eatonville Community and started work. Among their efforts:

- Decided to produce a festival to honour Hurston, her works, ideals and ethics.
- Agreed to include a strong humanities component.
- Attracted well-known speakers and authors to the event.
- Recruited sponsors to help with everything from marketing to operations.

Results

- Kennedy Boulevard was not widened and the community retains it small-town ambiance.
- The annual Hurston Festival draws visitors from around the country. Many return each year for the festival.
- More than 800 volunteers assist with planning the event.
- Estimates show that the January festival brings $3 million into the county.

A Cultural Mosaic: Chicago's Neighbourhood Tours

The Setting

Just beyond Chicago's famed downtown are ethnic neighbourhoods where cultural traditions are celebrated and preserved. But these neighbourhoods faced problems common to many large cities declining employment and infrastructure. As the city's Department of Cultural Affairs (DCA) staff worked with arts organizations in these neighbourhoods, it became clear that they wanted these areas to become viable cultural attractions for visitors.

What Happened Next

In 1991, DCA started with a grant from the National Endowment for the Arts to produce brochures and exhibits. From there, things started to happen:

- Development of van tours of the neighbourhoods.
- Targeted marketing to conference delegates.
- Coordinated 25 cultural partners to develop Chicago Neighbourhood Tours.
- Created the Chicago Neighbourhood Gifts Project.

- Created a series of themed tours highlighting aspects of the city's history.
- Hired and trained local residents as tour guides.

Results

- CNT offers 19 unique tours that employ more than 50 guides.
- Local artists have enjoyed increased exposure and sales.
- As many as 12 per cent of tour guests return to shop at neighbourhood stores.
- 83 per cent of tour guests live in or near Chicago.
- Guest surveys indicate a 92 per cent approval rating.
- An increased sense of community pride is evident in the neighbourhoods.

More than Lobsters, Lighthouses and L.L. Bean: Maine's Statewide Cultural Tourism Programme

The Setting

Although Maine is proud of being famous for lobsters, lighthouses and L.L. Bean, citizens knew there was even more that could be shared with visitors. The Maine Arts Commission and the Maine Office of Tourism took the first step by organizing a workshop for representatives of arts organizations, museums, state agencies, chambers of commerce, historical societies and businesses to discuss cultural heritage tourism.

What Happened Next

Following the initial workshop, a Task Force was appointed to begin building partnerships and seeking ways to build cultural heritage tourism. Among the results were:

- Expanded partnership to include the Maine Humanities Council and Historic Preservation Commission.
- The four agencies formed the Arts and Heritage Tourism Partnership and contributed funds for grants.
- Conducted a statewide inventory of arts and heritage groups.

- Created the Mid-Coast Arts and Heritage Map.
- Created an out-of-state marketing campaign.
- Created the staff position of Arts and Heritage Tourism Consultant.

Results

- Some museums experienced an 80 per cent increase in attendance.
- Publicity was generated in such publications as The New York Times.
- $3.6 million was awarded by the state legislature in 1999 for the New Century.
- Community Programme, providing funding through matching grants and direct services.
- The investment of state dollars leveraged $10 million in outside funding.

Renewing a Revolution

The Setting

In a place with no history of tourism, a place that considered tourism a poor relation to manufacturing, a pioneering spirit and Entrepreneurial insight brought together disparate interests to forge a new form of industry that is rebuilding the region's economic strength—heritage tourism.

Residents and elected officials laughed at Bob Billington in 1985, when he suggested that tourism could play a role in revitalizing the Blackstone River Valley's flagging economy. This was, after all, the corridor along which the Industrial Revolution had taken root and prospered in America some 200 years earlier. The 24 towns between Worcester, Massachusetts, and Providence, Rhode Island, had once boasted the lion's share of industrial output so that around the world, Blackstone Valley became synonymous with manufacturing innovation and excellence throughout the 19th century and into the next. But that was then and this was now.

After decades of shifting industrial trends that caused a steady attrition of manufacturers from the valley, the Blackstone communities were at the tail end of every economic resurgence that touched New England. Nothing seemed to work; the region had no apparent means of putting itself back into the economic and cultural mainstream. But while the jobs went south along with the economy, the physical legacy of industry remained along the Blackstone: the canal, hundreds of multi-story brick mill buildings, mill housing and towns, mill institutions such as hospitals and schools, and dozens of small lakes, ponds and dams created to power the historic mills. The physical evidence of the people who formed the valley's culture was deteriorating as was the enthusiasm of their descendants for this once-proud region.

In the 1980's, Bob Billington worked in his family's gift products factory, and there he saw the need for new retailing opportunities. He formed an outlet association with other Rhode Island manufacturers and, before he knew it, became involved in tourism. Soon, Bob realized that he had discovered his calling and cobbled together the money to devote all his time to the newly formed Blackstone Valley Tourism Council (BVTC). Two years later, Rhode Island ushered in a new tourism era when it levied its first room tax, and the council was designated as a regional tourism agency. Despite these advances, there was much skepticism among local residents for the idea that heritage tourism could really work.

But Billington and an increasingly larger number of other individuals knew there was treasure hidden beneath the years of disuse and neglect in the valley towns. In tandem with the council's efforts, a valley-wide movement to create a National Heritage Corridor got underway. The partnership between Massachusetts and Rhode Island to create the heritage area became formidable with the respective state legislative and congressional delegations supporting the effort. Groups on both sides of the state line became active proponents for the designation. Finally, these new heritage partners succeeded in getting the area from Worcester to Providence designated by Congress as a National Park Service (NPS) National Heritage Corridor in 1986. The area is managed by a commission that unifies the work of the NPS, two state governments, dozens of local municipalities, businesses, non-profit historical and environmental organizations, educational institutions, and private citizens. Blackstone Valley thus became the second such designated area in the country and, believe it or not, was on its way to becoming a tourist destination.

> "During the 1980's we spoke hundreds of times to dozens of different groups and at each engagement, there would always be some snickers from the audience when we talked about tourism in the Blackstone Valley. Today, it's different. Local officials use the word themselves in their policy discussions and in the press."
>
> — Bob Billington, Blackstone Valley Tourism Council President

What Happened Next

With the National Heritage Corridor designation in place, a new tone emerged in the valley. People began to see the region from a new perspective; the Blackstone River Valley suddenly became a place of national significance. The Department of Transportation in both Massachusetts and Rhode Island erected the well-known brown public resource signs along the nearby Interstate highways. Visitors' curiosity was aroused and residents were also influenced by this tangible recognition.

The NPS began its work by listening. It held workshops and public meetings and gave presentations all around the valley to understand what it was that valley residents wanted and to convey to residents the impressive value of the corridor's resources. Early on, according to Michael Creasey, executive director of the Corridor Commission, it became clear that infrastructure investment would be one of the Park Service's main goals. "We focused on things we could build that would make a difference for residents and visitors," says Creasey. This approach has resulted in more than $18 million of federal investment, but more impressive, that $18 million has been matched 10-to-1 by local and regional support. Projects have included visitor centres, rehabilitation of old mill buildings, new parks and recreational facilities.

The BVTC took a similar approach in its work as it pursued something that, at the time, seemed like a wild idea: boat rides on the Blackstone Canal. "We needed to define the valley for the visitor and it seemed that connecting them to the Blackstone River and Canal was the most important thing," says Billington. Maybe so, but it wasn't an easy sell since the waterways flowed past industrial development, not bucolic fields and woods. This was not a river with a romantic or recreational reputation. Still, the BVTC with the support of the Park Service raised the necessary funds, designed, and, in 1993, built the Blackstone Valley Explorer, a light, low-draft riverboat able to be moved easily by land from point to point and also able to move through the often shallow waters of the river and canal. The Council began offering scheduled exploration cruises and chartered events. They parked the boat prominently and promoted it to everyone within earshot. Soon, it was a hit. The Explorer began to demonstrate to residents that people would actually pay to see the Blackstone and could have some fun along the way.

Building on that success, BVTC purchased an old trolley car in 1996 from a Providence company, refurbished it, and renamed it the Blackstone Valley Trolley. With its brightly painted advertising, the trolley began to appear up and down the valley. It has become a favourite for its Sunday afternoon wanderings through the historic neighbourhoods of the Blackstone Valley communities.

In 1997, BVTC launched its second vessel, the Spirit of the Blackstone Valley. Built on a relationship that began during Slater Mill's 200th anniversary in 1993, the Council began a relationship with the community of Belper in the Amber Valley of Derbyshire, England, the first industrialized town in the world and ancestral home of Samuel Slater, founder of the first textile mill in Pawtucket, Rhode Island in the 1790s. This connection resulted in the Valley's first international marketing and tour package. It took the Council until May of 2000 to raise the funds to launch an authentically built English canal boat named the Samuel Slater in honour of the father of the American Industrial Revolution. Now, all three boats ply the waters of the Blackstone throughout the visitor season. Through the Blackstone Valley National Heritage Corridor, the NPS has become an active player in the valley's economic development. The NPS has supported the development of visitor centres in Uxbridge, Massachusetts, and in Woonsocket and Pawtucket, Rhode Island. In Woonsocket, the visitor centre is in the newly developed Museum of Work and Culture. The museum, a joint project of the NPS and the city of Woonsocket, focusses on the traditions and implications of work in life.

Finally, the NPS has played a key role in assisting local communities with a wide variety of resource protection and management projects. Part of the corridor's annual budget is devoted to grants to local communities to help them move their own projects forward. The Corridor Commission did much visioning work with communities in the early days, creating 14 vision plans for the region. To date, 10 of those plans have been implemented. "This process encouraged people to blend heritage resource management with more current or modern forms of economic development," says Executive Director Creasey.

> "No one person has made the Blackstone Valley Heritage Corridor a success. This project brought a multitude of people together to build the Heritage Corridor from the ground up. Thanks to these dedicated 'believers,' together we have been able to accomplish what no one could have done on their own."
>
> — Michael Creasey, Executive Director,
> Blackstone Valley National Heritage Corridor

Making the Most of Opportunities

Collaborate: "What one person can do to affect the world is small. We need a lot of collaboration to make it all happen," declares Billington. Putting minds and efforts together has, indeed, resulted in strong tourism and economic development in the valley. Local businesses, organizations, communities, volunteers, regional and state tourism and planning agencies, and state and federal agencies have all come together to forge a new industry to rebuild the Blackstone River Valley into a thriving area.

Find the Fit between the Community and Tourism: A critical aspect of the Heritage Corridor programme is the idea that communities are taking the lead in project development with the state and federal agencies backing them up. This has allowed cities and towns to decide whether and how they want more tourism.

Make Sites and Programmes Come Alive: The tourism organizations in both Massachusetts and Rhode Island have made it easier—and more fun—for visitors and local residents to get around and enjoy the attractions of the valley. Cruises through historic waterways on replica riverboats take visitors into the moment, helping them experience an older, slower way of life, work, and transportation.

Focus on Quality and Authenticity: A key to the valley's success has been working with the authentic resources in place in the corridor. Being selected as a National Heritage Corridor early on created pride and desire among local activists to live up to that honour by approaching all their tourism-related goals with quality in mind.

Preserve and Protect Resources: Protection of historic structures, stone walls, open spaces of important farming landscapes, and the adaptive use of old mills and downtown structures have all ensured that the Blackstone of the future will resemble the Blackstone of today.

Results

- During the first 10 months of operation beginning in September of 1999, the Blackstone Valley Visitor Centre in downtown Pawtucket, Rhode Island attracted more than 75,000 visitors.
- In its first year of operation in 2000, the Museum of Work and Culture in Woonsocket, Rhode Island, took in 35,000 visitors, and the visitor centre at Riverbend Farm in Uxbridge, Massachusetts, drew 30,000 people.
- BVTC board of directors established the Blackstone Valley Legacy Trust to obtain private and public financial support for future development projects for the Blackstone Valley Tourism Council. The Trust invests funds for the benefit of the valley.
- BVTC joined other tourism and environmental groups in supporting passage of a $50 million Rhode Island state bond issue for open space protection. During the last 15 years, the river's environmental health has improved so greatly that the number of fish species has soared from just two to the 33 species that now are present.
- The Blackstone Valley Explorer, the Spirit of the Blackstone Valley and the Samuel Slater have provided interpretive, cultural, environmental and recreational boat tours on the river to more than 150,000 people from 1993 to 2000.

Breaking out of the Box: The Tourism Role of Heritage Areas

County boundaries, state lines and city limits. All too often, collaborative tourism efforts are defined by these arbitrary political jurisdictions. These boundaries are meaningless for visitors and often make it challenging for sites in a region to work together. Heritage areas provide a mechanism to link communities and sites together based on geographical or thematic connections that make sense from the visitor's perspective. In this way, heritage areas provide a way to work across traditional boundaries to protect, enhance, and promote a region.

As of 2001, there are 23 National Heritage Areas in the U.S., each designated by an individual act of Congress. Almost all receive National Park Service funding to help get the heritage areas up and running so that they can become self-sustaining. The Alliance of National Heritage Areas estimates that there are another 170 local and state heritage areas across the nation. For more information on how to start a heritage area, order the Information Series booklet Getting Started in Heritage Area Development at http://www.culturalheritagetourism.org/successStories/www.nthp.orgor find out about the Alliance of National Heritage Areas at www.nationalheritagearea.org.

A Niche in the Northwoods: Michigan's Great Outdoors Culture Tour

The Setting

Michigan's upper Great Lakes region has long attracted visitors to enjoy outdoor activities like hiking, canoeing and camping. What they didn't find out about was the region's culture and heritage. Travel industry studies revealed a strong connection between culture and outdoor adventures and found that visiting state and national parks ranked as high priorities with cultural heritage travellers. The opportunity was waiting to be developed.

What Happened Next

In 1997, the Michigan Humanities Council decided to take cultural programming to the people. In the summer of 1998, the first Great Outdoors Culture Tour was produced. Action steps included:

- A pilot programme determined the success of the project.
- The Michigan Council for Arts and Cultural Affairs joined the project as a financial sponsor.

- Local hosts at state parks, forests and campgrounds identified programmes suited to their sites.
- Local hosts promoted the programme locally to visitors and residents.

Results

- 18 story-tellers, musicians, historical role-players, dancers and cultural interpreters presented programmes.
- The programme grew from 85 performances in 1998 to 94 in 2000.
- Programmes were held in state parks, national parks and forests, historical museums, community parks and children's summer camps.
- A Culture Tour logo was designed and collateral materials created to promote the programme.
- In 2000, the programmes attracted 8,500 people, a 42 per cent increase from the first year.
- The programme received the 2000 "Windows on the Past" national heritage award for excellence from the Chief of the U.S. Forest Service.

Montana Reins in Wide Open Spaces: The Yellowstone Heritage Partnership

The Setting

The wide open spaces of Montana, North Dakota and Wyoming hold within their boundaries federally managed land, Indian reservations and a fascinating heritage. The long distances between attractions proved to be a challenge in attracting visitors. How could organizers capitalize on the area's culture and heritage and draw some of the three million visitors who come to Yellowstone National Park each year?

What Happened Next

The Western Heritage Centre took the lead in organizing a coalition of historical, arts and cultural facilities as well as humanities scholars and community representatives. Working together, the Yellowstone Partnership took several action steps:

- *Developed an exhibit our Place in the West*: Places, Pasts and Images of the Yellowstone Region from 1880-1940.
- Offered a series of presentations by scholars on the history of the area.
- *Published Along the Yellowstone*: A Guide to Historic Sites in the Yellowstone Region to interpret the area for visitors.
- Created a series of regional cultural loop tours and additional exhibits.

Results

- The Explore the Yellowstone exhibit has been in 15 communities in the three-state region and has been seen by more than 20,000 people.
- The Yellowstone Partnership has more than 40 representatives from public and private interests.
- Partners secured $200,000 in grants for sites in the partnership region.

Building Bridges to Success

The Setting

Most rural communities lack large-scale, marquee tourist attractions. Instead, rural areas tend to be dotted with small, dispersed sites that offer varying degrees of information, activities and services. How can you package your scattered attractions into a viable destination that has real economic and civic impacts? The Seaway Trail in New York is one of the nation's most successful National Scenic Byways thanks to its development as a destination travel corridor.

The Seaway Trail, New York State's National Scenic Byway, is 454 miles of scenic driving along Lake Erie, the Niagara River, Lake Ontario and the St. Lawrence River. Lighthouses have guided voyagers through these waters for hundreds of years. And now, through the broad marketing spectrum of the Seaway Trail, these sentinels of safety have served as another type of beacon—

attracting travellers in search of history, recreation, relaxation, and scenic touring to their communities. And when travellers come, economic development follows.

But the real picture of economic development along the Seaway Trail is broader than heritage tourism alone. Over the last two decades since its dedication in 1978, the Seaway Trail has provided the foundation for a strong rural development strategy that encompasses eight major resource themes: coastal recreation, natural resources, history of the coast, peoples of the coast, coastal agriculture, international coastline, water-related industry, and commercial shipping. By partnering with U.S. federal agencies and departments, Seaway Trail has evolved into a long-term tool for economic growth through rural tourism.

> "The mission of Seaway Trail, Inc., is to increase tourism revenues and to enhance the economic well-being and quality of life in New York State's Seaway Trail corridor by managing and marketing it as a leading scenic byway."
>
> — Seaway Trail Mission Statement

What Happened Next?

It was the bridge that started it all. The seven-mile Thousand Islands Bridge, dubbed "the bridge from nowhere to nowhere," was built in 1938 to connect Canada and the United States along the most direct land-travel route between Washington, D.C. and Ottawa. Planned as a device to raise revenues through tolls and to increase tourism to the largely unknown Thousand Islands, the bridge put the region on the map and provided a reason for people to pass through the area.

Watching this progress with a keen eye was Vince Dee, a restaurateur in the St. Lawrence Seaway region. Dee recognized an opportunity to capitalize on the tour buses that now plied the route from New York City to Canada along the bustling Thousand Islands Bridge. He was the first person in upstate New York to tap the group tour market out of the city and it led to financial success for his business.

It was many years in the making, but Vince Dee developed first his own tourism trade and then turned his attention to his neighbours and the region. Looking across the St. Lawrence River for inspiration, Dee found a great tourism model to emulate: the Canadian Heritage Highway, a travel route stretching from Windsor, Ontario, to the Gaspé Peninsula in Quebec. Dee worked with area business owners to establish, in 1978, the 80-mile-long Seaway Trail and its non-profit arm, the Seaway Trail Foundation, a 501(c)(3). Dee, who was the trail's acknowledged visionary and its president until his death in 1995, called the Seaway Trail, "A string of jewels showcasing the communities close to the shoreline." Soon after its establishment, wayfinding signs placed by the New York State Department of Transportation marked the route for travellers.

In the early 1980s, the Seaway Trail conducted resource inventories. Through these efforts came the realization that the route contained 27 historic lighthouses, which in turn, caused the trail's marketers to sit up with interest. Brochures were produced to help visitors find and enjoy the lighthouses and, as people began visiting them, the lighthouse managers realized they were part of a dispersed, regional tourism product. In 1980, Seaway Trail published a guidebook to the lighthouses, the first in a series. Since then, the trail has developed guidebooks to sites pertaining to the War of 1812, a Wildguide to Natural History that illustrates the area's flora, fauna, and natural lands; Along the Trail and Into the Past, detailing architecture and history along the trail; and trail bicycling adventures. The Black River-St. Lawrence Resource Conservation and Development Project and others contracted with the Natural Resources Conservation Service for assistance in publishing The Nautical Seaway Trail, a boater's atlas and guide to waterfront services as well as several agri-tourism guides. The original vision of the Seaway Trail as a multimodal corridor was coming to fruition as these brochures emphasized walking, biking, driving and boating.

A new era for the Seaway Trail began in 1983, when it was accorded National Recreational Trail status by the U.S. Department of the Interior. The following year, the trail was extended to Niagara Falls and then, in 1986, it was extended to the Pennsylvania border, bringing it to a total of 454 miles. For each of these incremental extensions, all the communities had to participate. This required hours and hours of meetings and presentations by the board of directors and the planning staff.

As successful as that effort was, it still did not answer the Seaway Trail's problem of a lack of budget. In 1985, the state legislature was creating new tourism committees in the senate and assembly. The chairs of these committees were representatives from the St. Lawrence corridor: Matt Murphy, a Democrat from Lockport, and John McHugh, a Republican from Watertown. Vince Dee knew both men. With their support, the Seaway Trail garnered $250,000 in 1986 from the state. The trail hired staff, including Director Teresa Mitchell, and embarked on an aggressive marketing and development campaign.

From there, the Seaway Trail hit a steady stream of home runs, including 1987's I Love NY summer festival, which the trail sponsored, proving to residents and travellers alike that the region had reached legitimate status as a tourism destination. In preparation for that festival, the town of Oswego, which housed the trail's office at the time, came to the realization that it had no tourism events with which to attract anticipated travellers. The town, rallied by Mayor John Sullivan, his wife Charlotte Sullivan, and community historian Rosemary Nesbitt, went to work and created Harborfest to celebrate its waterfront heritage. More than a decade later, the four-day Harborfest is featured as one of the top New York State events by the American Bus Association with annual attendance in the tens of thousands.

While attending a conference on outdoor recreation in 1989 in Washington, D.C., Mitchell became aware that while the trail was accomplishing much on its own, it had failed to take advantage of potential federal funding sources. She got busy networking and eventually hooked up with officials at the Federal Highway Administration (FHWA) who were crafting legislation for the new National Scenic Byways Programme. Going back home, Mitchell prompted the Seaway Trail to lobby the New York legislature for a state-authorized byway designation, which then opened the door for federal recognition and a portion of the millions of dollars of available funding.

In 1996, the Seaway Trail was one of the first 20 roads designated as a National Scenic Byway or an All American Road. The U.S. Secretary of Transportation recognizes roads for their outstanding qualities. The corridor must possess distinctive archeological, cultural, historic, natural, recreational or scenic qualities.

Since that time, the Seaway Trail has garnered $1.9 million in grant funds from the National Scenic Byways programme. But, funding isn't the only reason an organization should seek federal designation, according to Mitchell. "A byway designation is as important as you want to make it. The more you use it, the more it benefits your organization. We have been able to make good use of the money that is available through the designation, but just as importantly, we have won recognition as being part of a larger, federally sanctioned programme. It brings prestige to your organization and helps it build important partnerships."

Making the Most of Opportunities

Collaborate: The only way that the original trail succeeded was through the collaboration of multiple jurisdictions, organizations and individuals. As the Seaway Trail has expanded to its full 500-mile length across New York and Pennsylvania, collaborations have developed between the two states, among various public and private entities, and with several federal agencies and departments. Overall success has come about largely through these cooperative efforts.

Find the Fit between the Community and Tourism: Towns and hamlets all along the Seaway Trail embraced tourism from both pride and economic standpoints. For communities that thought they had nothing to offer visitors, the trail emboldened them to turn to their natural and man-made histories and develop tourism infrastructure as well as attractions. In Sackets Harbor, new restaurants and shops handle the influx of visitors.

Make Sites and Programmes Come Alive: Activities that celebrate the trail's natural wonders, such as fishing, boating, agritourism and bird watching, are enhanced by Seaway Trail guidebooks. While at the many historic sites along the route, interpreters and reenactors demonstrate 18th and 19th centuries ways of life, ranging from Colonial infantry drills to 19th century style gardening.

Focus on Quality and Authenticity: The Seaway Trail contains myriad authentic resources from coastal wildlife habitats to scenic vistas, forests to farms, and historic architecture to cultural activities from a diverse international population. From marketing materials and trailblazing signs to official guidebooks and Journey, the trail's annual periodical, the Seaway Trail's assets are represented to the public with excellence.

Preserve and Protect Resources: By drawing attention to the area's vast natural and man-made resources, Seaway Trail has urged and promoted their preservation. Public and private organizations and individual citizens all along the 454-mile trail in New York have taken measures to preserve and protect resources ranging from lighthouses to wildlife refuges, and War of 1812 forts to swamps and wetlands. Leading by example, the Seaway Trail undertook the rehabilitation of the 1817 Union Hotel in Sackets Harbor's main square for use as offices and an information centre.

Results

- The Seaway Discovery Centre, which opened in July 2000, attracted 3,000 visitors in its first-half year, raising $7,000 in admissions and $27,000 in gift shop revenues.
- The bipartisan support that created the Seaway Trail line item in the state budget has continued since 1986 to the present because the trail is seen by legislators as one of the state's major tourism success stories.
- Partnerships with renowned national organizations have helped Seaway Trail develop sought-after tourism programmes. Working with the American Automobile Association, the trail has developed a "participating retailer" effort that offers discounts at trail sites for card-carrying AAA members. Pairing with Elderhostel, the Seaway Trail is sponsoring a variety of travel programmes aimed at that organization's members, who are all 55 years of age or older. In return, Seaway Trail is able to market to Elderhostel's membership of 175,000.
- An agreement in 1996 with the State of Pennsylvania authorized use of the name 'Seaway Trail' through the 50-mile route along Lake Erie to the Ohio border. In December 2000, representatives from convention and visitors bureaus in Ohio approached the folks at the Seaway Trail for advice on creating or extending the trail through their state along Lake Erie. Mitchell says it is not inconceivable that in the not-too-distant future a trail may extend all the way around the Great Lake shores to Duluth, Minnesota. All participating states and trails could take advantage of the

important Scenic Byways designation and work on cross promotions of their subsections of the trail.

- Agritourism along the trail is a growing industry. It promotes tourism to farms, festivals, historic farm sites, museums, and agricultural gift shops.

Scenic Byway Designations

Scenic Byway Designations Scenic byways can be designated at the local, state, or national level. Some are called heritage routes. Others may be called rustic roads or backcountry byways, although some of these designations differ slightly. The U.S. Forest Service began a National Forest Service Scenic Byway designation programme in 1988. In 1991, the U.S. Department of Transportation established its National Scenic Byways Programme, whereby roads may be designated as National Scenic Byways or All-American Roads, and now are promoted collectively as America's Byways. U.S. DOT also provides grants to states for by-way projects and development of a state by-way programme. For more information call 1-800-4BYWAYS or check out http://www.culturalheritagetourism.org/successStories/www.byways.org.

Ashley River Road is an 11-mile National Scenic Byway just outside Charleston, South Carolina. The by-way traverses a National Register Historic District that traces the history of European and African settlement, commerce, and industry from colonial times to the present. Citizens, landowners, businesses, and historic foundations have come together to safeguard the road and the special resources along it from encroaching growth and development. Contact the Ashley River Coalition at (843) 769-2600 or check out http://www.culturalheritagetourism.org/successStories/www.ashleyriver.org/mission.html.

Crowley's Ridge Parkway is a 212-mile National Scenic Byway located in northeast Arkansas and southeast Missouri. The by-way follows a natural ridge created during the Ice Age by action of wind and water. Rock was eroded and windblown loess collected on the ridge, forming this unique land form. A partnership among universities, businesses, and citizens to tend the 198-mile Arkansas portion of the by-way is led by Arkansas Delta By-ways, headquartered at Arkansas State University in Jonesboro. The Regional Commerce and Growth Association in Cape Girardeau is the principal contact for the 14-mile portion in Missouri. Check out http://www.culturalheritagetourism.org/successStories/ www.deltabyways.com, or for more information about the Arkansas segment, call (870) 910-8080. For more information about the Missouri segment, call (573) 334-4142.

Volcanic Legacy Scenic Byway is a 140-mile by-way in south central Oregon. This diverse All-American Road skirts lakes and wetlands, traverses ranches and croplands, and takes travellers to the "top of the world" on the rim of Crater Lake (National Park). The by-way was created by a unique group of partners and stakeholders that include representatives of tourism, transportation, national forests, Klamath Tribes, recreation, natural resources, and other community interests. The Winema National Forest has been instrumental in providing leadership and support for the by-way steering group.

Shaping Craft Heritage Trails in Western North Carolina: Handmade in America

The Setting

The mountains of western North Carolina, besides providing breathtaking scenery, are home to equally breathtaking displays of artistic talent. Artists and craftspersons work in every media: pottery, blown glass, woodworking, weaving and more—some following traditions handed down for generations and some recently relocated here for the inspiration the area provides. But could these artists and craftpersons help improve the area's severely distressed economy?

What Happened Next?

Handmade in America, a non-profit formed in 1993, designed the concept of a heritage trail which guided visitors to the studios of the artists and craftspeople. The organizations many action steps included:

- Researched the profile of heritage travellers in the region.
- Received a three-year organizational development grant and engaged hundreds of citizens in the planning process.

- Developed a system of trails and published a guidebook, The Craft Heritage Trails of Western North Carolina.
- Developed selection criteria for inclusion on the trails, focusing on high quality.
- Provided training to increase business entrepreneurial thinking.

Results

- More than 500 sites are included in the guidebook. Several editions of the guidebook have been printed, with new listings added each time.
- Response cards shows that 94 per cent of trail visitors purchase crafts.
- 78 per cent of businesses on the trail report increased sales.
- New trails have been created including trails focused on tours of gardens and the countryside.
- Handmade in America has become a national model for innovative cultural heritage tourism development.

Commerce and Canals: The Delaware and Lehigh National Heritage Corridor

The Setting

As with most settlements, this area of Pennsylvania grew up in the early 19th century around transportation routes. In this case, it was the Lehigh and Delaware Rivers and the series of canals that were developed to transport coal from the mines to other cities. By the 1930s, this mode of transportation became obsolete, and in the years to come, communities and businesses dried up. Was there something that could be done to save this part of the area's history?

What Happened Next

Friends of the Delaware Canal was formed in 1982. In the ensuing years, efforts included:

- A master plan was devised for the corridor's rehabilitation.
- The Delaware and Lehigh National Heritage Corridor was designated by Congress in 1988.

- A 10-year Management Action Plan was created in 1993.
- Plans were developed for moving visitors through the region.
- Research was conducted to document and interpret important historical stories.
- Preservation and conservation plans were developed.
- Economic development plans focused on quality of life improvements.

Results

- In 1993, the Corridor Visitors Centre was completed.
- The National Canal Museum was developed in Easton, and more than 100 new businesses opened.
- National heritage area designation was given to two state parks.
- Heritage area designation has helped attract $54 million in investments in 13 years.
- Audubon's Lehigh Auto Tour was developed through collaboration of the Environmental Protection Agency, Pennsylvania Department of Community Affairs Bureau of State Parks, Carbon County and the D&L Heritage Corridor Commission.

From Furs to Factories to Tourism: The Tennessee Overhill Heritage Association

The Setting

The three counties in this region of Southeast Tennessee that make up the Tennessee Overhill (so named for the 18th century Cherokee towns located over the mountains from the Carolina colonies) were as economically distressed as any could be—once thriving company towns and farms were quietly fading. But the remnants remained—from Cherokee fur-trading days to the coming of gold and copper mines and the railroad. The area was already drawing tourists for recreation. Could the region's heritage be appealing to visitors as well?

What Happened Next?

A group of local visionaries realized they had an important story to tell and formed the Tennessee Overhill Association. In 1990, the National Trust for Historic Preservation began a Heritage Tourism Initiative. Tennessee was selected as one of four states to participate, and the Overhill area was chosen as a pilot area. As part of the initiative the Overhill began work:

- Outreach programmes were designed to build pride among residents.
- Driving tour brochures were developed.
- A folklorist completed an inventory of all traditional artists and art forms in the area.
- Programmes were created to celebrate African-American heritage.
- An agriculture trail was developed.
- Assistance was provided to develop new museums and upgrade existing ones.

Results

- The association was permanently established with representatives from the three counties.
- New cabins, lodges, retreats and B&Bs have opened.
- Partnerships have been developed with local recreational companies to develop promotional packages.
- Travel writers are hosted on a regular basis.
- In 1996, the Overhill Association published a directory of arts and artists in preparation for the upcoming Olympic Whitewater Competition on the Ocoee River.
- Many historic buildings have been restored, and interest in preservation has increased.

Travelling with the Ghosts of Conflict Virginia Civil War Trails

The Setting

Civil War sites abound in history-rich Virginia. But finding them and interpreting them was a job left to the visitor. Many war-related places were unknown outside their vicinities and others faced possible destruction by commercial and residential development. Wasn't there some way to save the sites at risk, capitalize on the vast untapped tourism potential, and make the tourists experience more pleasant and informative?

What Happened Next?

The Virginia Civil War Trails (VCWT) initiative was launched in 1997 to develop and market Civil War trails in Virginia. VCWT efforts to date include:

- developing and installing trailblazer signs.
- producing engaging, user-friendly brochures.
- developing and installing interpretive signs.
- hosting a toll-free number for visitor inquiries.
- sending out visitor information.
- placing print and media advertisements.
- producing a VCWT website at http://www.civilwar-va.com/
- maintaining trails.

Results

- Visitors can now experience the story of the Civil War in Virginia.
- The programme brings visitors to previously unvisited parts of the state.
- The trails build community pride and grassroots support for Civil War preservation.
- Visits to Virginia's Civil War sites increased from 500,000 in 1996 to 580,000 in 1997.
- 50 new waysides have been created to provide vantage points for Civil War sites.
- The VCWT programme has grown to include trails in MD, NC, SC, WV & DC.
- VCWT served as the model for a new Civil War Trails organization in Georgia.

Culture, Corridors and Cars

The Setting

In Washington State, federal and state agencies with seemingly disparate missions have worked together to support an audio-tape tour and booklet project that serves their shared goals: using the state's cultural heritage to enhance the experience of driving selected routes. Although developed primarily as an educational tool and conservation programme to identify and preserve diverse cultural traditions, the project has grown into one that also contributes to economic development through heritage tourism.

From Native peoples like the Skokomish and Klallam to those of African, European, Latino, or Asian descent, Washington State contains a potpourri of cultures and traditions. The stories, music, crafts, songs, dances, and customs of these disparate cultures make up what Willie Smyth calls the "invisible landscape."

Smyth is manager of the Washington State Arts Commission (WSAC) Folk Arts Programme. His programme's goal is to develop ways to recognize and preserve the state's diverse expressions of cultural heritage and to encourage public awareness of and appreciation for these traditions. The challenge is to document and present them through exhibits, festivals, recordings and publications. The problem is that not only are these folk art traditions unknown and unseen by most people, they're often widely scattered in little travelled areas.

Folklorist Jens Lund knows a lot about Washington's past. He knows there are songs and legends and untold stories about oyster farmers, lumber mill workers, loggers, orchard growers, salmon fishermen, and ship's carpenters. Lund knows that the multi-faceted state population has produced arts and crafts from Native woodcarvings and woven baskets by artisans like Hazel Pete of the Chehalis Indian Reservation, to Finnish weavings like those by Mary Koski of Aberdeen, and Norwegian rosemaling, a traditional form of decorative painting handed down and practiced by people like Shari Underwood of Brady. Lund also knows that without preservation efforts, many of these traditions will fade from time and memory.

Willie Smyth thought it was time to "bring the invisible landscape alive in an area where the natural beauty is evident." But he needed help. Happily, it was available—but from an unlikely source.

> "The Arts Commission's idea to capture the incredibly rich and diverse heritage of these corridors was easy to support. It

enabled our state to bring to life the invisible landscapes of the past for travellers to better understand the sense of place they are experiencing today."

— Judy Lorenzo, Washington State Department of Transportation

What Happened Next?

Through the non-profit Northwest Heritage Resources, Willie Smyth contracted with Jens Lund to begin the lengthy process of inventorying and documenting cultural traditions in rural areas of the state. Early fact gathering showed a surprising diversity of cultures not even Lund or Smyth expected. They brainstormed and decided that a combined informational guide and audio-tape would be a satisfactory way to capture the essence of so many cultural treasures.

"We chose the tape and booklet format for the self-guided tour because it brings together such colourful traditional arts as songs, crafts, narratives, and music from Washington communities and presents them in an informative and accessible way to both locals and the public," explains Smyth. When drivers play the tape while following the tour, they hear the words and music of the residents featured in the booklet. In this way, the local residents speak directly to their visitors.

Looking for funding support, they began to consider a somewhat untraditional source. They approached Judy Lorenzo at the Washington State Department of Transportation (WSDOT), who is in charge of promoting the state's designated Heritage Corridors. These are scenic, older routes that often get bypassed by speedier, but often less interesting, Interstate highways. As director of that programme, Lorenzo must find ways to preserve the unique scenic character along the routes and help travellers get information about natural, cultural and historic features near them.

After considering the Folk Arts Programme proposal, Lorenzo approved WSDOT's grant of $25,000 for the first Washington Heritage Tour. Othello to Omak is a 153-mile, south-north drive through central Washington that traverses ranch lands, farmlands, arid landscapes strewn with boulders, passes the 400-foot-high, four-mile-wide canyon at Dry Falls, the Upper Grand Coulee and the Grand Coulee Dam, and winds through the Colville Indian

Reservation and forests of ponderosa pine. Lund conducted the cultural resource inventory for that area—interviewing people like Jess Goodwin, a cowboy poet; Rev. Frank Andrews, who tends the grave of his great-uncle, Chief Joseph of the Nez Perce; and traditional Mexican folk artist, Arminda Saldivar—which netted hundreds of hours of taped interviews and performances by singers, musicians, and story-tellers, as well as thousands of photographs.

Lund then edited the vast accumulation of information into a cohesive, compact package. He began with the audio-editing. "One of the hardest parts of the R&D process is choosing which sound clips to use from the huge selection that we come away with," he explains. "Sometimes the most significant things aren't as interesting as the little, quirkier things. It's a balancing act to provide important historical information with entertaining folklore." Much of what gets cut from the tour tape is written into the accompanying booklet.

WSDOT also provided technical assistance for the booklet by mapping and identifying roads, towns, lakes and other landmarks, one of the most challenging aspects of this endeavour. At Jack Straw Productions, sound engineer Tom Stiles mixed the narrator's voice along with the clips from the taped interviews and other audio material.

Each tape tour takes from one to two years to bring to completion. Before the tapes and booklets are printed, Lund conducts extensive field testing by actually driving the tours using the audio-tape and the booklet. Completed tapes and booklets are sold through bookstores and museum gift shops, and can be purchased from Northwest Heritage Resources. Up to 20 copies of the tour sets are provided to Washington's public library system, along with order forms for residents who want to purchase their own copies.

Three more heritage driving tours were conceived, researched, tested, produced, and marketed in partnership with WSDOT and the National Endowment for the Arts. One of these tours, the Olympic Peninsula Loop tour, was supported by a joint grant programme known as the National Endowment for the Arts/U.S. Forest Service Arts and Rural Community Assistance Initiative. The Forest Service partnered in the tour since the Olympic National Forest is on the Peninsula. Along this tour in the Hoquiam River

Valley, travellers will see the great stands of forests and hear the history of the logging industry on the peninsula from the earliest methods using double-bit axes and crosscut saws (known as "misery whips" or "Swede fiddles") to today's massive machines that do everything from cutting to limbing, bucking, and loading logs. Visible along the route are remnants of logging railroads and river pilings that once moored great rafts of logs as they were assembled for towing. Travellers will hear from Diane Ellison, a world champion "birler," or competition log roller in the 1960s, who travelled the world over to demonstrate the sport.

Plans are underway for three tours along the state's more heavily travelled Interstate highways. Since these are not Heritage Corridors, WSDOT won't be participating. Instead, WSAC will consider corporate funding possibilities.

Making the Most of Opportunities

Collaborate: The partners helped shape the rural auto tours in Washington. WSAC's goal was refined by WSDOT's interest in focusing the tours along specific corridors *versus* broad regions. The DOT provided a level of expertise with the mapping of resources that would have been difficult to achieve by the Folk Arts Programme. On the Olympic Peninsula, the U.S. Forest Service's participation through Rural Community Assistance funding ensured that the tour focusses on the significance of wood and timber-dependent lifestyles. Ongoing support from the National Endowment for the Arts has also played a critical role.

Find the Fit between the Community and Tourism: Lund literally took to the streets, visiting museums, radio stations, parks, bars and workplaces to find his subjects for the tours. In one community after another, he talked to the locals, asked who had folkways to share, or songs to sing, stories to tell. It was an organic process that relied heavily on the willingness of people to participate, and the information found in one locale often led him to the next. Thus, the shape of the tour route at times was determined by his subjects, while keeping within a predetermined framework for the overall tour.

Make Sites and Programmes Come Alive: The tape tours include oral histories and interviews with local folk artists and often feature obscure art forms and cultural traditions. For visitors who don't have the time to seek out locals, the tapes help them gain a better understanding of unique cultural heritage traditions. "In Soap Lake, in the centre of the state, I heard an astonishingly beautiful Russian choir at the Slavic Brethren Church," says Lund. "They are an economically stressed community, yet the voices of the people are filled with hope and wonder. It was a fantastic surprise and one I was delighted to find and share with travellers."

Focus on Quality and Authenticity: In sifting through a vast amount of information that can be included in each tour, a folklorist selects information that provides an accurate representation of the diverse folk traditions along each route. Quality is essential, and only clear recordings and high quality photographs are included in the final product.

Preserve and Protect Resources: Not only do the tape/booklet tours capture and acknowledge significant Washington state folk art traditions, the research preceding the production of the tours results in thousands of documents, photographs and a wealth of audio-taped information. What can't be included in the tours due to space constraints becomes a valuable resource, managed by WSAC, for teachers, researchers, and others who wish to trace the history and heritage of the state.

Results

- What began as an effort to recapture cultural traditions has evolved into a significant tourism tool, mainly through direct sales and online marketing. WSDOT's study of one of the Eastern Washington tours concludes that 30 per cent of the tour purchasers travelled that route specifically to use the tour guide. WSAC estimates the figures to be much higher in remote areas. The tours bring people to an area they might not otherwise visit and encourages them to stay there longer, with recommendations in the guidebooks for additional places to visit.
- The partnerships WSAC forged during this process opened the door for many more collaborative efforts between non-profit agencies, state agencies and federal agencies. The programme has a strong endorsement from Lorenzo, who says, "It was an honour for the Department of Transportation to contribute to this effort, and I

commend the Arts Commission for its passion and teamwork."

- Due to the quality and success of these tours, WSAC has provided assistance on at least 10 similar projects across the country including ones in Utah, Kentucky and Maryland.
- The tape tours are already shared with libraries statewide, but the Folk Arts Programme is not stopping there. They are planning to disseminate their inventoried heritage traditions through the development of a CD-ROM and searchable database.

A CASE STUDY OF MRSC

The Municipal Research and Services Centre (MRSC) is a non-profit, independent organization created in 1969 to continue programmes established in 1934 under the Bureau of Governmental Research at the University of Washington. In 1997, Washington counties joined cities in funding MRSC, and in 2007, special districts were added. Our mission is "working together for excellence in local government through professional consultation, research and information services."

MRSC is governed by a volunteer board of directors drawn from local government and the community-at-large. MRSC does not engage in political activity. We do work in cooperation with the Association of Washington Cities and the Washington State Association of Counties, and the Washington Association of County Officials, advocacy organizations for cities and counties.

Individual cities and counties pay no fees for MRSC programmes. Instead, programmes are cooperatively funded out of a small portion of the cities' distributions of the Liquor Board profits and the counties' distribution of the liquor excise tax. Funding is provided through a biennial contract with the Municipal Research Council, a state agency. Services are already paid for so do not hesitate to use them.

The Council has 14 members: two appointed by the President of the Senate; two appointed by the Speaker of the House; the director of the Department of Community, Trade and Economic Development; six city and town officials appointed by the Association of Washington Cities, two county officials appointed by the Washington State Association of Counties, and one county official appointed by the Washington Association of County Officials.

At least one city or town official is from a city having a population of twenty thousand or more; at least one from a city having a population of one thousand five hundred to twenty thousand; and at least one from a town having a population of less than one thousand five hundred. The terms of legislators, city, town, or county officials is dependent upon continuance in elective office. Members serve two year terms.

RESOURCE MANUAL FOR CULTURAL HERITAGE TOURISM

A. Partners in Tourism: US National Partners

- Alliance of National Heritage Areas.
- American Association of Museums.
- Americans for the Arts.
- Cultural and Heritage Tourism Alliance.
- Federation of State Humanities Council.
- National Assembly of State Arts Agencies.
- National Association of African American Heritage Preservation.
- National Conference of State Historic Preservation Officers.
- National Geographic Society.
- National Trust for Historic Preservation.
- Travel Industry Association of America.
- Tourism Works for America.

B. Partners in Tourism: Federal American Corresponding Partners

- Advisory Council on Historic Preservation.
- National Endowment for the Arts.
- National Endowment for the Humanities.
- Institute of Museum and Library Services.
- President's Committee on the Arts and Humanities.
- U.S. Department of Agriculture.
- Forest Service.
- Natural Resources Conservation Service.

- U.S. Department of Interior.
- Bureau of Land Management.
- National Park Service.

C. US-based and Affiliated Cultural Heritage Tourism Organizations

1. Alliance of National Heritage Areas.
2. American Association for State and Local History.
3. American Association of Museums.
4. American Bus Association.
5. American Institute for Conservation of Historic and Artistic Works.
6. American Planning Association.
7. American Society of Travel Agents.
8. Americans for the Arts.
9. America's Byways Resource Centre.
10. Association for Living Historical Farms and Agricultural Museums.
11. Association for Preservation Technology International.
12. Association of African American Museums.
13. The Foundation Centre.
14. The Getty Conservation Institute.
15. Heritage Preservation.
16. Institute of Museum and Library Services.
17. International Association of Convention and Visitors Bureau.
18. Land Trust Alliance.
19. National Alliance of Preservation Commissions.
20. National Assembly of State Arts Agencies.
21. National Association of State Development Agencies.
22. National Conference of State Historic Preservation Officers.
23. National Endowment for the Arts.
24. National Endowment for the Humanities.
25. National Historical Publications and Records Commission.
26. National Park Service.
27. National Scenic Byways Programme.
28. National Tour Association.

29. National Trust for Historic Preservation.
30. Preservation Action.
31. Rails-to-Trails Conservancy.
32. Scenic America.
33. Society of American Travel Writers.
34. Travel Industry Association of America.
35. Travel and Tourism Research Association.
36. U.S. Department of Agriculture Rural Development.
37. U.S. Department of Transportation.
38. United States Tour Operators Association.
39. World Tourism Organization.
40. World Travel and Tourism Council.
41. Cross Reference Index.

Alliance of National Heritage Areas

The Alliance of National Heritage Areas is a collaboration of the congressionally designated regions that represent the stories of nationally significant and distinct aspects of America's heritage. The Alliance advocates, facilitates and celebrates excellence and co-operative initiatives which: Enhance the quality of life for citizens and their communities; Attract national and international visitors to those communities; Provide distinguished examples of sustainable destination development for our nation. The goals of the Alliance are:

(*i*) To create and enhance strategic links among National Heritage Areas for their mutual benefit.

(*ii*) To educate key constituencies, including our communities and the public at large, about successes and opportunities associated with NHAs and to communicate successes in: natural resource conservation; historic preservation; community revitalization; economic development; recreation enhancement; the arts; folklife; education; and interpretation.

(*iii*) To create a federal platform for NHAs upon which both collective and individual issues are articulated.

(*iv*) To develop and support entrepreneurial activities with the private sector in support of sustainable NHAs development.

(*v*) To encourage formation of additional alliances and partnerships.
(*vi*) To enhance organizational capacity in support of NHAs and national heritage partnerships through advancement of collective research, public policy, promotion and management initiatives.

American Association for State and Local History

The American Association for State and Local History (AASLH) is a membership organization comprised of individuals, agencies, and organizations acting in the public trust, engaged in the practice of history, and representing a variety of disciplines and professions. Its goal is to strengthen the field of state and local history by sharing information, answering questions, providing training, and serving as a professional networking source. AASLH provides individuals, communities, and organizations worldwide with information, publications, and training to save and celebrate their heritage. Its services benefit history professionals and volunteers working in historical societies, museums, historic sites, parks, libraries, archives, historic preservation organizations, schools and colleges.

American Association of Museums

The American Association of Museums (AAM) promotes professional standards by improving the quality of museum programmes, services, and operations. AAM is a representative and advocate for museums, promoting understanding of the responsibilities, functions, and needs of museums before political, corporate, foundations, and community leaders throughout the nation. It also provides professional development opportunities through publications and meetings for museum professionals, trustees and volunteers.

American Bus Association

The American Bus Association (ABA) is the trade association of the intercity bus industry with approximately 800 motor coach owners and tour company members in the U.S., Canada and Mexico. Its members operate charter, tour, regular route, airport express, special operations, and contract services (commuter, school, transit). Another 3,000 members are travel and tourism organizations and suppliers of bus products and services who work in partnership with the North American motor coach industry. The ABA represents the U.S. bus industry in Washington, DC, facilitates relationships between the North American motor coach industry and all related segments of the travel and supplier industry, and creates awareness of the motor coach industry among consumers in North America. Annual programmes include: Institute of Industry Advancement Educational Seminars, Certified Travel Industry Specialist Programme, International Driving Championship, Golden Wrench Award, Business and Education Conference, ABA Scholarship Programme, Destinations Magazine Guide Awards, and the American Bus Marketplace. The American Bus Marketplace is a group travel industry business event. North American motorcoach and tour owners and operators (buyers) meet with representatives of the travel industry (sellers) in pre-scheduled appointments. Motorcoach and tour operators use the opportunity to obtain information on attractions, lodging, and restaurants as possible stops for charters and tours. Travel industry members (sellers)—convention and visitors bureaus, state and provincial tourism offices, restaurants, attractions, hotels and motels—entice operators to bring them motorcoach charters and tours.

The ABA publishes Destinations magazine, a monthly magazine for tours and travel (advertising accepted), and several newsletters and membership directories.

American Institute for Conservation of Historic and Artistic Works

The American Institute for Conservation (AIC) of Historic and Artistic Works is the national organization of conservation professionals which sponsors conferences and publishes and sells a variety of conservation-related periodicals. Its non-profit foundation, Foundation of the American Institute for Conservation (FAIC) of Historic and Artistic Works, offers educational programmes, grants to conservators, and a conservator referral system. A general bibliography on conservation, and guidelines for selecting a conservator, are available on request.

American Planning Association

The American Planning Association (APA) is a non-profit public interest and research organization representing 31,000 professional planners, elected officials, and citizens involved with urban and rural planning issues. APA' s main office in Chicago houses our conference, education, membership, publications and research departments. The Washington, DC, office house the government affairs, public affairs and outreach offices. In addition, our members across the country are organized into 46 states and regional chapters and 17 topical or special interest divisions. Among the latter are the Resort and Tourism Division, the Urban Design and Preservation Division, and the Transportation Planning Division. APA's website (www-planning-org) helps individuals access information about current projects, publications, upcoming conferences, chapter and division websites, and other useful resources—Recent research reports relating to cultural heritage tourism include:

(*i*) Parks, Recreation and Open Spaces: An Agenda for the 21st century.
(*ii*) Aesthetics, Community Character, and the Law.
(*iii*) Traffic Sheds, Rural Highway Capacity, and Growth Management.
(*iv*) Principles of Smart Development.
(*v*) Gambling, Economic Development and Historic Preservation.
(*vi*) Saving Face: How Corporate Franchise Design can Respect Community Identity.

American Society of Travel Agents (ASTA)

The American Society of Travel Agents (ASTA) is a voluntary trade association whose primary mission is to enhance the professionalism and profitability of member travel agents through effective representation in industry and government affairs, education and training, and by identifying and meeting the needs of the travelling public. Most travel professionals and students can also join. ASTA is the world's largest travel trade association.

ASTA Foundation offers scholarships to any travel and tourism student attending school in the United States or Canada. Grants range from $500 to $3,000; approximately $30,000 is available annually. Some geographic and eligibility requirements apply. Most application deadlines are in mid-June or July, some are year-round. ASTA provides reference or research assistance to its members through a toll-free hotline.

Americans for the Arts

Americans for the Arts is the nation's leading arts information clearinghouse, with a 40-year record of objective arts industry research. As the nation's arts advocacy organization, it is dedicated to representing and serving local communities and creating opportunities for every American to participate in and appreciate all forms of the arts. Americans for the Arts provides research and information, professional development, advocacy, policy and visibility programmes and services.

America's Byways Resource Centre

America's Byways Resource Centre provides support and assistance to coordinators for designated All-American Roads, National Scenic Byways, State Scenic Byway programmes, or other organizations or public agencies involved with a designated National Scenic Byway or All-American Road. The centre provides help on everything from organization to marketing, funding advice to networking. The Centre:

- (*i*) offers specific assistance, information, expertise and connections for scenic byways.
- (*ii*) conducts and shares research and case studies about byways.
- (*iii*) provides connections to a network of scenic byway experts.
- (*iv*) provides education and training resources.
- (*v*) facilitates communication between scenic byway contacts.
- (*vi*) provides resources from the National Clearinghouse Library.

Association for Living Historical Farms and Agricultural Museums

From its founding in 1970, the Association for Living History, Farm and Agricultural Museums (ALHFAM) has been the central international service organization for those involved in living historical farms, agricultural museums and outdoor museums of history and folklife—ALHFAM encourages information sharing about current historical interpretation methods applicable to agricultural and rural history; encourages research, presentation and publication on historic agriculture, rural society, folklife and the farm environment; stimulates the exchange of ideas, artifacts and information; identifies sources of livestock, plant stock, skills and processes for use in living history farms and other interpretive programmes; and provides standards and guidance for management and operation of living historical farms and related facilities.

The Bulletin, published quarterly, updates members on individual and institutional activities, educational and professional training opportunities, annual meeting plans, and the availability of artifacts, replicas, and publications—Annual meetings are held in the U.S. and Canada.

Association for Preservation Technology International (APTI)

The Association for Preservation Technology International (APTI) is a multi-disciplinary membership organization dedicated to advancing the application of technology to conservation of the built environment. APTI offers the technical information published in the Bulletin, a quarterly Journal of Preservation Technology, and a referral service for technical assistance on products, manufacturers, suppliers and individual professionals.

Association of African American Museums (AAAM)

The Association of African American Museums (AAAM) is a non-profit membership organization serving the interests and needs of black museums and cultural institutions, and black museum professionals throughout the nation. Established as the single representative and principal voice of the African American museum movement, AAAM seeks to strengthen and to advocate the interests of institutions and individuals committed to the preservation of African derived cultures. In additions to its other services, the organization publishes *African American Heritage Directory*, a directory of black museums and related institutions, in collaboration with Howard Johnson Hotels.

The Foundation Centre

The Foundation Centre is an independent national service organization established by foundations to provide an authoritative source of information on foundation and corporate giving. Since 1956, the Foundation Centre has done this by maintaining a comprehensive and up-to-date database on foundations and corporate giving programmes, by producing directories, and by analyzing trends in foundation support of the non-profit sector. It publishes *The Foundation Directory*, the classic reference work for grant seekers, and more than 60 other directories, guides, and research reports. Information from the database is available electronically through custom searching and online services and on CD-ROM. As a vital component of its mission, the Foundation Centre offers information free to the public at five Foundation Centre Libraries (New York, Washington DC, Atlanta, Cleveland and San Francisco) and approximately 200 cooperating collections across the country (nine in Pennsylvania). Through a programme of orientations and educational seminars, the Foundation Centre introduces thousands of grant seekers each year to the funding research process. Cooperating Collections contain a core collection of the Centre's reference works and have staff trained to direct grant seekers to appropriate funding information resources. Many maintain books and reports on local funders and IRS returns for foundations located in their state.

The Getty Conservation Institute

The Getty Conservation Institute works internationally to advance conservation in the visual arts. The Institute serves the conservation community through scientific research, education and training, model field projects, and the dissemination of information. The Institute is a programme of the J. Paul Getty Trust, an international cultural and philanthropic institution devoted to the visual arts and the humanities.

Heritage Preservation

Heritage Preservation works to ensure the preservation of America's collective heritage for present and future generations. Programmes and publications provide advice and guidance on the proper care and maintenance of historic documents, books and archives, works of art, photographs, architecture, monuments, natural science specimens, and family heirlooms—Heritage Preservation works with its members, the nation's leading museums, libraries and archives, historic preservation organizations and historical societies, to inform the public of the need to preserve our collective heritage.

Institute of Museum and Library Services (IMLS)

The Institute of Museum and Library Services is a federal agency that supports museums' education role through grant programmes that encourage outstanding museum management and comprehensive collections care practices. IMLS is the only federal source of operating support for this diverse group of education institutions. Eligible institutions include:

> Aquariums; arboretums and botanical gardens; art museums; children's museums; general museums; historic houses and sites; history museums; nature centres; natural history and anthropology museums; planetariums; science and technology centres; and specialized museums and zoos. Grant categories include general operating support, conservation project support, museum leadership initiatives, professional services programmes, museum assessments; and conservation assessments—Assessment grants are available on a first-come, first-served basis. All other grants are made through a competitive national peer review process with application deadlines throughout the year.

International Association of Convention and Visitor Bureaus (IACVB)

The International Association of Convention and Visitor Bureaus represents more than 500 member bureaus in 30 countries. The association was founded in 1914 to promote sound professional practices in the solicitation and servicing of meetings and conventions.

The IACVB provides public relations for the industry publishes a monthly newsletter and annual membership directory, offers educational programmes for members, runs the online Convention Industry Network (CINET) with a broad spectrum of data on client meetings, and conducts three "Destinations Showcase" trade show events where members exhibit their destinations to meeting professionals. The IACVB Foundation was founded in 1993 to meet the needs of the destination management community and its clients by facilitating research, scholarship, and philanthropy and providing recognition and visibility for the destination management profession. The IACVI3 publishes the "*IACUB News*" membership news magazine 6 times per year, and an E-News e-mail twice a month.

Land Trust Alliance

The Land Trust Alliance is the national organization of land trusts. Through the Alliance, these 1,200 grassroots organizations enhance their ability to protect land—by learning from one another, gaining access to vital information and technical expertise, building public awareness about their work and acquiring financial and political support for their open space protection. Established in 1982, LTA publishes books, a quarterly magazine and a newsletter; sponsors an annual conference and other educational forums; develops and disseminates reports and data of interest to the land trust community; and represents the land trust community in Washington on public policy matters affecting land conservation.

National Alliance of Preservation Commissions (NAPC)

The National Alliance of Preservation Commissions builds strong local preservation programmes through education, information and advocacy. NAPC publishes. *The Alliance Review* newsletter; produces technical seminars and conferences, regional events, and an annual meeting and workshops held in conjunction with the National Trust's Annual Preservation Conference; maintains an information resource centre and a database of historic preservation commissions in the United States.

National Assembly of State Arts Agencies (NASAA)

The National Assembly of State Arts Agencies is the membership organization of the nation's 56 state and jurisdictional arts agencies. NASAA's mission is to advance and promote a meaningful role for the arts in the lives of individuals, families and communities throughout the United States. NASAA empowers state arts agencies through strategic assistance that fosters leadership, enhances planning and decision-making and increases resources. Each year, some 28,000 grants and programmes sponsored by state arts agencies benefit citizens in 5,600 communities, reaching almost every county in the U.S. Grants range from support for theatres and dance companies to heritage organizations and cultural centres. Resources for cultural tourism include grants for artists and organizations, as well as assistance in marketing, planning, professional development, cultural and community convenings to name a few. Examples of these activities can be found at NASAA's Website, as well as a directory of state arts agencies.

National Association of State Development Agencies (NASDA)

The National Association of State Development Agencies provides a reference point for officials and other groups to access information on state economic development and to obtain the viewpoint of state development agencies on various matters. Member agencies generally are state commerce departments, or other state government offices with economic development responsibilities.

National Conference of State Historic Preservation Officers

The National Conference of State Historic Preservation Officers is the professional association of the State Government officials who carry out the national historic preservation programme as delegates of the Secretary of the Interior pursuant to the National Historic Preservation Act (16 USC 470). The State Historic Preservation Officers (SHPOs) locate and record historic properties, nominate significant historic properties to the National Register, foster historic preservation programmes at the local government level and the creation of preservation ordinances, provide matching funds for preservation projects, comment upon preservation projects under consideration for the federal rehabilitation tax credit, review all federal projects for impact on historic properties under Section 106 of the Act and the regulations of the Advisory Council on Historic Preservation, and provide technical assistance on restoration and other preservation activities to federal agencies, state and local governments, and the private sector.

The State Historic Preservation Office is a source for information for heritage tourism projects including research assistance, restoration grants, loans, and state and federal tax incentives.

National Endowment for the Arts

The National Endowment for the Arts recognizes, encourages, and supports the excellence and diversity of our nation's artistic creativity and accomplishments. The majority of the NEA's grants are awarded in the following areas: Creativity, Creating and presenting high quality artistic work; Organizational Capacity: Developing strong and effective arts organizations; Access: Making the arts available to all; Arts Learning: Children and youth learning in and through the arts—Heritage/Preservation: Preserving our cultural heritage. Many of the arts activities that the Endowment supports attract tourists, for example, dance, music, theatre, folk and traditional arts and the design arts (including urban planning and design, historic preservation and landscape architecture).

In addition, Challenge America, a new initiative, offers grants for Community Arts Development projects involving partnerships between arts organizations and community groups that highlight the potential of the arts as a focus for the development of cultural tourism or cultural districts, make a community more livable by addressing civic design issues, and the development of community cultural plans.

Some funding and other opportunities for cultural heritage tourism projects include:

- *Grants to Organizations*: Access www.nea.gov/guide/.
- *NEA*: Forest Service Arts and Rural Community Assistance Initiative (available only in specified states; www.arts.endow.gov/paitnei/Rural-html.

- *Cultural Funding*: Federal Opportunities http://www.arts.endow.gov/federal.html. A searchable database of cultural projects funded by non-cultural federal agencies.

National Endowment for the Humanities

The National Endowment for the Humanities supports research, education, and public programmes in the humanities. The Division of Preservation and Access supports documentation and cataloguing activities, the stabilization of material culture collections, and the preservation of US newspapers. The Division of Public Programmes supports historic site interpretation, museum, and library exhibitions, printed materials, multi-media projects, radio and television programmes, reading and discussion groups, and other public programmes. The Office of Challenge Grants assists non-profit institutions in developing new sources of long-term support for the humanities through grants for institutional endowments, construction, renovation, and other activities. The Office of Federal/State Partnerships provides funds that enable state humanities councils in every state and territory to support and conduct local and statewide programmes for the public in museums, libraries, schools, and other community sites.

National Historical Publications and Records Commission

The National Historical Publications and Records Commission is a federal agency that makes grants for the preservation and publication of historically important manuscripts and archives. Eligible projects include those to collect, preserve, edit, and/or publish the papers of outstanding persons or other significant historical documents relating to U.S. history. Grants can be made to state and local agencies, non-profit organizations, colleges and universities, and to individuals. The average grant amount is $50,000.

National Park Service (NFS)

The mission of the National Park Service is to lead America's conservation movement, including the conservation of natural, historical, and recreational resources. Many of these objectives are expressed in activities the NFS commonly refers to as its partnership programmes. These include Recreation, Trails and Conservation Assistance programmes, and the various historic preservation programmes through which the NFS gives grants, administers the rehabilitation tax credit programme and provides other forms of aid or recognition of important resources in the culture of our nation. National Park Service programmes and activities include:

(*a*) *National Historic Landmark Programme*: Advisory services, technical assistance, and counselling to study and identify national historic landmarks. A bronze plaque and certificate are presented to selected landmarks at a formal ceremony.

(*b*) *National Register of Historic Places*: The National Register of Historic Places is the official list of the Nation's cultural resources worthy of preservation and is part of a national programme to coordinate and support public and private efforts to identify America's historic and archeological resources. Properties include districts, sites, buildings, structures and objects. Nominations to the National Register are made through State Historic Preservation Offices.

(*c*) *Rivers, Trails and Conservation Assistance Programme*: Provides technical assistance to help citizens and community leaders plan and advance locally-led nature-based recreation development and environmental, historic and cultural conservation.

Preservation publications for owners of historic buildings, landscapes, and national historic landmarks, including information on preservation techniques, interpretation and documentation. Various publication listings are available on the NFS Website. (www.cr.nps.gov).

Technical assistance on evaluation and protection (architectural, archaeological, historical and interpretation) of nationally significant resources includes publications, the Internet, and training courses.

National Scenic Byways Programme

The Federal Highway Administration's National Scenic Byways Programme promotes the recognition and enjoyment of America's memorable roads. The National Scenic Byways (NSB) Programme was established under the Intermodal Surface Transportation Efficiency Act of 1991, and reauthorized in 1998 under the Transportation Equity Act for the 21st Century (TEA-21). Under the programme, the U.S. Secretary of Transportation recognizes certain roads as National Scenic Byways or All-American Roads based on their archaeological, cultural, historic, natural, recreational and scenic qualities. There are 72 such designated byways in 32 states. The Federal Highway Administration promotes the collection as America's Byways.

National Tour Association

The National Tour Association is the premier packaged travel association in North America with a membership that includes nearly 650 American and Canadian tour companies; nearly 2,400 tour suppliers such as hotels, attractions, restaurants, air lines, motorcoach companies and others; and approximately 800 destination marketing organization members, such as state and provincial tourism offices, convention and visitor bureaus and Chambers of Commerce. NTA facilitates contacts between tour operators, travel suppliers and destination marketers and provides its members with education by the experts in travel planning, marketing and service delivery—NTA funds and supports research projects designed to improve packaged travel in ways that will enhance the experience for all participants. NTA's research programme is largely carried out by a separate, non-profit organization called the National Tourism Foundation. Working through its representative in Washington, DC, and an active government relations committee of its members, NTA participates actively in tourism-related deliberations within the legislative and executive branches of the federal government, especially about issues that affect the group tour and packaged travel industry. NTA publishes Courier magazine, its monthly membership magazine (advertising accepted). All of NTA's members must abide by a strict code of ethics that protects both members and the travelling public. Each member tour company is covered by a $250,000 consumer protection plan and is required to carry at least $1 million in professional liability, errors and omissions insurance.

National Trust for Historic Preservation

The National Trust for Historic Preservation is a non-profit organization which provides leadership, education and advocacy to save America's diverse historic places and revitalize our communities-Managed from a headquarters in Washington, DC and eight regional and field offices, the National Trust works with national and state agencies involved in preservation and with thousands of community groups in all 50 states. It serves these bodies and the preservation movement generally through the following functions:

- (*i*) provides technical advice and financial assistance to non-profit organizations and public agencies engaged in preservation;
- (*ii*) sponsors educational programmes, technical workshops, and an annual preservation conference;
- (*iii*) serves as an advocate for protection of the country's heritage in the courts and with legislative and regulatory agencies;
- (*iv*) sponsors programmes to demonstrate how preservation can stimulate community revitalization and economic development;
- (*v*) owns and operates 20 historic house museums and
- (*vi*) publishes five periodicals in addition to books, brochures, and educational materials about a variety of preservation topics.

The National Trust has a variety of programmes that can assist local preservation and heritage tourism efforts such as the Heritage Tourism Programme, the National Main Street Centre, the Rural Heritage Programme, the Historic Hotels of America Programme and the Community Partners Programme. It also has several funding programmes that can assist local preservation efforts. These are administered through the Trust's regional offices.

(*a*) *The Heritage Tourism Programme:* It is a fee-for-service programme. The programme helps historic sites, communities, states and federal agencies develop and market a wide variety of tourism programmes. To strengthen the ties between heritage and tourism, it secures partnerships between preservation entities and the travel industry. The programme produces publications and videos, including Getting Started: How to Succeed in Heritage Tourism and is currently spearheading a national cultural heritage tourism initiative, Share Your Heritage, on behalf of Partners in Tourism.

(*b*) *The National Main Street Centre*: It is a fee-for-service programme that provides access to experts with knowledge of every aspect of commercial district revitalization and historic preservation. The Centre links hundreds of downtown revitalization programmes into a strong network.

(*c*) *The Rural Heritage Programme*: It assists rural constituents to respond to rural preservation issues by providing information and access to resources; oversees production of "Your Town" workshops; works on issues such as heritage areas and scenic byways.

(*d*) *Historic Hotels of America (HHA)*: It identifies quality hotels that have faithfully maintained their historic integrity, architecture and ambience. These hotels are promoted nationally and internationally to those who prefer historic settings for their leisure and business travel. Member hotels in this programme must be located in a building that is at least 50 years old and listed in, or eligible for, the National Register of Historic Places or recognized locally as having historic significance. Current membership totals more than 170 hotels and resorts in 42 states, the District of Columbia, and Puerto Rico. Hotels range in size from the eight room American Hotel in Sag Harbor, New York to the Waldorf-Astoria in New York City with 1,407 room. A directory of member hotels is available for purchase.

Financial Assistance

The regional offices provide financial assistance for numerous preservation projects throughout the regions through the National Trust's grant and loan programmes:

(*i*) *The Preservation Services Fund*, which provides matching grants to non-profit organizations, universities and public agencies to support project planning, development of preservation education programmes, or conferences and workshops.

(*ii*) *The Johanna Favrot Fund*, which provides grants to non-profit organizations, government agencies, for profit businesses and individuals for projects that contribute to the preservation or the recapture of an authentic sense of place.

(iii) *The Cynthia Woods Mitchell Fund* for Historic Interiors, which provides grants to non-profits and government agencies for projects that assist in the preservation, restoration and interpretation of historic interiors.

(iv) *The National Preservation Loan Fund,* which provides below-market rate loans to non-profit organizations and public agencies to help preserve properties listed in or eligible for inclusion in the National Register.

(v) *The Inner-City Ventures Fund,* which provides matching grants and low-interest loans to non-profit community organizations to help them revitalize their historic neighbourhoods as a benefit to low and moderate income residents.

Preservation Action

Preservation Action, founded in 1974, is the national non-profit grassroots lobby for historic preservation. It coordinates a network of citizens, preservation professionals, historians, commercial investors and community leaders working together to advocate for our architectural heritage. It works to strengthen local preservation efforts by supporting federal legislation to:

> Protect the craftsmanship and beauty of our architectural heritage for generations to come; invest in historic neighbourhoods, towns and cities; restore and reuse historic structures; rehabilitation of historic structures as high quality housing for all income levels; celebrate and promote the history and diversity of our communities; and make "smart growth" work or for the re-growth of our urban centres, small towns and historic neighbourhoods. Preservation Action publishes a weekly online legislative update, quarterly newsletter and, as appropriate, in-depth policy briefings.

Rails-to-Trails Conservancy

Established in 1985, the Rails-to-Trails Conservancy (RTC) is a national non-profit public charity with more than 100,000 members. Its mission is to enhance America's communities and countryside by converting thousands of miles of abandoned rail corridors, and connecting open space, into a nationwide network of public trails. RTC is based in Washington, DC, with six field offices across the country. RTC carries out a programme of technical assistance, public education, advocacy, negotiation, corridor preservation, regulatory action and corridor assessments. Through a nationwide network of contacts in the recreation, transportation and conservation communities, RTC notifies trail advocates and local governments of upcoming railroad abandonments; assists public and private agencies in the legalities of trail corridor acquisition; provides technical assistance to private citizens as well as trail planners and managers on trail design, development and protection; and publicizes rails and greenways issues throughout the country.

Scenic America

Scenic America is the only national non-profit organization dedicated solely to protecting natural beauty and distinctive community character. Scenic America provides technical assistance across the nation and through nine states affiliates (CA, FL, KY, MI, MO, NC, TX, TN, VA) on scenic byways, billboard and sign control, context-sensitive highway design, wireless telecommunications tower and overhead utility location, transportation enhancements, and other scenic conservation issues. Scenic America advances our #1 goal, to build a citizen movement for scenic conservation, through education, site-specific projects in various states, grassroots organization, and publications on preserving scenic beauty, open space, and quality of life.

Society of American Travel Writers (SATW)

The Society of American Travel Writers is a not-for-profit professional association of writers, photographers, editors, electronic media and film journalists, film lecturers and public relations representatives. Its purposes are the mutual support and professional advancement of its members, as well as to serve the travelling public. It exists to promote unbiased, accurate and interesting reporting on travel destinations, facilities and services, and on consumer issues directly affecting the travelling public. In magazines and newspapers, travel books and guides, radio and television programmes, the Society's members strive to provide readers, viewers and listeners complete, accurate and interesting information on travel destinations, facilities and services. The Society works to raise the standards of the profession. In addition, it seeks to guard the right of freedom to travel and to encourage conservation and preservation of historic sites and natural wonders. Membership is by invitation from sponsors only.

Travel Industry Association (TIA) of America

The Travel Industry Association of America is a national, non-profit unifying organization representing the common concerns of all components of the U.S. travel industry. As an umbrella organization for the industry, TIA includes both public and private sectors. Its primary role is to take a leadership position with major industry developments and initiatives in marketing, government policy, research and analysis, and public education. Its annual "International Pow-Wow-"convention brings together 1500 of the world's largest inbound USA international tour operators at the world's largest inbound "visit USA" marketplace. TIA members are able to join specialized attractions councils as well as attend educational seminars. Its Domestic, International and Economic Research studies are dedicated to providing up-to-date marketing and economic information to the U.S. travel industry.

Travel and Tourism Research Association

The Travel and Tourism Research Association is a membership organization that serves as an international forum for the exchange of ideas and information; promotes and disseminates high quality, credible, and effective research; fosters the development of travel and tourism research and related curricula in institutes of higher education; and advocates for the effective use of research in the decision making process of professionals in the travel and tourism industry. The organization sponsors conferences and provides workshops, seminars, and conferences that help members maintain or enhance their professional skills.

U.S. Department of Agriculture Rural Development

USDA Rural Development is helping fulfill the promise and overcome the problems of the nation's rural heartland. USDA Rural Development was created in 1994 when rural economic and community development programmes that had been splintered among various USDA agencies were forged into a new mission area. With this action, the Farmers Home Administration, Rural Development Administration, Rural Electrification Administration and Agricultural Cooperative Service passed into history, but their tradition of service to America is being carried on by USDA Rural Development.

USDA's Rural Development mission area is committed to helping improve the economy and quality of life in all of rural America. Financial programmes support such essential public facilities and services as water and sewer systems, housing, health clinics, emergency service facilities and electric, telephone and telecommunication services. Economic development is promoted by supporting loans to businesses through banks and community-managed lending pools. Technical assistance and information is provided to help agricultural and other cooperatives get started and improve the effectiveness of their member services. And technical assistance is offered to help communities undertake community empowerment programmes. Each year, USDA Rural Development programmes create or preserve tens of thousands of rural jobs and create or improve more than 65,000 units of quality rural housing. To multiply the impact of its programmes, USDA Rural Development is working with state, local and Indian tribal governments, as well as private and non-profit organizations and user-owned cooperatives. Rural Development programmes are administered through Rural Utilities Service (RUS), the Rural Business-Cooperative Service (RBS) and the Rural Housing Service (RHS). Detailed information and applications for financial assistance are available through Rural Development State Offices.

The following are most relevant to tourism:

(*a*) *Rural Utilities Service*: The mission of the RUS is to serve a leading role in improving the quality of life in rural America by administering its Electrification, Telecommunications, and Water and Waste Disposal Programmes in a service-oriented, forward looking, and financially responsible manner. The Distance Learning and Telemedicine Programme is designed to encourage, improve, and make affordable the use of telecommunications, computer networks and related technology for rural communities to improve access to educational and/or medical services.

(*b*) *Rural Business-Cooperative Service*: The mission of RBS is to enhance the quality of life for all rural Americans by providing leadership in building competitive businesses (including rural business cooperatives) that can build sustainable economic communities, compete successfully in domestic arena, and develop emerging market opportunities in the international arena. RBS objectives are to invest its financial resources and technical assistance in businesses and communities, and to build partnerships that leverage public and private resources to stimulate rural economic activity. RBS programmes include:

(*i*) *Business and Industrial (B&I) Guaranteed Loans*:
Purpose: To improve, develop or finance business, industry and employment and to improve the economic and environmental climate in rural communities; including pollution abatement and control. This purpose is achieved through bolsters the existing private credit structure through guarantee of quality loans which will provide lasting community benefits. This type of assistance is available to businesses located in areas outside any city with a population of 50,000 or more and its immediately adjacent urbanized or urbanizing area. Eligible entities include corporations, partnerships, cooperatives, federally recognized Indian tribes, individuals, and other legal entities.

(*ii*) *Business and Industry Direct Loans*: The Business and Industry Direct Loan Programme provides loans to public entities and private parties who cannot obtain credit from other sources. Loans to private parties can be made for improving, developing, or financing business and industry, creating jobs, and to improve the economic and environmental climate in rural communities (including pollution abatement). This type of assistance is available in rural areas (this includes all areas other than cities of more than 50,000 people and their immediately adjacent urban or urbanizing areas). Eligible entities include cooperatives, corporations, partnerships, trusts or other profit or non-profit entities, Indian tribes or federally recognized tribal groups, municipalities, counties, and any other political sub-division of a state or individuals.

(*iii*) *Intermediary Relenting Programme Loans*:
Purpose: To finance business facilities and community development projects in rural areas including dries with a population of less than 25,000. This is achieved through loans made by RBS to intermediaries who provide loans to ultimate recipients for business facilities and community development projects. Eligible intermediaries include public bodies, non-profit corporations, Indian tribes and cooperatives.

(*iv*) *Rural Business Enterprise Grants*:
Purpose: To help public bodies, non-profit corporations, and federally recognized Indian Tribal groups finance and facilitate development of small and emerging private business enterprises located in areas outside the boundary of a city of 50,000 or more and its immediately adjacent urbanized or urbanizing area. Funds may be used to finance and develop small and emerging private business enterprises. Costs that may be paid from grant funds include the acquisition and development of land and the construction of buildings, plants, equipment, access streets and roads, parking areas, utility and service extensions; refinancing; fees for professional services; technical assistance and training associated with technical assistance; start-up operating costs and working capital; providing financial assistance to a third party; production of television programmes to provide information to rural residents; and creation, expansion, and operation of rural distance learning networks.

(*v*) *Rural Economic Development Loans and Grants*:
Purpose: To finance rural economic development and rural job creation projects that are based on sound economic and financial analyses. Loans and grants are made to RUS electric and telephone borrowers who use the funds to provide financing for business and community development projects. Loans are provided to finance abroad array of projects, including for profit businesses.

Grants are targeted to certain purposes such as community development assistance, education and training for economic development, medical care, telecommunications for education, job training or medical services, business incubators, and technical assistance. RUS borrowers may receive financing for grant purposes through either a grant to establish a revolving loan fund or a combination loan and grant.

(*vi*) *Rural Housing Service*: The Rural Housing Service has various programmes available to aid in the development of rural America. Rural Housing programmes are divided into three categories: Community Facilities (CF), Single Family Housing (SFH.) and Multi-Family Housing (MF). These programmes were formerly operated by the Rural Development Administration and the Farmers Home Administration.

(*vii*) *Community Facilities Loans*

Purpose: To construct, enlarge, extend, or otherwise improve community facilities providing essential services in rural areas and towns with a population of 50,000 or less. The funds are available to public entities such as municipalities, counties, special—purpose districts, Indian tribes, and corporations not operated for profit. RHS also guarantees community facility loans made by banks or other eligible lenders.

(*viii*) *Office of Community Development*: The Office of Community Development administers the Empowerment Zones and Enterprise Communities (EZ/EC) programme that provides economically depressed rural areas and communities with real opportunities for growth and revitalization. It's mission: to create self-sustaining, long-term economic development in areas of pervasive poverty, unemployment, and general distress, and to demonstrate how distressed communities can achieve self-sufficiency through innovative and comprehensive strategic plans developed and implemented by alliances among private, public, and non-profit entities.

1890, 1862 and 1994 Land-Grant Institutions: This initiative is a cooperative effort between USDA and historically black land-grant universities to develop income-producing projects for underdeveloped rural communities.

U.S. Department of Transportation

The U.S. Department of Transportation's Federal Highway Administration oversees the Transportation Enhancements (TE) programme, which began in 1991. The focus of these state administered funds is to address environmental, cultural, economic, and social conditions in an effort to create a more balanced transportation system. There are 12 specific TE categories and among them is support for historic preservation and scenic and historic highway programmes, which have supported a number of cultural heritage tourism projects. Transportation enhancements are federal-aid reimbursement activities; TE is not a grant programme. In most cases, the federal government pays 80 per cent of the project cost, and the project sponsor is responsible for the remaining 20 per cent, also called the matching funds.

United States Tour Operators Association (USTOA)

The United States Tour Operators Association, founded in 1972, is a professional organization representing the tour operator industry. USTOA's Active Members, whose tours encompass the entire globe, are among the world's leading tour operators. To become an Active Member of USTOA, a tour operator is required to have a total of 18 references from a variety of industry sources and financial institutions, and must meet specific minimums in terms of tour passengers and/or dollar volume. The company must also be in business at least three years under the same management in the U.S. and must carry a minimum of $1 million professional liability insurance. Another important membership requirement is adherence to USTOA's strict code of ethics, which is framed by a pledge to encourage and maintain the highest standards of professionalism, integrity and service. In addition to these requirements, all active USTOA members must participate in USTOA's $1 Million Consumer Protection Plan.

World Tourism Organization (WTO)

The World Tourism Organization is the world's leading

international organization in the field of travel and tourism and is an inter-governmental organization and proficient partner of the United Nations and its specialized agencies. Its overall objectives are: economic development; international understanding; peace; prosperity; universal respect; observance of human rights; and fundamental freedoms. Membership includes 133 countries, with six territories as Associate Members and 350 Affiliate Members.

WTO offers seven activity areas: Marketing Intelligence and Promotional Techniques, Statistics and Economic Evaluation of Tourism, Human Resource Development, Sustainable Development of Tourism, Cooperation for Development, Quality of Tourism Development, and Communications and Documentation.

World Travel & Tourism Council (WTTC)

Established in 1990, the World Travel and Tourism Council is a global coalition of industry chief executive officers promoting the case for travel and tourism at the highest level of government/public policy. WTTC includes major international companies from the accommodation, catering, recreation, transportation and travel service sectors of the world's largest industry.

4

Cultural and Heritage Tourism in India: An Overview

UNDERSTANDING CULTURAL AND HERITAGE TOURISM IN INDIA

From time since immemorial, India has been considered to be a land with rich cultural heritage. Centuries after centuries, this country has seen rulers like Rajputs, Moughals, English, Portuguese. Besides, various religions also flourished at different times in this country like Buddhism, Jainism etc. All these factors have played their role in making an impact on the culture of this country. One can find the traces of different cultures in music, dance, architecture, festivities, languages spoken, traditional beliefs and customs, food and many more like these. It is the development in these aspects of life that makes the heritage of India one of the most vibrant and most exhaustive. We believe in the continuity and dynamism of Indian cultural heritage and it is our endeavour to help people from world over get acquainted with same. And there cannot be a better way to understand this than to experience it. Travel to India with our cultural tour packages and understand why this heritage has withstood thousands of years and still going strong.

Music

Classical music of India has its roots beliefs of the people and an amalgamation with other systems has not erased this source. Careful intonation has always been at the core of Indian classical music. The chanting of sacred words and phrases like Om required total precision because these chants were part of what it took to maintain the order of the universe.

Dances

India offers a number of classical dance forms, each of which can be traced to different parts of the country and representing the culture of a certain region or a group of people. The beginning of the contemporary styles of classical dances can be traced to the period 1300-1400 A.D. The dance forms range from temple dances like Bharatnatyam, Oddissi and Mohiniyattam, to Kathakali, symbolizing the victory of truth over falsehood. Kathak and Kuchipudi are means to recite religious and mythological tales to the accompaniment music, mime and dance. Manipuri, and Dandiya Raas represents the celebration of Radha-Krishna's togetherness.

Art and Crafts

The talent of the Indian artisans' is till date visible in the age-old monuments/constructions. The sculptures boast of their creativity and hard work. The numerous sculptures on temple walls are all hewn out of hard rock and last to date. Rock-cut architecture was perfected by the Buddhists, and was followed by several Hindu rulers. In Southern India Pallavas excelled in this art form.

The sculptures or idols in temples are made of granite and the Utsava Murthis are made of Bronze and Panchaloha. Apart from these, there are the huge Iyyanar statues and horses exist in South Indian villages.

ASSOCIATION WITH RAILWAY TOURISM IN INDIA

India has the largest network of railways in the world. It is one of the most convenient and popular mode of transport for travelling in India. Indian Railways offer you a heat of options when you choose to explore India by train. There is the most exclusive and royal—'palace on wheels', which takes you into the world of royal life. Then there are fast and comfortable Rajdhanis and Shatabdis. Besides, there are hundreds of trains available which covers almost whole of India. We, therefore, offer you an exclusive opportunity to see and explore India with Indian Railways, which is the most enduring symbol of British Raj. We as your Travel Agent to India would strive to make you aware of India that is spellbounding, exotic, and full of oriental charms.

North India by Rail

(12 Nights/13 Days)—Delhi, Jodhpur, Jaisalmer, Jodhpur, Udaipur, Jaipur, Agra, Delhi.

Indo-Nepal by Rail

(17 Nights/18 Days)—Delhi, Jodhpur, Jaisalmer, Jodhpur, Udaipur, Jaipur, Agra, Varanasi, Kathmandu, Delhi.

Golden Triangle by Rail

(05 Nights/6 Days)—Delhi, Jaipur, Agra, Delhi.

Central India Train Tour

(10 Nights/11 Days)—Delhi, Jaipur, Agra, Gwalior, Khajuraho, Varanasi, Delhi.

Western India by Rail

(Duration: 14 Nights/15 Days)—Mumbai (Bombay), Ahmedabad, Udaipur, Jodhpur, Jaisalmer, Jodhpur, Jaipur, Agra, Delhi.

West/South India by Rail-I

(Duration: 12 Nights/13 Days)—Mumbai (Bombay), Aurangabad, Hyderabad, Chennai (Madras), Mysore, Bangalore, Mumbai (Bombay).

West/South India by Rail-II

(Duration: 17 Nights/18 Days)—Mumbai (Bombay), Aurangabad, Hyderabad, Chennai (Madras), Trichy, Madurai, Periyar, Cochin, Bangalore, Mysore, Bangalore, Mumbai.

South India by Rail

(Duration: 13 Nights/14 Days)—Chennai (Madras), Madurai, Periyar, Trivandram, Cochin, Bangalore, Mysore.

CONNECTING WITH YOGA AND MEDITATION

Modern age life has given too many news things to us. It has made our lives easier in many ways. But more than that, it has also increased the stress levels, the complexities and mental pressure under which we keep going on. What we immediately do not realize is the impact of living such a life-style on our health. But those who do care about their lives and want to live it the healthy way, what could be a better way to de-stress from the distresses of life than to relax in the soothing and therapeutic balm of India's Yogic and Meditational practices. India is internationally renowned for its ancient healing practices and alternative therapies. For more than thousands of years now, we have followed our own indigenous healing systems and medicinal practices such as Ayurveda, Naturopathy and Pranic Healing to name just a few. It is no wonder then that people from all over the world are turning to the Indian sub-continent for guidance towards a more spiritually satisfying way of life. Yoga and Meditation are just such indigenous twin techniques of self-realization and purification. One incomplete without the other, they help an individual to develop a sense of physical, mental, emotional as well as spiritual well-being. Yoga in all its forms tries to create harmony of the body with the mind and soul. It is a very general term that encompasses many different disciplines ranging from the purely physical to the purely spiritual, and is a truly original Indian concept. Many people believe that Yoga and meditation are mystic arts that demand complete devotion to the exclusion of everything else. However, the truth is that Yoga and Meditation are not the hard taskmasters they are often made out to be. Yoga and Meditation can easily be incorporated into our daily lives, requiring no more than a few minutes, if not more, everyday. Their benefits on the other hand are wide-ranging and restorative. For instance, meditation has proven to be highly effective in treating psychological conditions, such as obsessive-compulsive disorder, depression, and anxiety, and Yoga is known to increase levels of self-confidence and memory. We have designed special Yoga and Meditation tour packages that will allow you to combine your holiday and travel to India with a truly uplifting and revitalizing experience. What could be better way to spend a vacation than to go on an inspiring health holiday that will leave you physically, mentally and spiritually refresh.

KARNATAKA PLAN

Karnataka has many unturned pages. Sadly, little has been done to make her well read and explored. With the state tourism department having picked up pace only in the past two years, Karnataka still has long way to go in terms of accessibility, infrastructure, conservation and preservation. For the year 2008, the department wants to throw open the doors to some well-known destinations that have so far been neglected and is planning some aggressive promotion. Tourism Director C. Somasekhara told *The Times of India* that the department would lay thrust on blending culture with tourism. Rs. 4 crore is being set aside to promote cultural activities in some lesser known destinations, including Karavali and Lakkundi. While tourism clubs are being initiated in all district and taluk schools so students are encouraged to act as guides, the department is also hosting district conclaves in Hassan, Mangalore, Udupi, Shimoga, Bidar, Uttar Kannada and Belgaum starting from December 27. These conclaves are stakeholders' meetings to decide on ways to promote district tourism. The state has some prime tourist destinations that have been crying for attention and the department plans to showcase them better to attract travellers.

Focus on Jog Falls

The department plans to pump water up to the mouth of the fall so that the falls are full and resplendent through the year. Presently they are full between September and December, but run dry the rest of the year. Rs. 5 crore will be spent on setting up machinery at 5 or 6 stages to pump up the water instead of letting it flow downstream. Landscaping—hardscaping and softscaping—will also be taken up at Rs. 3.10 crore, by the Karnataka Housing Board.

Works at Sadhankeri Lake, Dharwad

This lake has gained much importance thanks to poet and Jnanpith awardee D.R. Bendre's continuous reference to it in his poems. The department wants to develop this lake because Bendre Bhavan and Bendre House, which are nearby, are visited by students and researchers regularly. The objective is to turn it into a tourist attraction while preserving the visiting bird species. Located right opposite the poet's house on the Dharwad-Goa highway, it will now be developed at a cost of Rs. 3.56 crore. The Centre has provided Rs. 3.08 crore, of which Rs. 2.46 crore has already been released. The comprehensive development plan is ready and the department along with the district administration will begin work soon. The foundation stone for the project will be laid on December 28.

Gaganachukki and Bharachukki Falls, Shivanasamudhra

The department has a Rs. 5 crore proposal to develop the two falls. This will involve providing ropeways, accommodation and other facilities. Rs. 2 crore has already been spent on setting up a guest house.

Tourism in Mangalore

The department, with the Karnataka State Industrial Infrastructure Development Corporation (KSIIDC), is developing an Acqua Marine Park, Golf Club and a ropeway from Tannir Bhavi to Sulthan Batheri. Of the Rs. 20 crore, Rs. 6 crore has been released, even as KSIIDC is carrying out the feasibility study.

Chamundi Hills, Mysore

Landscaping, provision of parking facilities, removal of encroachments, etc, will be part of the overall development plan for the Hills. The department is spending Rs. 13.78 crore.

Belur and Halebid

A detailed report on the concept 'Heritage Passport' will be prepared by mid-February, with members of UNESCO and town planning authority chalking out a circuit that will include Somanathapura and Banavara, apart from Belur and Halebid. Traveller can buy a passport and get a guided tour to the four places, apart from food and accommodation facilities. Heritage houses are being identified to turn into hotels, while tanks and lakes built in the Hoysala period will be improved.

Kuppalli Smaraka, Kuppalli Shimoga

The Kuvempu Prathishthana will be developed into a tourism centre under a Rs. 50 lakh project. A museum and a research centre will be built, apart from providing accommodation facilities.

Janapada Loka, Mysore Road

Rs. 1 crore is being spent on developing a museum and crafts centre to showcase the local arts and crafts in Janapada Loka. Both the structures will come up side-by-side. The blueprint is being readied.

Homestays

A nodal agency will regulate and monitor all homestays in the state, with more being planned in Chikmagalur, Shimoga and Coorg. Only those listed under the department will be promoted rigorously. Accommodation facilities will be provided in two categories—Gold and Silver.

INDIA RELATED TOURISM STATISTICS

Table 4.1: Foreign Tourist Arrivals in India, 1996-2006

Year	*Foreign Tourist Arrivals (in million)*	*Percentage Change Over the Previous Year*
1996	2.29	8.0%
1997	2.37	3.5%
1998	2.36	–0.4%
1999	2.48	5.1%
2000	2.65	6.9%
2001	2.54	–4.2%
2002	2.38	–6.3%
2003	2.73	14.7%
2004	3.46	26.7%
2005	3.92	13.3%
2006*	4.45	13.5%

*Provisional.
Source: Bureau of Immigration.

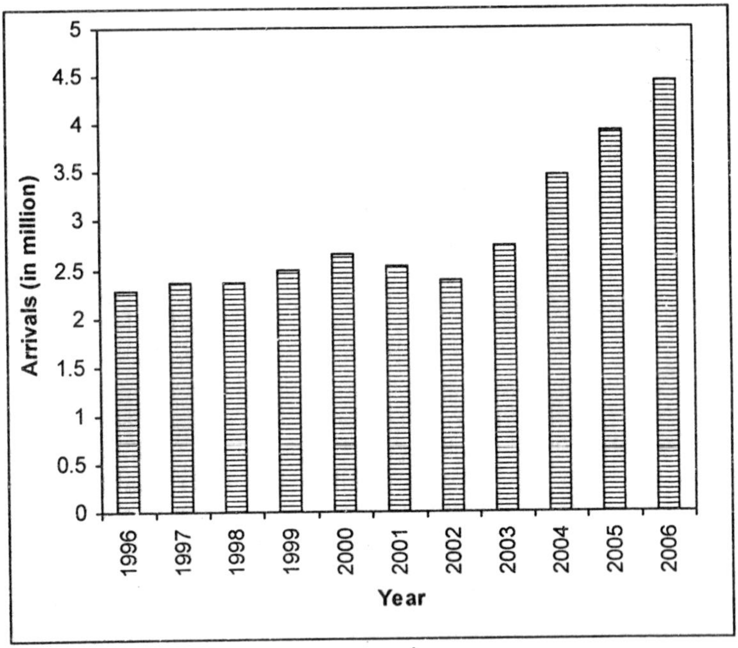

Chart 4.1: Foreign Tourist Arrivals in India, 1996-2006

Table 4.2: Month-wise Foreign Tourist Arrivals in India, 2005-07 (January-July)

Month	*2005*	*2006 (PR)*	*2007**	*Percentage Change 2006/05*	*Percentage Change 2007/06*
January	385977	459489	532088	19.0%	15.8%
February	369844	439090	498806	18.7%	13.6%
March	352094	391009	444186	11.1%	13.6%
April	248416	309208	333945	24.5%	8.0%
May	225394	255008	267758	13.1%	5.0%
June	246970	278370	310104	12.7%	11.4%
July	307870	337332	377474	9.6%	11.9%
Total (January-July)	2136565	2469506	2764361	15.6%	11.9%

PR—Provisional Revised.
* Provisional.

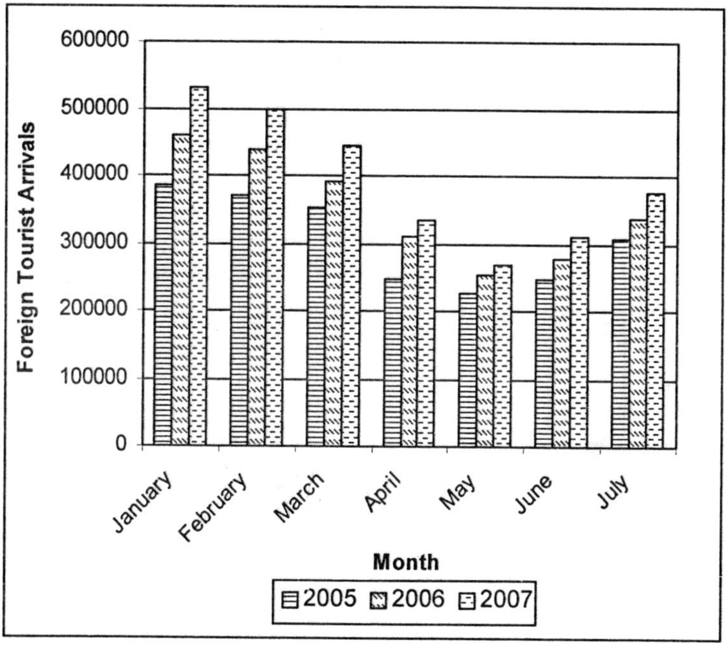

Chart 4.2: Month-wise Foreign Tourist Arrivals in India, 2005-07 (January-July)

Table 4.3 (a): Foreign Exchange Earnings (in US$ Million) from Tourism in India, 1996-2006

Year	*Earnings (in US$ million)*	*Percentage Change Over the Previous Year*
1996	2832	9.6%
1997	2889	2.0%
1998	2948	2.0%
1999	3009	2.1%
2000	3168	5.3%
2001	3042	–4.0%
2002	2923	–3.9%
2003	3533	20.9%
2004	4769	35.0%
2005*	5731	20.2%
2006*	6569	14.6%

* Provisional.

Source: Reserve Bank of India.

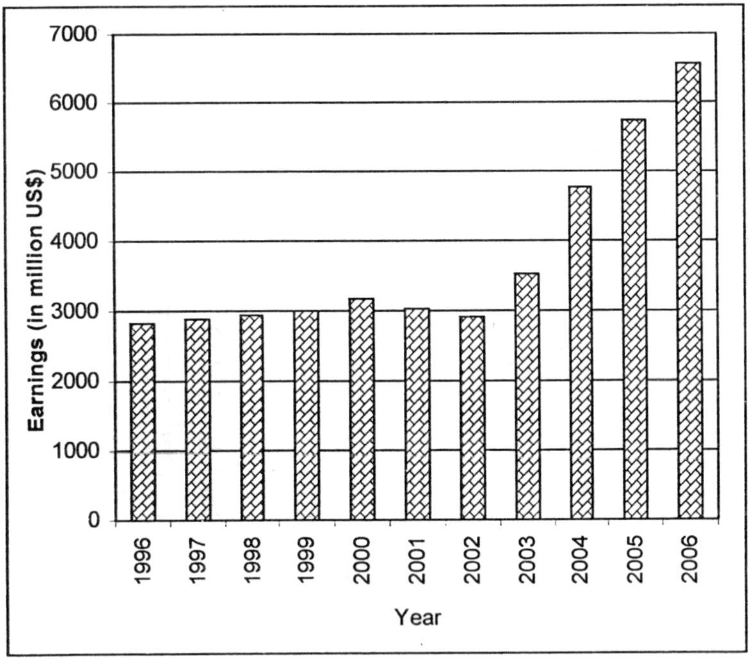

Chart 4.3 (a): Foreign Exchange Earnings (in US$ Million) from Tourism in India, 1996-2006

Table 4.3 (b): Foreign Exchange Earnings (in Rs. Crore) from Tourism

Year	*Earnings (in Rs. Crore)*	*Percentage Change Over the Previous Year*
1996	10046	19.2%
1997	10511	4.6%
1998	12150	15.6%
1999	12951	6.6%
2000	14238	9.9%
2001	14344	0.7%
2002	14195	–1.0%
2003	16429	15.7%
2004	21603	31.5%
2005*	25172	16.5%
2006*	29604	17.6%

* Provisional.

Source: Reserve Bank of India.

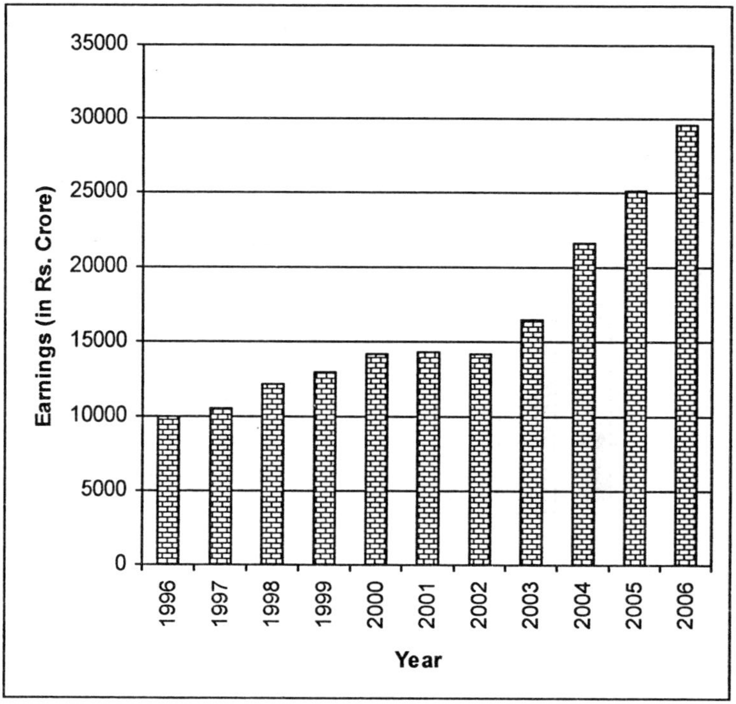

Chart 4.3 (b): Foreign Exchange Earnings (in Rs. Crore) from Tourism in India, 1996-2006

Table 4.4 (a): Month-wise Foreign Exchange Earnings (in US$ Million) from Tourism in India, 2005-2007 (January-July)

Month	*Earnings (in US$ million)*			*Percentage Change Over the Previous Year*	
	2005*	2006*	2007*	2006/05	2007/06
January	532.19	632.43	744.58	18.8%	17.7%
February	536.07	594.64	680.41	10.9%	14.4%
March	505.74	547.17	636.05	8.2%	16.2%
April	378.38	473.44	554.66	25.1%	17.2%
May	333.15	368.56	455.64	10.6%	23.6%
June	375.47	420.80	518.49	12.1%	23.2%
July	470.08	522.70	703.63	11.2%	34.6%
Total (January-July)	3131.08	3559.74	4293.46	13.7%	20.6%

* Provisional.

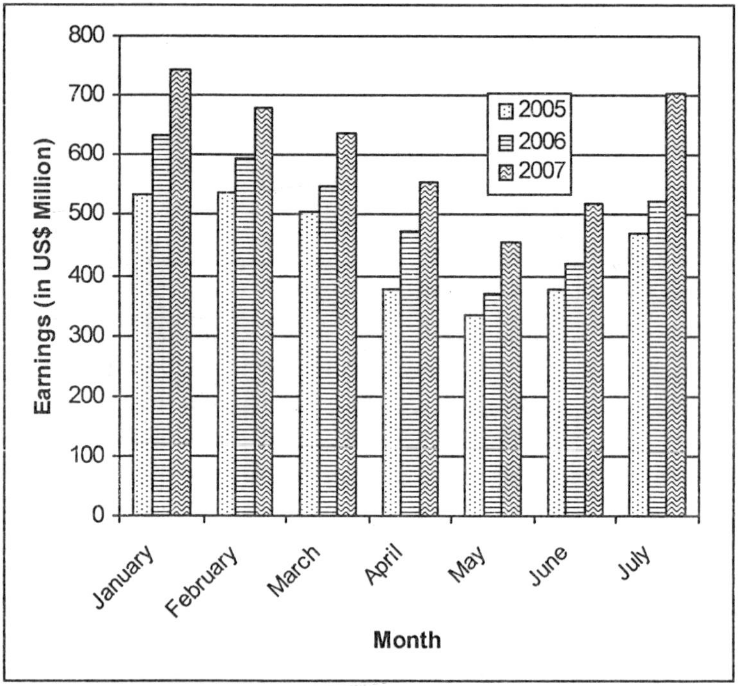

Chart 4.4 (a): Month-wise Foreign Exchange Earnings (in US$ Million) from Tourism in India, 2005-07 (January-July)

Table 4.4 (b): Month-wise Foreign Exchange Earnings (In Rs. Crore) from Tourism in India, 2005-2007 (January-July)

Month	*Earnings (in Rs. Crore)*			*Percentage Change Over The Previous Year*	
	*2005**	*2006**	*2007**	*2006/05*	*2007/06*
January	2326.20	2722.07	3299.51	17.0%	21.2%
February	2343.18	2635.98	3003.95	12.5%	14.0%
March	2210.62	2434.32	2798.96	10.1%	15.0%
April	1649.96	2127.44	2341.18	28.9%	10.0%
May	1452.72	1673.91	1858.51	15.2%	11.0%
June	1637.29	1937.38	2111.74	18.3%	9.0%
July	2048.78	2427.04	2844.72	18.5%	17.2%
Total (January-July)	13668.75	15958.14	18258.57	16.7%	14.4%

* Provisional.

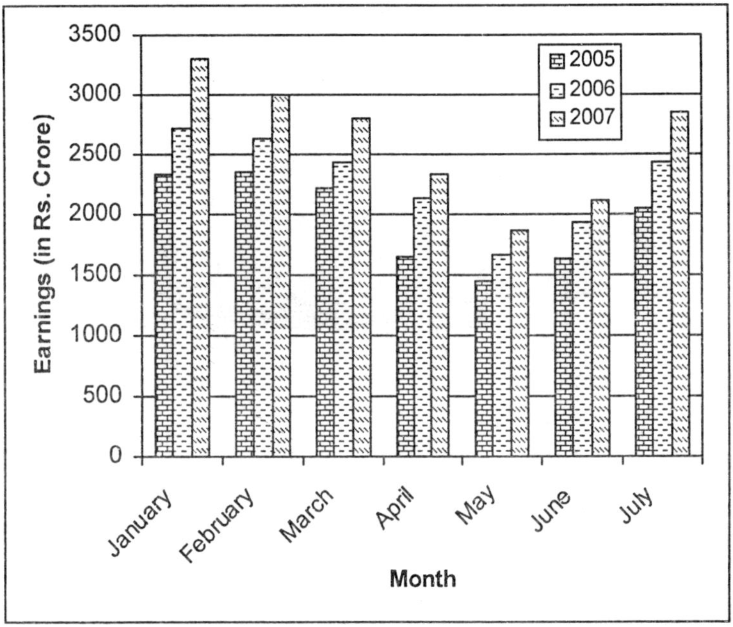

Chart 4.4 (b): Month-wise Foreign Exchange Earnings (in Rs. Crore) from Tourism in India, 2005-07 (January-July)

Table 4.5: Top 10 Source Countries for Foreign Tourist Arrivals to India in 2006

Source Country	*Foreign Tourist Arrivals (in million)**	*Percentage Share*
UK	0.734	16.5%
USA	0.697	15.7%
Canada	0.177	4.0%
France	0.175	3.9%
Germany	0.157	3.5%
Srilanka	0.155	3.5%
Japan	0.119	2.7%
Australia	0.110	2.5%
Malaysia	0.107	2.4%
Nepal	0.092	2.1%
Total of top 10 countries	2.523	56.7%
Others	1.925	43.3%
All Countries	4.447	100.0%

* Provisional.

Source: Bureau of Immigration.

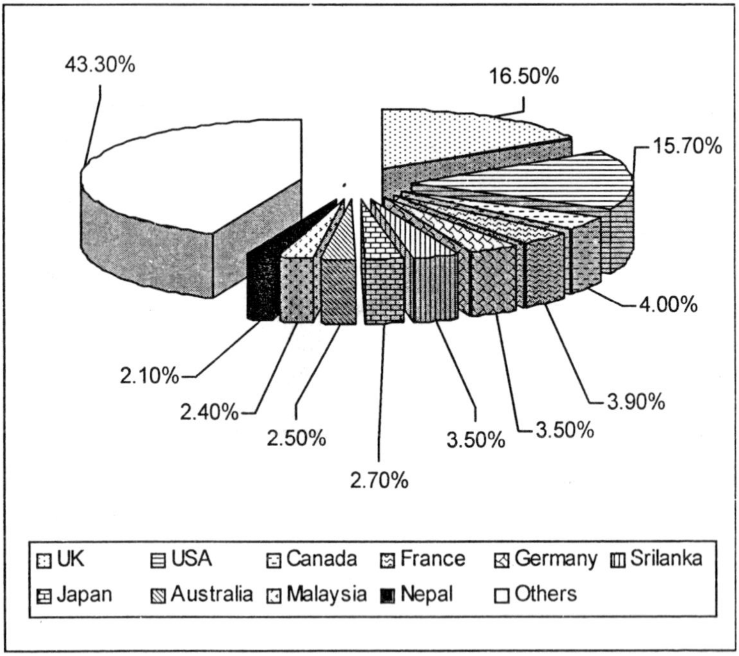

Chart 4.5: Percentage Share of Top 10 Source Countries for Foreign Tourist Arrivals to India in 2006

Table 4.6: Outbound Visits of Indian Nationals, 1996-2006

Year	*No. of Outbound Visits (in Million)*	*Percentage Change Over the Previous Year*
1996	3.46	13.3%
1997	3.73	7.8%
1998	3.81	2.1%
1999	4.11	7.9%
2000	4.42	7.5%
2001	4.56	3.2%
2002	4.94	8.3%
2003	5.35	8.3%
2004	6.21	16.1%
2005	7.18	15.6%
2006*	8.34	16.2%

* Provisional.
Source: Bureau of Immigration.

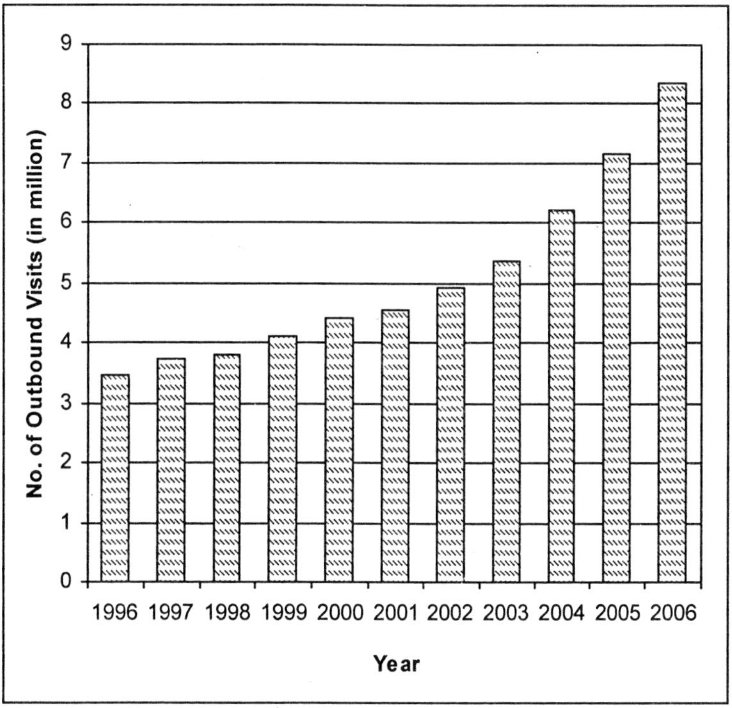

Chart 4.6: Outbound Visits of Indian Nationals, 1996-2006

Table 4.7: Domestic Tourist Visits to all States/ UTs in India, 1996-2006

Year	*No. of Domestic Tourist Visits (in million)*	*Percentage Change Over the Previous Year*
1996	140.12	2.5%
1997	159.88	14.1%
1998	168.20	5.2%
1999	190.67	13.4%
2000	220.11	15.4%
2001	236.47	7.4%
2002	269.60	14.0%
2003	309.04	14.6%
2004	366.23	18.5%
2005	390.47	6.6%
2006*	461.16	18.1%

* Provisional.
Source: State/UT Tourist Departments.

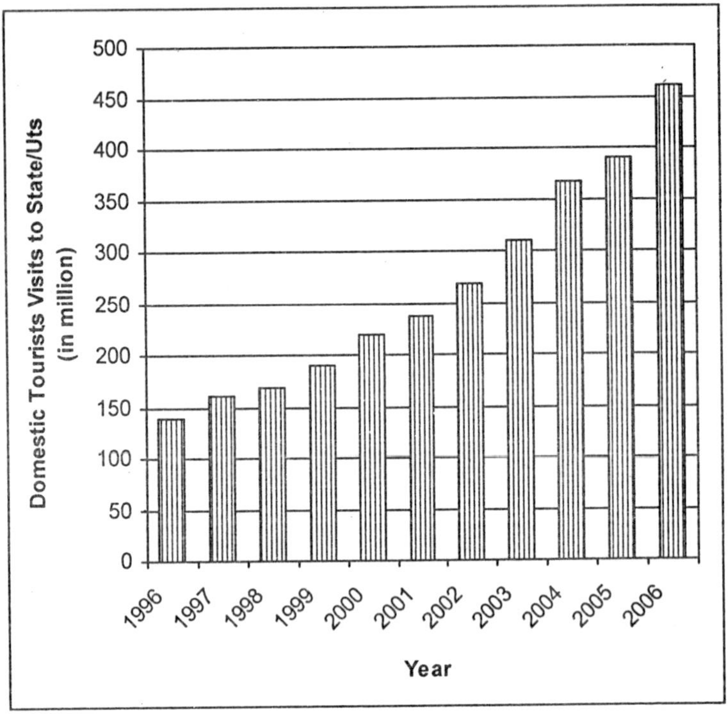

Chart 4.7: Domestic Tourist Visits to all States/UTs in India, 1996-2006

Table 4.8: Foreign Tourist Visits to All States/UTs in India, 1996-2006

Year	*No. of Foreign Tourist Visits to all States/UTs (in million)*	*Percentage Change Over the Previous Year*
1996	5.03	8.4%
1997	5.50	9.3%
1998	5.54	0.7%
1999	5.83	5.2%
2000	5.89	1.0%
2001	5.44	–7.6%
2002	5.16	–5.1%
2003	6.71	30.0%
2004	8.36	24.6%
2005	9.94	18.9%
2006*	11.40	14.7%

* Provisional.

Source: State/UT Tourism Departments.

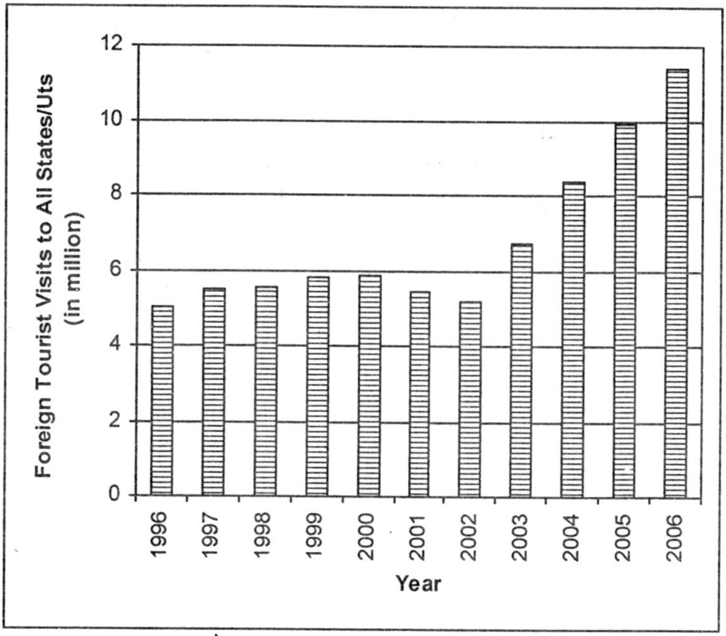

Chart 4.8: Foreign Tourist Visits to all States/UTs in India, 1996-2006

Table 4.9: Top 10 States/UTs of India in Domestic Tourist Visits in 2006

Rank	*Domestic Tourist Visits**	
	State	*Percentage Share*
1.	Andhra Pradesh	24.2%
2.	Uttar Pradesh	22.9%
3.	Tamil Nadu	12.7%
4.	Karnataka	7.8%
5.	Rajasthan	5.1%
6.	Maharashtra	3.7%
7.	Uttarakhand	3.6%
8.	West Bengal	3.4%
9.	Gujarat	2.5%
10.	Madhya Pradesh	2.4%
	Total of top 10	88.3%
	Others	11.7%
	Total	100.0%

* Provisional.
Source: State/UT Tourism Departments.

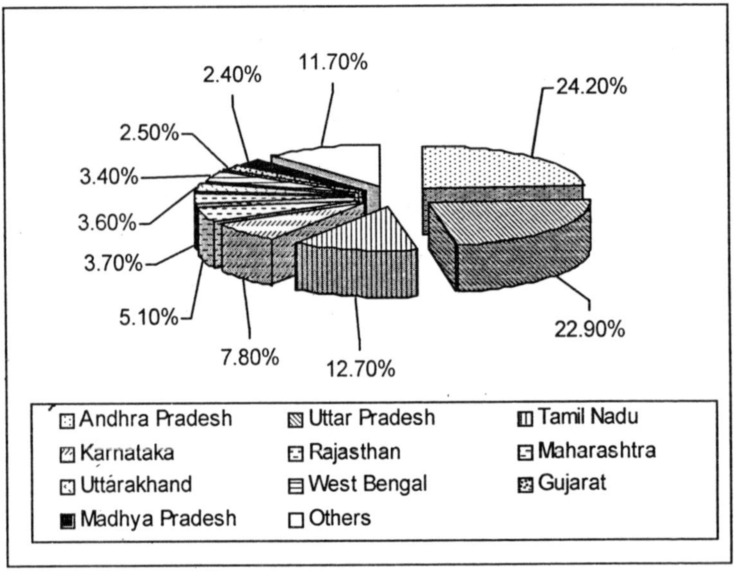

Chart 4.9: Percentage Share of Top 10 States/UTs in Domestic Tourist Visits in 2006

Table 4.10: Top 10 States/UTs of India in Foreign Tourist Visits in 2006

Rank	*Foreign Tourist Visits**	
	State	*Percentage Share*
1.	Delhi	17.3%
2.	Maharashtra	14.5%
3.	Uttar Pradesh	11.6%
4.	Rajasthan	10.7%
5.	Tamil Nadu	9.1%
6.	West Bengal	8.8%
7.	Andhra Pradesh	5.9%
8.	Karnataka	4.4%
9.	Kerala	3.8%
10.	Goa	3.3%
	Total of Top 10	89.4%
	Others	10.6%
	Total	100.0%

* Provisional.

Source: State/UT Tourism Departments.

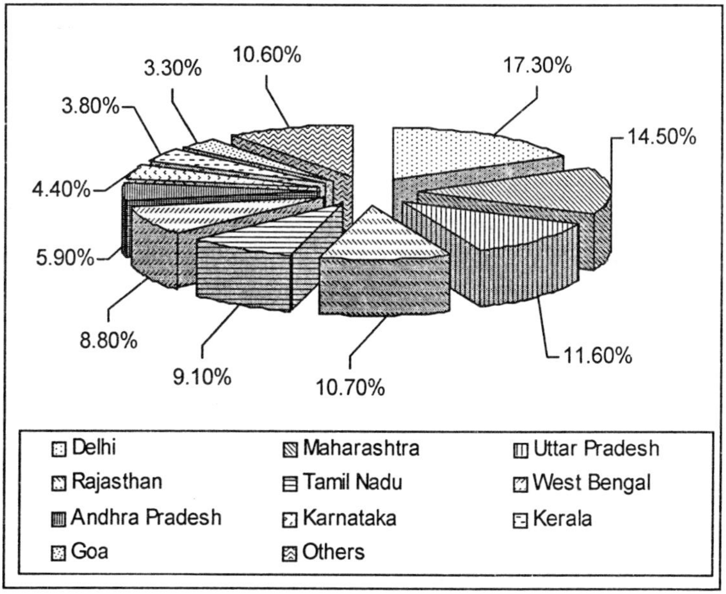

Chart 4.10: Percentage Share of Top 10 States/UTs in Foreign Tourist Visits in 2006

Table 4.11: Share of India in International Tourist Arrivals in World, 1996-2006

Year	*International Tourist Arrivals in World (in million)*	*Foreign Tourist Arrivals in India (in million)*	*Percentage share of India*
1996	573.5	2.3	0.40%
1997	597.5	2.4	0.40%
1998	616.0	2.4	0.39%
1999	639.5	2.5	0.39%
2000	686.7	2.6	0.38%
2001	686.0	2.5	0.36%
2002	706.4	2.4	0.34%
2003	693.2	2.7	0.39%
2004	761.0	3.5	0.46%
2005	802.0	3.9	0.49%
2006*	842.0	4.4	0.52%

* Provisional.

Source: Tourism Market Trends 2005 Edition (WTO) for the years upto 2003, WTO Barometer June, 2007 for other years.

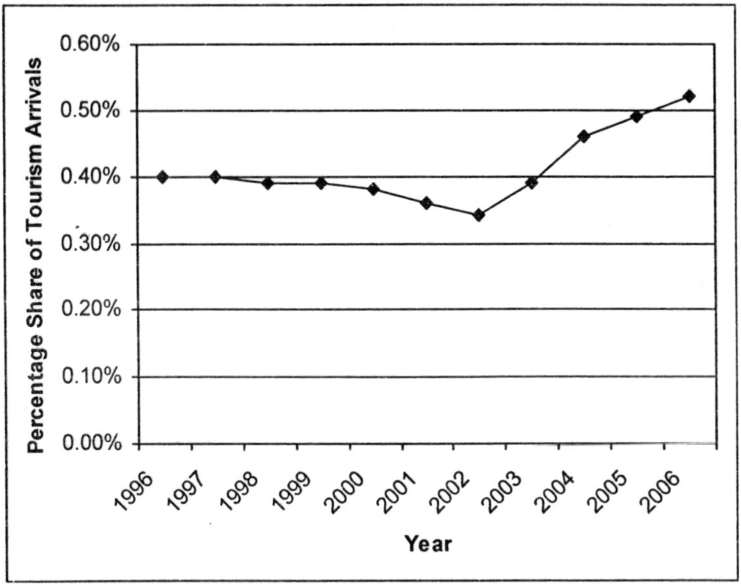

Chart 4.11: Percentage Share of India in International Tourist Arrivals in World, 1996-2006

Table 4.12: Share of India in International Tourism Receipts in World, 1996-2006

Year	*International Tourism Receipt in World (in US$ billion)*	*Tourism Receipt in India (in US$ billion)*	*Percentage share of India*
1996	450.5	2.8	0.63%
1997	454.2	2.9	0.64%
1998	451.7	3.0	0.65%
1999	465.7	3.0	0.65%
2000	483.8	3.2	0.66%
2001	472.3	3.0	0.64%
2002	487.0	2.9	0.60%
2003	533.1	3.5	0.66%
2004	633.0	4.8	0.75%
2005	678.0	5.7	0.85%
2006*	735.0	6.6	0.89%

* Provisional.

Source: Tourism Market Trends 2005 Edition (WTO) for the year up to 2003, WTO Barometer June 2007 for other years.

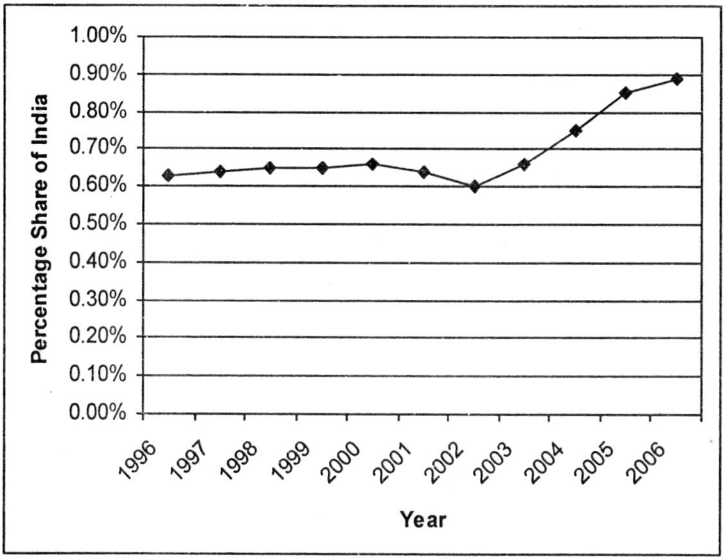

Chart 4.12: Percentage Share of India in International Tourism Receipt in World, 1996-2006

Table 4.13: Top 10 Countries of the World and India in International Tourist Arrivals in 2006

Rank	*Country*	*International Tourist Arrivals* (In Million)*	*Percentage Share*
1.	France	79.1	9.39%
2.	Spain	58.5	6.95%
3.	USA	51.1	6.07%
4.	China	49.6	5.89%
5.	Italy	41.1	4.88%
6.	UK	30.1	3.57%
7.	Germany	23.6	2.80%
8.	Mexico	21.4	2.54%
9.	Austria	20.3	2.41%
10.	Russian Federation	20.2	2.40%
	Total of Top 10 countries	395.0	46.91%
	India	4.4	0.52%
	Others	442.6	52.57%
	Total	842.0	100.00%

* Provisional.

Source: WTO Barometer June, 2007.

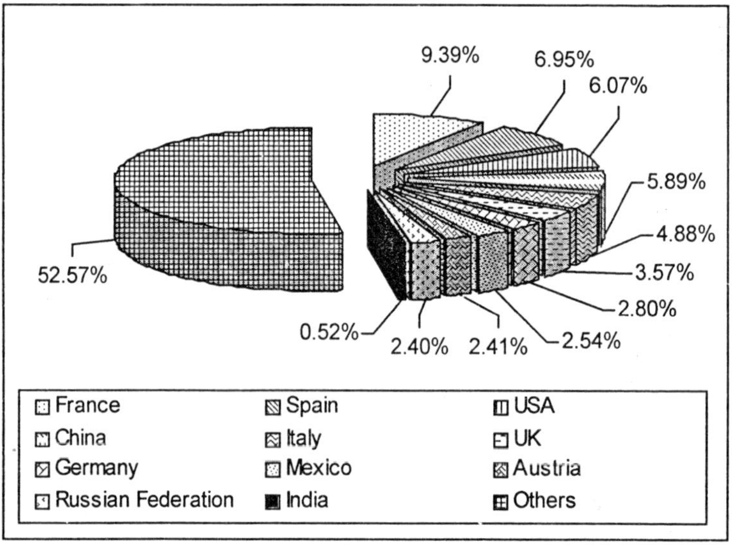

Chart 4.13: Percentage Share of Top 10 Countries of the World in International Tourist Arrivals (in million) in 2006

Table 4.14: Top 10 Countries of the World and India in International Tourism Receipts in 2006

Rank	*Country*	*International Tourism Receipts* (in US$ billion)*	*Percentage Share*
1.	USA	85.7	11.7%
2.	Spain	51.1	7.0%
3.	France	46.3	6.3%
4.	Italy	38.1	5.2%
5.	China	33.9	4.6%
6.	UK	33.5	4.6%
7.	Germany	32.8	4.5%
8.	Australia	17.8	2.4%
9.	Turkey	16.9	2.3%
10.	Austria	16.7	2.3%
	Total of Top 10 countries	372.8	50.7%
	India	8.9	1.2%
	Others	353.3	48.1%
	Total	735.0	100.0%

* Provisional.

Source: WTO Barometer June, 2007.

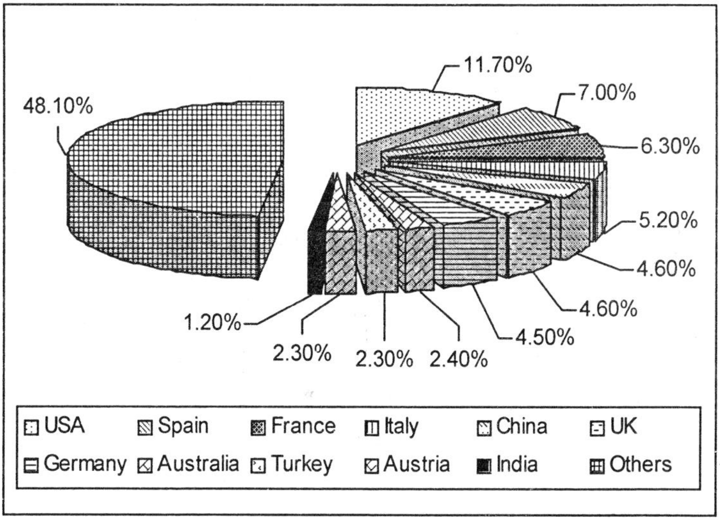

Chart 4.14: Percentage Share of Top 10 Countries of the World in International Tourism Receipts (in US$ billion) in 2006

Table 4.15: Economic Benefits of Tourism

Indicators	*Year*	*India*	*World*
Contribution of Tourism to GDP*	2002-03	5.83%	10.0% (2002)
	2003-04	5.90%	10.2% (2003)
	2004-05	6.11%	10.4% (2004)
	2005-06	NA	10.6% (2005)
Employment in Tourism Sector*	2002-03	38.6 million (8.27%)	198.098 million (7.8%) (2002)
	2003-04	41.8 million (8.78%)	194.562 million (7.6%) (2003)
	2004-05	NA	214.697 million (8.1%)
	2005-06	NA	221.568 million (8.3%)

* Direct as well as indirect contribution of tourism.

Note:

1. *India figures*: For 2002-03 based on Tourism Satellite Account (TSA) 2002-03. For other years, estimated using TSA 2002-03.
2. *World figures*: World Tourism & Travel Council (WTTC).
3. Figures within parentheses for employment indicate percentage share in total employment.

DELHI TOURISM

Delhi, the capital of India, can easily be symbolized with a lotus where each petal represents different era and milestones of the history. Starting from the ages of Mahabharata to the British rule, Delhi has been always the most preferred destination for the power seekers whoever wished to start their legacy in India. The city is thus studded with mementos and edifice carrying reminiscence of the bygone era.

Being the third-largest city and capital of India, no wonder, Delhi has gained the position of North India's industrial hub. It presents a nice montage of the modern and ancient life where Old Delhi carries the heritage of the 17th and 19th centuries and New Delhi boasts of modern city life. Once the capital of Mughals, Old Delhi is adorned with cenotaphs, mausoleums, mosques and forts all narrating the saga of Muslim History. But if you think this is all about Delhi, then you are mistaken, as the splendour of New Delhi is yet to discovered. With the advent of British rulers, a need of new capital was needed and thus Sir Edwin Lutyens came into limelight with a new version of Delhi with imperial architecture and government buildings creating New Delhi. Delhi, combining both Old and New Delhi seem to never lose its charming mystery with the passage of time.

The bustling markets of Delhi need special mention to feel the warmth of the city. From the traditional jewellery and garments to modern electronic goods, Delhi markets are the dream destination of the shopalcoholics. Delhi cuisine is another identity that explores the hidden flavour of Delhi culture. Its said *dilwalon ki shahar* (city of warm hearted people) loves to steal the heart of people by feeding them. Be it *Mughlai Paratha* or *Shammi Kabab*, the heritage of Delhi cuisine dates back to Mughal era. The delicious street foods of Delhi vendors find their mention in the pages of history and on the screens of celluloid.

Once you come and taste the fragrance of this heritage city, it's for sure that you are destined to come here again and again. The warm and melting hospitality of the city will surely steal your heart and you never know when Delhi becomes the most favourite destination of yours in the world.

KHAJURAHO TOURISM

Situated in the northern part of Madhya Pradesh, the town of Khajuraho has been recognized as a world heritage site by UNESCO. The town is famous for its imperial temples. The temples were built by the rulers of Chandela dynasty between 10th and 11th centuries. The construction of the temple just took around 100 years to complete. There were around 85 temples in the area but now only 22 exist. Rest are nothing more than ruins. They sure have gained popularity due to the erotic sculptures carved on the walls. However, such sculptures cover only a small portion. The major share of sculptures are depicting the daily life of people in the rural India.

If you thought that there are only temples to see in Khajuraho, then you are mistaken. There is more to the town than these one of a kind temples. Visit the town in the month of February and March and you can be a part of the renowned Khajuraho Dance Festival. The festival witnesses performances by many great exponents of Indian classical dances like Kathak, Kuchipudi, Bharatnatyam, Odissi, and Manipuri Dance. And after you are through with the attractions in the town, you can move out to nearby sites like the famous Panna National Park and many appealing waterfalls. The climate here is not very different from other parts of Madhya Pradesh. It is sweltering in summers and extremely pleasant in winters. Although it is worth a visit at any time of the year, but September to March season is by far the best.

Main Attractions

Khajuraho Temples

The biggest tourist attractions of Khajuraho are the many temples that adorn the face of this unique town. Temples of Khajuraho are the greatest artistic gift given by the Chandela Kings to the world. The walls of these temples are carved with erotic statues and sculptures. Temples have been divided into three group, Western Group, Eastern Group and Southern Group according to their location in the town.

The Western Group

This is clearly the most important section of Khajuraho temples. It is here that you will find the biggest and most intricate temples of all. The Kandriya Mahadev which is dedicated to Lord Shiva is the largest temple in Khajuraho towering to a height of 31 m. In the Sanctum Sanctorum, there is a lingam. Do notice the ceilings and pillars of the temple that are magnificently carved. Other well-known temples in the group are Chaunsat Yogini temple, Lakshmana temple and Matangeshwara temple. The Chandela Kings were Lord Vishnu's ardent devotees, so you will find many temples dedicated to Lord Vishnu. The most important of them is Varaha temple, famous for the 9 feet high Boar statue.

The Eastern Group

There are mostly Hindu and Jain temples in the eastern group. They are situated closer to Khajuraho temple. Parsvanath temple, which is the largest Jain temple, has the most scintillating structure in the group. Ghantai temple is another famous Jain temple in the group. The images on the walls depict day-to-day lives of people. The three Hindu temples in the group are Brahma, Vamana and Javari temples.

The Southern Group

The southern group is also called Jain group of temples. They are situated 5 km to the southeast of the town. Chaturbhuj temple and Duladeo temple are the most important of all. Chaturbhuj temple has a massive structure of Lord Vishnu inside the sanctum.

Other Attractions

When you are visiting Khajuraho, apart from the major temples, look out for some other attractions as well. Most of these attractions are few kilometres away from Khajuraho. The main attraction is definitely Panna National Park that is one of the major wildlife parks in Madhya Pradesh. The park is rich in flora and fauna and is famous for the exquisite surroundings. The park is around 20 km away from Khajuraho. Also explore Ken Gharial sanctuary that is 24 km away. The park is the natural habitat of long snouted alligators. Pandava Water Fall which is around 30 km from Khajuraho, is the favourite picnic spot for the locales. It is said that Pandavas spent the major part of their exile here. Temples of Khajuraho are surely a spellbinding sight, but leaving Khajuraho without visiting these attractions lying around the town, is a big loss for tourist who are looking for perfect amalgamation of history and nature.

Where to Stay

Khajuraho is certainly the most famous city of Madhya Pradesh. Due to the temples here, it receives tourists from all over the world in a huge number. And to accommodate them, many hotels have been opened. You will find high-end luxury hotels like Taj Chandela and Radisson Jass Hotel alongside good budget hotels like Hotel Clark and Hotel Usha Bundela. Most of these hotels are situated close to the temples.

Getting There

By Air

Khajuraho has its own domestic airport, which receives regular flights from Delhi and Agra. Both Indian Airlines and Private flight operators have their flights coming in and out of Khajuraho.

By Rail

The nearest railway station is at Mahoba which is at a distance of 64 km from here. Other close by station is at Harpalpur at a distance of 94 km.

By Road

Khajuraho is well-connected to all the cities of Madhya Pradesh. There is regular bus service Gwalior, Bhopal Jabalpur and Agra.

Local Transport

For getting around in the town you can hire a taxi or a cycle rickshaw. But the best way to explore the town is by taking a ride in a tonga (Horse Carriage).

PUSHKAR MELA

Pushkar At A Glance	
Population	13,000
Area	9.8 sq. km.
Temperature	Max. 45° C, min. 25° C (summer); max. 22° C, min. 8° C (winter)
Ideal time to visit	October to March
State	Rajasthan
Fair dates for 2005	November 12th to 15th
STD code	014581
PIN code	305022

Pushkar Location

The sacred and beautiful town of Pushkar lies in a valley some 14 km from Ajmer, Rajasthan. Believed to be one of the oldest Indian towns, Pushkar is grandly nestled between three hillocks and sand dunes. This provides a perfect setting to the world famous camel and religious fair at Pushkar. The Pushkar Camel Fair is amongst the largest cattle fairs in the world. This annual camel festival attracts thousands of tourists from all over the world.

Climate

Situated in the Thar Desert of Rajasthan, Pushkar offers an extreme climate. During summer months, the mercury, sometimes, rises as high as 45°C while in winters it plummets to as low as 10°C. Like all other parts of the Thar Desert, Pushkar also does not get much rain during the monsoons. That is the reason why the period between October to March is considered the best to visit Pushkar.

Importance of Pushkar

According to the Hindu mythology, Pushkar is among the five Dhams, held to be the most sacred (other four being Badrinath, Puri, Rameswaram and Dwarka). According to legends, Lord Brahma (the creator of the world), in search for his abode on earth, performed the utmost spiritual Vedic yagna at Pushkar. Pushkar is the only place to have a Brahma temple. It is said that no pilgrimage is complete without a holy dip in the sacred waters of the Pushkar Lake. Pushkar is called "The Gayatri Dham", the source of the "Gayatri Mantra". Along with the Brahma temple, there are numerous other temples and palaces in Pushkar city.

GOKARNA

Gokarna/Gokarnam Mahabaleswarar is a popular pilgrimage in Karnataka. The literal meaning of 'Gokarna' is 'the ear of the cow' and is so named because of the ear-shaped confluence of two rivers. However, according to the popular belief, it is named so to commemorate Lord Shiva's emergence from the ears of a cow. It is an important Hindu pilgrimage centre and also a famous Sanskrit-learning centre. 200 km from Mangalore, the place has been mentioned in Gokarnam Purana, where it is said that mere visit to the place liberates one from hundreds of sins including the deadliest ones such as 'brahma-hatya' (the killing of a Brahmin or a pious person). It also mentions that even a glimpse of the Atma-linga, one of the popular shrines of the city, helps one to attain salvation and frees one from the cycle of births and rebirths. The popular solitary beaches here are Kudle beach with a beautiful white sand beach surrounded by palm trees about a kilometre long, Om beach, which is so-named because of its shape like the auspicious Om sign and Half-moon and Paradise beaches where one can enjoy the moonlight on the soft sands by the seaside. However, the star of all the sacred and tourism sites of the region is the Mahaballeswara temple dedicated to Lord Shiva or Rudra, often referred to as the Kashi of the South. According to a legend, Lord Rudra went to Patalaloka for penance on the advice of Lord Brahma and returned through the ear of Mother Earth, often symbolized as a cow. Since the place served as the womb for him, it is also known as Rudra Yoni or Adi Gokarna. It holds a special religious significance and is one of the three 'Siddhi Kshetras', the other two being Pushkar and Shaligram.

BADAMI CAVE TEMPLES

The Badami cave temples are known for their wonderful architecture. Have a look at Badami cave temples of Karnataka. The erstwhile capital of early Chalukyas, Badami is known for its beautiful carved cave temples belonging to 6th and 7th centuries. Wedged between two rocky hills at the mouth of a ravine, the four rock-cut cave temples display the full range of religious sects that evolved in India. Overlooking the sandstone caves, is an artificial lake lined with four temples on its shores. While three of the temples belong to Vedic faith, the fourth and natural cave is the only Jain temple at Badami. Out of the three Hindu temples, two are dedicated to Lord Vishnu while one is dedicated to Lord Shiva. The beautiful carvings, paintings and bracket figures depict Lord Narasimha (with the face of a lion and body of a man), Lord Vishnu Hari Hara (half-Shiva and half-Vishnu), Vishnu Narayana sitting or reclining on Shesh Nag or Ananta (Eternity) and various other figures and scenes from Hindu mythology. Each of the cave temples have a sanctum, a hall, an open verandah and pillars adorned with spectacular carvings and sculptures. The architectural style can be said to be a blend of Indian Nagara style and the South Indian Dravidian style. The beautiful murals and the masterpieces found in these caves include the well-renowned idol of 18-armed Lord Nataraja (Shiva), which seems to strike 81 poses when observed closely. Cave 4 or the last cave houses the idol of 24th Tirthankara, Mahavira seated against a cushion in the inner sanctum. It is said that the construction of the world-famous Elephanta and Ellora caves were inspired by the Badami caves. The other shrines worth visiting at Badami are the the shrine of Nagamma, the local serpent goddess, on the bank of the ancient Bhutnatha lake, and the two Shiva temples where Lord Shiva can be seen sitting in a rare pose of leaning back besides the water in the inner sanctum.

SOMNATHPUR TEMPLE

The Somnathpur temple in Karnataka is dedicated to Lord Krishna. The temple of Lord Krishna on the shores of River Kaveri situated in the tiny village of Somnathpur is said to be the last and the grandest of Hoysala monuments. This Kesava Temple was built about 740 years ago in 1268 and displayed all the former riches and splendor of the Hoysala architectural style as evident in their temples at Belur and Halebid (then Dvarasamudra). According to the stone inscription in old Kannada at its entrance, it was built during the reign of Narasimha III by his celebrated army commander, Somnath, after whom the temple and the village was named. However, the king bestowed Somnath with his generous donations to help him set up a grand temple to glorify Hoysala craftsmanship and also sanctioned an annual grant of 3,000 gold coins for the temple's upkeep and maintenance. The best and legendary sculptors who were hired for the construction of the temple included the famous Mallitamma, Ballayya, Chaudayya, Bharmayya, Kamayya and Nanjayya. It is said that Mallitamma contributed 40 out of the 194 carved images on the outer walls. Strangely, the images are signed unlike the practices of the time but similar to other Hoysala temples at Belur and Halebid. The main shrine is centrally located and is stellar in shape. Out of the beautiful carved idols that once housed the three sanctums of the temple, idol of Kesava is missing today. However, one can still witness the beauty of idols of Janardhana and Venugopala. Since, earliest Hoysala monarchs were Jains and later they turned to Vaisnavism and Shaivism, they had general tolerance of all faiths. The temple at Somnathpur is unique in design, has fabulous stone carvings and are perfect in symmetry.

SANEESWARA TEMPLE

Sri Saneesvara/Shaneesvara temple in Mandapally village of Andhra Pradesh is dedicated to Saneeshwara Bhagwan situated in a small village called Mandapalli, 38 km from Rajamundy, in the East Godavari District of Andhra Pradesh, this famous temple is one of the rare ones with Saneeshwara Bhagwan as its presiding deity. Also known as Sri Mandeswara Swami temple and Someswara temple, it is said that Saturn himself consecrated the Linga representing Lord Shiva here. The other deities of the temple are Bhrameswara and Nageswara enshrined in the form of black stone Shiva Lingas. The small temple has some interesting legends attached to it. A great and benevolent sage 'Dhadichi' undertook a great sacrifice of donating his valuable spinal cord for Lord Indra's 'Vajra', so that he can relieve the people from the tyranny of the demon Kartabha by killing him using this weapon. However, the sons of the demon known as Aswartha and Pippala vowed revenge against the people and the gods alike and broke havoc in Mandapalli. They tortured people and sages and brought forth untold miseries on them. Touched by their disheartening state, sage Agastya approached Lord Shaneeswar or Saturn, who is also the Lord of Dharma (Righteousness) and the Son of God Surya, who was doing penance at the time to get the powers to kill those demon brothers. Shani (Saturn) stated that till the prayers and penance is completed, he wouldn't have enough strength to fight and get rid of the demons. However, he relented when sages agreed to give their 'Tapasshakti' (power of penance) to him. Then, he fought and killed the demons and relieved the people and the sages from their long tyrannical rule. There were rejoicings and everybody praised Saturn in many words. Sage Agastya and the other sages showered him with blessings and boons while Saturn installed a 'Shiva Linga' known as 'Someswara' or 'Mandeshwara' to mark his victory, around which the Saneeshwara temple is built.

SREE SAILAM TEMPLE

Sree Sailam/Sri Sailam temple of Kurnool district in Andhra Pradesh is a popular temple. Situated in the thick, deep forests of Nallamalai hills in the Kurnool District of Andhra Pradesh, Sree Sailam temple is one of the most ancient and sacred places in South India. Standing on the shores of River Krishna known as 'Pataalganga' here on the Rishabhagiri hill, it is also known by the names of Sri Giri, Sriparvata, Rudra Parvata and Seshachalam. Its reference can be found in several texts and Puranas. The presiding deities of the temple are Sri Mallikarjuna Swami and his consort Bharamaramba (incarnations of Shiva and Parvati). The lingam here is said to be one of the twelve Jyotirlingams in the country. The sculptural beauty of the temple is exemplary and there are about 116 inscriptions in and around it. Unlike other temples in Andhra Pradesh, people of any caste or creed can worship in this temple and touch the deity. Historically, this temple has been associated with the Chalukyan kings, Krishnadevaraya of Vijayanagara and Chatrapati Shivaji along with Adi Shankaracharya and the Buddhist pilgrims, Fahiyan and Hieun T`sang who have made references to it in their extensive travelogues. Both the Hindus and the Buddhists consider this place sacred. According to the popular legend, Vrishabha, the sacred bull mount of Lord Shiva performed penance here until Lord Shiva and Parvati appeared before him as Mallikarjuna and Bharamaramba. The other shrines that are enclosed within the Sreesailam temple premises are Sahasra Linga, Panchapandava temples and Vata Vriksha.

TIRUPATI TEMPLE

The Tirumala Tirupati Balaji temple dedicated to Lord Venkatesvara is a popular temple in Andhra Pradesh. Said to be the world's richest temple, the Tirumala Tirupati Balaji temple is situated on the Tirumala hill on the outskirts of Tirupati in the Chittoor district of Andhra Pradesh. Famous all over the world as a significant pilgrimage place, this ancient temple of Sri Venkateswara, the Lord of Seven Hills, is so-called as Tirumala hill is a cluster of seven hills known as Seshachalam or Venkatachalam at an altitude of 2,800 ft. above the sea level. The grand history of the temple spans over several centuries and it is the backbone of the pilgrimage and tourism industry of Andhra Pradesh. A fine example of Dravidian temple architecture, the Tirumala temple received generous offerings from the great dynasties like the Pallavas of Kanchipuram, the Cholas of Tanjore, the Pandyas of Madurai and the Kings and chiefs of Vijayanagara. The Gopuram of the temple is splendid. Elaborate rituals and modes of worship as stated by the saint Ramanujacharya and followed in the temple even today. However, the most popular and well-known customs of the temple are anointing the idol with camphor and the offering of the hair by the pilgrims who visit the place. For the latter, one should go to the licensed barbers only. The gold-plated 'Vimana' (Cupola) over the sanctum sanctorum is known as 'the Ananda Nilayam'. Along with the idols of the deities, this temple also houses statues of Vijayanagara king Krishnadevaraya and his consorts, and Todarmal, the minister of Akbar. The principal deity, Lord Venkateswara is also known as Venkataramana, Srinivasa and Balaji and is said to have attributes of Vishnu and Shiva, the preserver and the destroyer of the world.

CHAYAVANESWARA TEMPLE

Chayavaneswara temple is one of the popular temples of Tamil Nadu. Two miles from Tiruvengadu, the magnificent Chayavaneswara temple is situated at Chayavanam in the Chaikadu district of Tamil Nadu. Just a mile away from Kaveripatnam, the place where the River Cauvery meets the sea, it is an important pilgrimage centre for the Hindus. Held in much reverence and sanctity, the pilgrims visit this temple after ablution at the confluence to offer their homage to the deity, Lord Chayavaneswara, and seek his blessings. According to Hindu customs, having a holy dip at the confluence of a river with the sea is religiously meritorious and absolves one of all the sins and makes one pure to meet the Supreme Lord. However, there is an absurd but interesting legend attached to the temple to state its significance. It is said that the temple is closely connected with Iyarpagai Nayanar, one of the sixty-three Nayanmars (Saivite saints) of the South. According to the legend, Nayanar used to contribute generously to the temples and was known for his charitable nature towards 'sadhus', especially, Saivite saints. He has earned a repute of feeding them well and satisfying all their desires. It is said that one-day an old man in the form of Saivite saint approached him and asked him to give his wife as a gift to him. Iyarpagai Nayanar instantly gratified the old man's request and without hesitation sent his wife to him. All the relatives and friends and society definitely found his act as morally degrading and they condemned him. However, he insisted that wife should follow the 'sadhu', which she did as a respect to him. Touched by his great devotion towards his devotees, Lord Shiva who has just come to test the faith of Nayanar revealed his true form blessed him with salvation.

KRISHNAPURAM TEMPLE

The Krishnapuram temple in Tamil Nadu is known for its sculptural magnificence. Six miles from Tirunelveli, Krishnapuram temple displays a sculptural splendor like none other. More than 300 years old, the figures in Arulnigu Venkatachalapati temple look as alive and young as ever. It is interesting to see that besides the usual statues of deities, the sculptures also depict scenes from the court life. Another unique feature of the temple is the musical pillars that emanate interesting sounds, when tapped. It encloses the temple of Lord Venkatachalapati installed here with amazing statues of Sri Devi and Bhoo Devi. The Mandam to the north of the temple is known as Veerappa Naick Mandapam with two beautifully carved elephants adorning its entrance. The six pillars at the Mandapam exhibit Puranic scenes with dexterity and look life-like. The stone for carving out the idols produce melodious musical sounds when struck at different places. One of the pillars depicts the story of the adventure of Bhimasena with Purushamrigam, a half-man and half-beast who an ardent devotee of Lord Shiva. The Bhima stole some of its milk for the 'yagya' to be performed by his elder brother when he was in deep penance and had to run for life when the creature came to know about it. With the help of the cunningness of Lord Krishna and finally, the righteous love of Yudhishthira for his younger brother, Bhima finally manage to escape from his death at the hands of the creature, who was impressed by the love of the brothers for each other. Another pillar shows a princess and a prince being abducted by a Kuravan and a Kuratti (gypsies) and rescued by a king or minister. Yet another pillar shows Arjuna with a flowing beard performing penance with bow and arrow in his hands.

KUMBESWARA TEMPLE

Kumbeswara temple is located at Kumbakonam in Tamil Nadu. It is dedicated to Lord Kumbeswara and Goddess Sri Mangalambigai. The largest and the oldest Shiva temple at Kumbakonam is dedicated to Lord Kumbeswara and Goddess Sri Mangalambigai. The temple is an architectural and sculptural gem with a 128-ft high Gopuram carved intricately. It houses a shrine of Adi Vinayaka (Lord Ganesha) and Navarathri Mandapam that enshrines a single block of stone on which all the 27 stars and 12 Rashis (zodiacs) have been carved out. The temple also enshrines a rare specimen of the image of Lord Subrahmanya with six heads and six hands with different kinds of weapons. The temple also has an extensive collection of silver 'vahanas' (chariots) that are used carry the deities around at festival times. It was originally built by a Chola ruler only to be renovated later by the Nayak King. However, some of the old antique idols are still enshrined here such as those of 'Sri Ambal', 'Sri Durgaiamman' and 'Sri Kirathamoorti'. According the legend that after the Great Floods, Lord Shiva set a 'Kumbam' (Pot) full of amirtham and seeds for creation afloat and proclaimed that the place where the pot touched the ground would be considered as the holiest places in the world. It came to rest at Kumbam, later deformed to 'Kumbakonam'. Lord Shiva appeared as a hunter and broke the pot with his arrow. While the divine nectar from the pot became the famous Mahamaham Tank, Shiva made a Shiva Linga out of the broken pot pieces and entered it. Thus he came to be known as Adi Kumbeswara and is said to be enshrined here in this temple. Unlike other temples, the Maha Linga here is not made up of granite stone. The great Mahamaham festival is celebrated in honour of the Lord once in every 12 years and attracts thousands of pilgrims.

MEENAKSHI TEMPLE

Meenakshi temple at Madurai in Tamil Nadu is revered all over India. Read more about the Meenakshi Amman temple at Madurai. Madurai, the oldest and second largest city of Tamil Nadu, is built around the Sri Meenakshi Sundareswara temple in a lotus-shape. The interesting legend attached to Madurai goes like this. Built in magnificent Dravidian architectural style, the Meenakshi temple has a religious icon of South India and is known for its fantastic and splendid sculptures. Once Indra killed a demon performing penance. However, he could not get rid of his guilt and wandered from place to place with a heavy heart. However, he felt a sudden relief surging through him while passing through a forest of Kadamba trees in Pandya land. On enquiry, he found out about the Shivalinga under a Kadamba tree beside a lake in the forest. He worshipped it in reverence and built a small temple around it. It is said that this Linga is still under worship at Meenakshi temple and the small shrine is known as 'Indra Vimana'. Much later, Dhananjaya, a merchant of Manavur, was passing through the forest and sought refuge during the night in the Indra Vimana. He felt asleep and yet found signs of worshipping when he woke up next morning. Surprised, he mentioned it to the Pandya ruler, Kulasekhara, in Manavur. Kulasekhara decided to build a temple and a city at the spot and thus originated Meenakshi temple and Madurai. The temple seems to be built between twelfth to the eighteenth century and has two main shrines, twelve Gopurams, a tank and innumerable Mandapas. Among the other Mandapas in the temple is the celebrated thousand pillared one.

MURUGAN TEMPLE

Murugan temple is located in Tirupporur town in Tamil Nadu. One of the 33 major temples of Tamil Nadu, the ancient temple of Lord Murugan at Tirupporur is 45 km from Chennai. It dates back to the times of Pallavas and is known by different names like Poriyur or Yuddhapuri or Samarapuri. There are many legends related to Tirupporur and one of them relates to Lord Shiva relieving Lord Vishnu and his consort Lakshmi from the curse of Kanva Rishi. This Lord Shiva and his son Murugan are worshipped here. According to the Sthalapurana, it was here that Lord Murugan with his consorts Valli and Devayanai granted protection to the demi-gods and explained the true meaning of Pranava or the real truth to them and Agastya Muni. Thus, the hill behind the temple is known as 'Pranava Malai', where Lord Vishnu is said to have worshipped Lord Shiva. Inscriptions dating back to as early as the 10th century and 12th centuries can be seen in the temple here. Tirupporur got lost into oblivion until it was rediscovered in the 17th century and was renovated by Chidambara Swamigal. The idol of Lord Murugan is said to be the 'Swayambhu Murti', (not made by the hands of a man) and was found by Chidambara Swamigalin in an anthill. The temple enshrines Skanda in several forms based on the legends of Skanda Puranam. To the east of the temple the 'Palmyra' tree and the anthill where the image of Skanda was found can be seen. The anthill is now covered with Kavacha (armor) and other jewels. The other things enclosed in the temple premises are a 24-pillared hall, a 30-pillared circular hall, a shrine to 'Vembadi Vinayaka' under a Neem tree, two sacred Teerthams—'Saravana Poigai' and 'Valliyar Odai' to the south of the temple, a Mandapam of four pillars and another Teertham known as 'Pranavamritam'.

KARTHIGAI DEEPAM

Karthigai Deepam is a popular festival of Tamil Nadu. Read further to know more about the Karthigai Deepam festival. The oldest festival of Tamil Nadu and South India, Karthigai Deepam has been mentioned and referred to in many ancient works of Tamil literature such as 'Tolkappiyam' that dates back to 2,000 or 2,500 BC, 'Jeevakachintamani', an epic written by Jain poet, Thiruthakka Thevar, in the Sangam period, 'Karnarpadu', 'Kalavazhi Narpadu' dating around 1,000 BC and 'Pazhamozhi'. It falls in the month of Karthigai when the star Krithigai is on the ascendant according to the Tamil Calendar on a full moon day. It is believed that Lord Muruga, the divine light of Lord Shiva, took his form during this month. The ten-days festival is also known as 'the Festival of Lights' and is said to be the extension of the Deepavali festival of India. In some communities, people keep doubling the number of lamps everyday from the day of Deepavali till Karthigai Deepam and thus the burning lamps present an enchanting spectacle during the night. People clean their houses and decorate them with 'Kolam' patterns on the festive occasion. It is only after the 'Deeparathana' (worship ritual) that the lamps are moved to all the parts of the house and lit to create the dreamy look that enchants everyone. During this festival, people also flock to the Annamali Hills (thus it also known as Annamalai Deepam) to worship the Bharani Deepam, the huge lamp that is lit early in the morning on the final day of the festival in the sanctum sanctorum of the shrine. It is said that the flame of the lame does not flicker on this day and reveals the form of Lord Muruga, reaching up to the sky. The Deepam actually a colossal circular metal vessel with a capacity to hold about 2,000 litres of ghee, a height of five and half feet and diameter of five feet. The wick of the lamp itself is made up of 30m of 'Ghada' cloth burnt using 2 kilos of camphor. It is claimed that on the night of 'Karthigai Pournami', when the lamp is lit it can be seen across an area of 35 kms around the shrine.

KAVADI FESTIVAL

Kavadi is a popular festival of Tamil Nadu. Read more on the Kavadi festival of Tamil Nadu. The festival dedicated to Lord Muruga (a form of Lord Shiva), 'Kavadi' is much more than fulfilling the vow to the Lord in exchange of some wish-fulfillment, it is one of the most awesome festivals of India that makes one wonder whether there is more to the world than one can sense through one's sense organs. The vows range from simpler ones to the painful ones, which are claimed to be the result of the supreme love for God. It is said that once the worldly wish is fulfilled, the devotee takes the Kavadi and in the process comes so close to God that he attains the supreme state of devotion. 'Kavadi' is actually a wooden stick with two baskets at each end that can be slung across the shoulder and is usually richly decorated with flowers, peacock feathers and even jewels and especially, brass bells that serve to announce the presence of the Kavadi-bearer nearby. During the Kavadi procession, Kavadi bearer has to follow many rules such as observing silence all the way. The two baskets hanging at either end of the Kavadi are filled with rice, milk and other such articles that have to be collected by begging. Some of the bearers walk barefooted from their homes to the shrine of Lord Muruga after elaborate ceremonies. The bearer has to wear 'Pandaram', which consists of a saffron-coloured cloth, a scarlet conical cap and a silver-capped cane silver-capped at both ends along with several 'Rudraksha Malas' (rosaries) to cover his bare chest. They observe celibacy and abstain from intoxicating drinks and substances and partake of 'Satwik' food, which is strictly vegetarian and has no oil or spices. However, the scene that strikes terror in the hearts is seeing devotees that pass a sharp little spear through their tongue that protrudes out of their mouth or a spear through their cheeks. They are said to be in a high state of religious fervor and can be seen dancing in ecstasy even through the live burning coals! Kavadi is carried all the way up to Palani Hills. The Ettukudi Kavadi festival is celebrated during the months of April or May.

NATYANJALI DANCE FESTIVAL

Natyanjali dance festival is an important annual event at Chidambaram in Tamil Nadu. The festival in the honour of the great Cosmic Dancer or Lord Natraja (a form of Lord Shiva) is held every year in Chidambaram during February or March. This five-day long festival starts from the auspicious occasion of the Maha Shivaratri day. According to the Hindu mythology, Lord Nataraja is the Lord of Dances and hence the festival features dance performances in the 'Prakara' of the magnificent Chidambaram temple, which is dedicated to Lord Shiva. The 1000-year old temple provides a fitting backdrop to the spectacular event taking place under the golden roof of the temple showing pillars that depict Lord Nataraja in the classic 108 poses from the classical dance form of Tamil Nadu known as Bharatanatyam. Renowned dancers from all over India pay their homage to the deity by performing in the honour of Lord Nataraja at Natyanjali festival.

The Department of Tourism of Government of Tamil Nadu, the Ministry of Tourism of Government of India and the

Natyanjali Trust of Chidambaram jointly organize this festival. One can almost feel the elation of the dancers as they go into a trance while performing with exquisite acumen and skill that comes with years of training and practice. The evocative 'Abhinaya' (acting) and the subtle movements of each of their body parts are worth seeing. Performing at the festival is considered one of the greatest honours offered to these classical dancers as they dance to create the 'Padams' and 'Varnams' in the course of creating an imaginary figure of the Lord Nataraja. The dance festival re-establishes music and dance as the universal language and while entertaining, it also makes the audience aware of the rich classical dance forms of India.

PONGAL FESTIVAL

Pongal is an important festival of Tamil Nadu. Read more on Pongal festival. The harvest festival of Tamil Nadu marks the withdrawal of the south-east monsoons and happy days of reaping of the harvest. Basically a rural festival, it is celebrated in the month of Thai (that falls in January) for four days. The two most popular legends associated with Pongal associates the first day of the festival to the event when Lord Krishna lifted the gigantic Govardhan Mountain on his little finger to shelter people from heavy rains and wrath of the Rain God, Indra. The third day of Pongal is said to be the day for animals as it was on this day that Lord Shiva ordered Nandi Bull to forever help humans with their farming activities as a punishment for mixing up the message he sent to the people of Earth. The most popular festival of Tamil Nadu, the month of Pongal is considered very auspicious for marriages and other kinds of activities. During the festival, Sun God is worshipped as a sustainer of life on Earth. The first day or 'Bhogi' is celebrated on January 13, the second day or 'Pongal' on January 14, the third day or 'Mattu Pongal' on January 15 and finally the fourth day or 'Thiruvalluvar Day' on January 16 every year. The last day is associated with the great Tamil author known as Thiruvalluvar who composed 1,330 verses of 'Thirukkural' on all the aspects of life. Pongal is so named after the rice pudding made up of freshly harvested rice, milk and jaggery. It is the New Year festival of the State and hence is associated with cleaning and burning of the rubbish from the past. 'Kolams' (Rangoli) drawn with rice flour to feed the insects in the front yards of the houses, new clothes, adorning cattles with beads, bells and flowers and painting and capping their horns with metals, delicious traditional cuisines, typical style of worshipping rituals and a procession taken out from the Kandaswamy Temple in Chennai along with the bull fights or Jellikattu in Madurai, Tanjore and Tiruchirrapalli and community meals are the chief highlights of Pongal.

5

International Charters for Promoting Cultural Tourism and Preserving Heritage Sites

Cultural tourism is that form of tourism whose object is, among other aims, the discovery of monuments and sites. It exerts on these last, a very positive effect insofar as it contributes—to satisfy its own ends—to their maintenance and protection. This form of tourism justifies in fact the effort which said maintenance and protection demand of the human community because of the socio-cultural and economic benefits which they bestow on all the populations concerned.

ICOMOS CULTURAL TOURISM CHARTERS

The following charters are important covenants in the preservation of built and natural resources, those elements that attract cultural tourists:

- ICOMOS Charter on Cultural Tourism.
- UNESCO World Heritage Convention.
- ICOMOS Charter on the Conservation of Historic Towns and Urban Areas.
- ICOMOS New Zealand Charter for the Conservation of Places of Historic Value.
- Venice Charter.

International Cultural Tourism Charter: Managing Tourism at Places of Heritage Significance

Eighth Draft, for Adoption by ICOMOS at the 12th General Assembly, Mexico, October 1999

Introduction

The Charter Ethos

At the broadest level, the natural and cultural heritage belongs to all people. We each have a right and responsibility to understand, appreciate and conserve its universal values.

Heritage is a broad concept and includes the natural as well as the cultural environment. It encompasses landscapes, historic places, sites and built environments, as well as biodiversity, collections, past and continuing cultural practices, knowledge and living experiences. It records and expresses the long processes of historic development, forming the essence of diverse national, regional, indigenous and local identities and is an integral part of modern life. It is a dynamic reference point and positive instrument for growth and change. The particular heritage and collective memory of each locality or community is irreplaceable and an important foundation for development, both now and into the future.

At a time of increasing globalisation, the protection, conservation, interpretation and presentation of the heritage and cultural diversity of any particular place or region is an important challenge for people everywhere. However, management of that heritage, within a framework of internationally recognised and appropriately applied standards, is usually the responsibility of the particular community or custodian group.

A primary objective for managing heritage is to communicate its significance and need for its conservation to its host community and to visitors. Reasonable and well-managed physical, intellectual and/or emotive access to heritage and cultural development is both a right and a privilege. It brings with it a duty of respect for the heritage values, interests and equity of the present-day host community, indigenous custodians or owners of historic property and for the landscapes and cultures from which that heritage evolved.

The Dynamic Interaction between Tourism and Cultural Heritage

Domestic and international tourism continues to be among the foremost vehicles for cultural exchange, providing a personal experience, not only of that which has survived from the past, but of the contemporary life and society of others. It is increasingly appreciated as a positive force for natural and cultural conservation. Tourism can capture the economic characteristics of the heritage and harness these for conservation by generating funding, educating the community and influencing policy. It is an essential part of many national and regional economies and can be an important factor in development, when managed successfully.

Tourism itself has become an increasingly complex phenomenon, with political, economic, social, cultural, educational, bio-physical, ecological and aesthetic dimensions. The achievement of a beneficial interaction between the potentially conflicting expectations and aspirations of visitors and host or local communities, presents many challenges and opportunities.

The natural and cultural heritage, diversities and living cultures are major tourism attractions. Excessive or poorly-managed tourism and tourism related development can threaten their physical nature, integrity and significant characteristics. The ecological setting, culture and lifestyles of host communities may also be degraded, along with the visitor's experience of the place.

Tourism should bring benefits to host communities and provide an important means and motivation for them to care for and maintain their heritage and cultural practices. The involvement and co-operation of local and/or indigenous community representatives, conservationists, tourism operators, property owners, policy makers, those preparing national development plans and site managers is necessary to achieve a sustainable tourism industry and enhance the protection of heritage resources for future generations.

ICOMOS, the International Council on Monuments and Sites, as the author of this Charter, other international organisations and the tourism industry, are dedicated to this challenge.

Objectives of the Charter

The Objectives of the International Cultural Tourism Charter are:

- To facilitate and encourage those involved with heritage conservation and management to make the significance of that heritage accessible to the host community and visitors.
- To facilitate and encourage the tourism industry to promote and manage tourism in ways that respect and enhance the heritage and living cultures of host communities.
- To facilitate and encourage a dialogue between conservation interests and the tourism industry about the importance and fragile nature of heritage places, collections and living cultures including the need to achieve a sustainable future for them.
- To encourage those formulating plans and policies to develop detailed, measurable goals and strategies relating to the presentation and interpretation of heritage places and cultural activities, in the context of their preservation and conservation.

In addition,

- The Charter supports wider initiatives by ICOMOS, other international bodies and the tourism industry in maintaining the integrity of heritage management and conservation.
- The Charter encourages the involvement of all those with relevant or at times conflicting interests, responsibilities and obligations to join in achieving its objectives.
- The Charter encourages the formulation of detailed guidelines by interested parties, facilitating the implementation of the Principles to their specific circumstances or the requirements of particular organisations and communities.

Principles of the Cultural Tourism Charter

Principle 1: Since domestic and international tourism is among the foremost vehicles for cultural exchange, conservation should provide responsible and well-managed opportunities for members of the host community and visitors to experience and understand that community's heritage and culture at first hand.

1.1 The natural and cultural heritage is a material and spiritual resource, providing a narrative of historical development. It has an important role in modern life and should be made physically, intellectually and/or emotively accessible to the general public. Programmes for the protection and conservation of the physical attributes, intangible aspects, contemporary cultural expressions and broad context, should facilitate an understanding and appreciation of the heritage significance by the host community and the visitor, in an equitable and affordable manner.

1.2 Individual aspects of natural and cultural heritage have differing levels of significance, some with universal values, others of national, regional or local importance. Interpretation programmes should present that significance in a relevant and accessible manner to the host community and the visitor, with appropriate, stimulating and contemporary forms of education, media, technology and personal explanation of historical, environmental and cultural information.

1.3 Interpretation and presentation programmes should facilitate and encourage the high level of public awareness and support necessary for the long-term survival of the natural and cultural heritage.

1.4 Interpretation programmes should present the significance of heritage places, traditions and cultural practices within the past experience and present diversities of the area and the host community, including that of minority cultural or linguistic groups. The visitor should always be informed of the differing cultural values that may be ascribed to a particular heritage resource.

Principle 2: The relationship between Heritage Places and Tourism is dynamic and may involve conflicting values. It should be managed in a sustainable way for present and future generations.

2.1 Places of heritage significance have an intrinsic value for all people as an important basis for cultural diversity and social development. The long-term protection and conservation of living cultures, heritage places, collections, their physical and ecological integrity and their environmental context, should be an essential component of social, economic, political, legislative, cultural and tourism development policies.

2.2 The interaction between heritage resources or values and tourism is dynamic and ever changing, generating both opportunities and challenges, as well as potential conflicts. Tourism projects, activities and developments should achieve positive outcomes and minimise adverse impacts on the heritage and lifestyles of the host community, while responding to the needs and aspirations of the visitor.

2.3 Conservation, interpretation and tourism development programmes should be based on a comprehensive understanding of the specific, but often complex or conflicting aspects of heritage significance of the particular place. Continuing research and consultation are important to furthering the evolving understanding and appreciation of that significance.

2.4 The retention of the authenticity of heritage places and collections is important. It is an essential element of their cultural significance, as expressed in the physical material, collected memory and intangible traditions that remain from the past. Programmes should present and interpret the authenticity of places and cultural experiences to enhance the appreciation and understanding of that cultural heritage.

2.5 Tourism development and infrastructure projects should take account of the aesthetic, social and cultural dimensions, natural and cultural landscapes, bio-diversity characteristics and the broader visual context of heritage places. Preference should be given to using local materials and take account of local architectural styles or vernacular traditions.

2.6 Before heritage places are promoted or developed for increased tourism, management plans should assess the natural and cultural values of the resource. They should then establish appropriate limits of acceptable change, particularly in relation to the impact of visitor numbers on the physical characteristics, integrity, ecology and biodiversity of the place, local access and transportation systems and the social, economic and cultural well-being of the host community. If the likely level of change is unacceptable the development proposal should be modified.

2.7 There should be on-going programmes of evaluation to assess the progressive impacts of tourism activities and development on the particular place or community.

Principle 3: Conservation and Tourism Planning for Heritage Places should ensure that the Visitor Experience will be worthwhile, satisfying and enjoyable.

3.1 Conservation and tourism programmes should present high quality information to optimise the visitor's understanding of the significant heritage characteristics and of the need for their protection, enabling the visitor to enjoy the place in an appropriate manner.

3.2 Visitors should be able to experience the heritage place at their own pace, if they so choose. Specific circulation routes may be necessary to minimise impacts on the integrity and physical fabric of a place, its natural and cultural characteristics.

3.3 Respect for the sanctity of spiritual places, practices and traditions is an important consideration for site managers, visitors, policy makers, planners and tourism operators. Visitors should be encouraged to behave as welcomed guests, respecting the values and lifestyles of the host community, rejecting possible theft or illicit trade in cultural property and conducting themselves in a responsible manner which would generate a renewed welcome, should they return.

3.4 Planning for tourism activities should provide appropriate facilities for the comfort, safety and well-being of the visitor, that enhance the enjoyment of the visit but do not adversely impact on the significant features or ecological characteristics.

Principle 4: Host communities and indigenous peoples should be involved in planning for conservation and tourism.

4.1 The rights and interests of the host community, at regional and local levels, property owners and relevant indigenous peoples who may exercise traditional rights or responsibilities over their own land and its significant sites, should be respected. They should be involved in establishing goals, strategies, policies and protocols for the identification, conservation, management, presentation and interpretation of their heritage resources, cultural practices and contemporary cultural expressions, in the tourism context.

4.2 While the heritage of any specific place or region may have a universal dimension, the needs and wishes of some communities or indigenous peoples to restrict or manage physical, spiritual or intellectual access to certain cultural practices, knowledge, beliefs, activities, artefacts or sites should be respected.

Principle 5: Tourism and conservation activities should benefit the host community.

5.1 Policy makers should promote measures for the equitable distribution of the benefits of tourism to be shared across countries or regions, improving the levels of socio-economic development and contributing where necessary to poverty alleviation.

5.2 Conservation management and tourism activities should provide equitable economic, social and cultural benefits to the men and women of the host or local community, at all levels, through education, training and the creation of full time employment opportunities.

5.3 A significant proportion of the revenue specifically derived from tourism programmes to heritage places should be allotted to the protection, conservation and presentation of those places, including their natural and cultural contexts. Where possible, visitors should be advised of this revenue allocation.

5.4 Tourism programmes should encourage the training and employment of guides and site interpreters from the host community to enhance the skills of local people in the presentation and interpretation of their cultural values.

5.5 Heritage interpretation and education programmes among the people of the host community should encourage the involvement of local site interpreters. The programmes should promote a knowledge and respect for their heritage, encouraging the local people to take a direct interest in its care and conservation.

5.6 Conservation management and tourism programmes should include education and training opportunities for policy makers, planners, researchers, designers, architects, interpreters, conservators and tourism operators. Participants should be encouraged to understand and help resolve the at times conflicting issues, opportunities and problems encountered by their colleagues.

Principle 6: Tourism promotion programmes should protect and enhance Natural and Cultural Heritage characteristics.

6.1 Tourism promotion programmes should create realistic expectations and responsibly inform potential visitors of the specific heritage characteristics of a place or host community, thereby encouraging them to behave appropriately.

6.2 Places and collections of heritage significance should be promoted and managed in ways which protect their authenticity and enhance the visitor experience by minimising fluctuations in arrivals and avoiding excessive numbers of visitors at anyone time.

6.3 Tourism promotion programmes should provide a wider distribution of benefits and relieve the pressures on more popular places by encouraging visitors to experience the wider cultural and natural heritage characteristics of the region or locality.

6.4 The promotion, distribution and sale of local crafts and other products should provide a reasonable social and economic return to the host community, while ensuring that their cultural integrity is not degraded.

ICOMOS International Scientific Committee on Cultural Tourism.

IDENTIFICATION AND CONSERVATION OF WORLD HERITAGE SITES

Heritage is our legacy from the past, what we live with today, and what we pass on to future generations. Our cultural and natural heritage are both irreplaceable sources of life and inspiration. Places as unique and diverse as the wilds of East Africa's Serengeti, the Pyramids of Egypt, the Great Barrier Reef in Australia and the Baroque cathedrals of Latin America make up our world's heritage. What makes the concept of World Heritage exceptional is its universal application. World Heritage sites belong to all the peoples of the world, irrespective of the territory on which they are located. The United Nations Educational, Scientific and Cultural Organization (UNESCO) seeks to encourage the identification, protection and preservation of cultural and natural heritage around the world considered to be of outstanding value to humanity. This is embodied in an international treaty called the **Convention concerning the Protection of the World Cultural and Natural Heritage**, adopted by UNESCO in 1972.

UNESCO's World Heritage Mission is to:

(*i*) encourage countries to sign the World Heritage Convention and to ensure the protection of their natural and cultural heritage;

(*ii*) encourage States Parties to the Convention to nominate sites within their national territory for inclusion on the World Heritage List;

(*iii*) encourage States Parties to establish management plans and set up reporting systems on the state of conservation of their World Heritage sites;

(*iv*) help States Parties safeguard World Heritage properties by providing technical assistance and professional training;

(*v*) provide emergency assistance for World Heritage sites in immediate danger;

(*vi*) support States Parties' public awareness-building activities for World Heritage conservation;

(*vii*) encourage participation of the local population in the preservation of their cultural and natural heritage;

(*viii*) encourage international cooperation in the conservation of our world's cultural and natural heritage.

WORLD HERITAGE LIST

The World Heritage List includes 851 properties forming part of the cultural and natural heritage which the World Heritage Committee considers as having outstanding universal value.

These include 660 cultural, 166 natural and 25 mixed properties in 141 States Parties. As of October 2006, 184 States Parties have ratified the World Heritage Convention.

Afghanistan

- Minaret and Archaeological Remains of Jam (2002).
- Cultural Landscape and Archaeological Remains of the Bamiyan Valley (2003).

Albania

- Butrint (1992, 1999, 2007).
- Museum-City of Gjirokastra (2005).

Algeria

- Al Qal'a of Beni Hammad (1980).
- Djémila (1982).
- M'Zab Valley (1982).
- Tassili n'Ajjer (1982).
- Timgad (1982).
- Tipasa (1982).
- Kasbah of Algiers (1992).

Andorra

- Madriu-Perafita-Claror Valley (2004, 2006).

Argentina

- Los Glaciares (1981).

- Jesuit Missions of the Guaranis: San Ignacio Mini, Santa Ana, Nuestra Señora de Loreto and Santa Maria Mayor (Argentina), Ruins of Sao Miguel das Missoes (Brazil) (1983, 1984).
- Iguazu National Park (1984).
- Cueva de las Manos, Río Pinturas (1999).
- Península Valdés (1999).
- Ischigualasto/Talampaya Natural Parks (2000).
- Jesuit Block and Estancias of Córdoba (2000).
- Quebrada de Humahuaca (2003).

Armenia

- Monasteries of Haghpat and Sanahin (1996, 2000).
- Cathedral and Churches of Echmiatsin and the Archaeological Site of Zvartnots (2000).
- Monastery of Geghard and the Upper Azat Valley (2000).

Australia

- Great Barrier Reef (1981).
- Kakadu National Park (1981, 1987, 1992).
- Willandra Lakes Region (1981).
- Lord Howe Island Group (1982).
- Tasmanian Wilderness (1982, 1989).
- Gondwana Rainforests of Australia (1986, 1994).
- Uluru-Kata Tjuta National Park (1987, 1994).
- Wet Tropics of Queensland (1988).
- Shark Bay, Western Australia (1991).
- Fraser Island (1992).
- Australian Fossil Mammal Sites (Riversleigh/Naracoorte) (1994).
- Heard and McDonald Islands (1997).
- Macquarie Island (1997).
- Greater Blue Mountains Area (2000).
- Purnululu National Park (2003).
- Royal Exhibition Building and Carlton Gardens (2004).
- Sydney Opera House (2007).

Austria

- Historic Centre of the City of Salzburg (1996).
- Palace and Gardens of Schönbrunn (1996).
- Hallstatt-Dachstein Salzkammergut Cultural Landscape (1997).
- Semmering Railway (1998).
- City of Graz—Historic Centre (1999).
- Wachau Cultural Landscape (2000).
- Fertö/Neusiedlersee Cultural Landscape (2001).
- Historic Centre of Vienna (2001).

Azerbaijan

- Walled City of Baku with the Shirvanshah's Palace and Maiden Tower (2000).
- Gobustan Rock Art Cultural Landscape (2007).

Bahrain

- Qal'at al-Bahrain—Ancient Harbour and Capital of Dilmun (2005).

Bangladesh

- Historic Mosque City of Bagerhat (1985).
- Ruins of the Buddhist Vihara at Paharpur (1985).
- The Sundarbans (1997).

Belarus

- Belovezhskaya Pushcha/Bialowieza Forest (1979, 1992).
- Mir Castle Complex (2000).
- Architectural, Residential and Cultural Complex of the Radziwill Family at Nesvizh (2005).
- Struve Geodetic Arc (2005).

Belgium

- Flemish Béguinages (1998).

- La Grand-Place, Brussels (1998).
- The Four Lifts on the Canal du Centre and their Environs, La Louvière and Le Roeulx (Hainault) (1998).
- Belfries of Belgium and France (1999, 2005).
- Historic Centre of Brugge (2000).
- Major Town Houses of the Architect Victor Horta (Brussels) (2000).
- Neolithic Flint Mines at Spiennes (Mons) (2000).
- Notre-Dame Cathedral in Tournai (2000).
- Plantin-Moretus House-Workshops-Museum Complex (2005).

Belize

- Belize Barrier Reef Reserve System (1996).

Benin

- Royal Palaces of Abomey (1985, 2007).

Bolivia

- City of Potosí (1987).
- Jesuit Missions of the Chiquitos (1990).
- Historic City of Sucre (1991).
- Fuerte de Samaipata (1998).
- Noel Kempff Mercado National Park (2000).
- Tiwanaku: Spiritual and Political Centre of the Tiwanaku Culture (2000).

Bosnia and Herzegovina

- Old Bridge Area of the Old City of Mostar (2005).
- Mehmed Paša Sokolović Bridge in Višegrad (2007).

Botswana

- Tsodilo (2001).

Brazil

- Historic Town of Ouro Preto (1980).
- Historic Centre of the Town of Olinda (1982).
- Jesuit Missions of the Guaranis: San Ignacio Mini, Santa Ana, Nuestra Señora de Loreto and Santa Maria Mayor (Argentina), Ruins of Sao Miguel das Missoes (Brazil) (1983, 1984).
- Historic Centre of Salvador de Bahia (1985).
- Sanctuary of Bom Jesus do Congonhas (1985).
- Iguaçu National Park (1986).
- Brasilia (1987).
- Serra da Capivara National Park (1991).
- Historic Centre of São Luís (1997).
- Atlantic Forest South-East Reserves (1999).
- Discovery Coast Atlantic Forest Reserves (1999).
- Historic Centre of the Town of Diamantina (1999).
- Central Amazon Conservation Complex (2000, 2003).
- Pantanal Conservation Area (2000).
- Brazilian Atlantic Islands: Fernando de Noronha and Atol das Rocas Reserves (2001).
- Cerrado Protected Areas: Chapada dos Veadeiros and Emas National Parks (2001).
- Historic Centre of the Town of Goiás (2001).

Bulgaria

- Boyana Church (1979).
- Madara Rider (1979).
- Rock-Hewn Churches of Ivanovo (1979).
- Thracian Tomb of Kazanlak (1979).
- Ancient City of Nessebar (1983).
- Pirin National Park (1983).
- Rila Monastery (1983).
- Srebarna Nature Reserve (1983).
- Thracian Tomb of Sveshtari (1985).

Cambodia

- Angkor (1992).

Cameroon

- Dja Faunal Reserve (1987).

Canada

- L'Anse aux Meadows National Historic Site (1978).
- Nahanni National Park (1978).
- Dinosaur Provincial Park (1979).
- Kluane/Wrangell-St Elias/Glacier Bay/Tatshenshini-Alsek (1979, 1992, 1994).
- Head-Smashed-In Buffalo Jump (1981).
- SGang Gwaay (1981).
- Wood Buffalo National Park (1983).
- Canadian Rocky Mountain Parks (1984, 1990).
- Historic District of Old Québec (1985).
- Gros Morne National Park (1987).
- Old Town Lunenburg (1995).
- Waterton Glacier International Peace Park (1995).
- Miguasha National Park (1999).
- Rideau Canal (2007).

Central African Republic

- Manovo-Gounda St Floris National Park (1988).

Chile

- Rapa Nui National Park (1995).
- Churches of Chiloé (2000).
- Historic Quarter of the Seaport City of Valparaíso (2003).
- Humberstone and Santa Laura Saltpeter Works (2005).
- Sewell Mining Town (2006).

China

- Imperial Palaces of the Ming and Qing Dynasties in Beijing and Shenyang (1987, 2004).
- Mausoleum of the First Qin Emperor (1987).
- Mogao Caves (1987).

- Mount Taishan (1987).
- Peking Man Site at Zhoukoudian (1987).
- The Great Wall (1987).
- Mount Huangshan (1990).
- Huanglong Scenic and Historic Interest Area (1992).
- Jiuzhaigou Valley Scenic and Historic Interest Area (1992).
- Wulingyuan Scenic and Historic Interest Area (1992).
- Ancient Building Complex in the Wudang Mountains (1994).
- Historic Ensemble of the Potala Palace, Lhasa (1994, 2000, 2001).
- Mountain Resort and its Outlying Temples, Chengde (1994).
- Temple and Cemetery of Confucius and the Kong Family Mansion in Qufu (1994).
- Lushan National Park (1996).
- Mount Emei Scenic Area, including Leshan Giant Buddha Scenic Area (1996).
- Ancient City of Ping Yao (1997).
- Classical Gardens of Suzhou (1997, 2000).
- Old Town of Lijiang (1997).
- Summer Palace, an Imperial Garden in Beijing (1998).
- Temple of Heaven: an Imperial Sacrificial Altar in Beijing (1998).
- Dazu Rock Carvings (1999).
- Mount Wuyi (1999).
- Ancient Villages in Southern Anhui—Xidi and Hongcun (2000).
- Imperial Tombs of the Ming and Qing Dynasties (2000, 2003, 2004).
- Longmen Grottoes (2000).
- Mount Qingcheng and the Dujiangyan Irrigation System (2000).
- Yungang Grottoes (2001).
- Three Parallel Rivers of Yunnan Protected Areas (2003).
- Capital Cities and Tombs of the Ancient Koguryo Kingdom (2004).
- Historic Centre of Macao (2005).
- Sichuan Giant Panda Sanctuaries (2006).

- Yin Xu (2006).
- Kaiping Diaolou and Villages (2007).
- South China Karst (2007).

Colombia

- Port, Fortresses and Group of Monuments, Cartagena (1984).
- Los Katíos National Park (1994).
- Historic Centre of Santa Cruz de Mompox (1995).
- National Archeological Park of Tierradentro (1995).
- San Agustín Archeological Park (1995).
- Malpelo Fauna and Flora Sanctuary (2006).

Costa Rica

- Talamanca Range-La Amistad Reserves/La Amistad National Park (1983, 1990).
- Cocos Island National Park (1997, 2002).
- Area de Conservación Guanacaste (1999, 2004).

Côte d'Ivoire

- Mount Nimba Strict Nature Reserve (1981, 1982).
- Taï National Park (1982).
- Comoé National Park (1983).

Croatia

- Historical Complex of Split with the Palace of Diocletian (1979).
- Old City of Dubrovnik (1979, 1994).
- Plitvice Lakes National Park (1979, 2000).
- Episcopal Complex of the Euphrasian Basilica in the Historic Centre of Poreč (1997).
- Historic City of Trogir (1997).
- The Cathedral of St. James in Šibenik (2000).

Cuba

- Old Havana and its Fortifications (1982).

- Trinidad and the Valley de los Ingenios (1988).
- San Pedro de la Roca Castle, Santiago de Cuba (1997).
- Desembarco del Granma National Park (1999).
- Viñales Valley (1999).
- Archaeological Landscape of the First Coffee Plantations in the South-East of Cuba (2000).
- Alejandro de Humboldt National Park (2001).
- Urban Historic Centre of Cienfuegos (2005).

Cyprus

- Paphos (1980).
- Painted Churches in the Troodos Region (1985, 2001).
- Choirokoitia (1998).

Czech Republic

- Historic Centre of Český Krumlov (1992).
- Historic Centre of Prague (1992).
- Historic Centre of Telč (1992).
- Pilgrimage Church of St. John of Nepomuk at Zelená Hora (1994).
- Kutná Hora: Historical Town Centre with the Church of St. Barbara and the Cathedral of Our Lady at Sedlec (1995).
- Lednice-Valtice Cultural Landscape (1996).
- Gardens and Castle at Kroměříž (1998).
- Holašovice Historical Village Reservation (1998).
- Litomyšl Castle (1999).
- Holy Trinity Column in Olomouc (2000).
- Tugendhat Villa in Brno (2001).
- Jewish Quarter and St. Procopius' Basilica in Třebíč (2003).

Democratic People's Republic of Korea

- Complex of Koguryo Tombs (2004).

Democratic Republic of the Congo

- Virunga National Park (1979).

- Kahuzi-Biega National Park (1980).
- Garamba National Park (1980).
- Salonga National Park (1984).
- Okapi Wildlife Reserve (1996).

Denmark

- Jelling Mounds, Runic Stones and Church (1994).
- Roskilde Cathedral (1995).
- Kronborg Castle (2000).
- Ilulissat Icefjord (2004).

Dominica

- Morne Trois Pitons National Park (1997).

Dominican Republic

- Colonial City of Santo Domingo (1990).

Ecuador

- Galápagos Islands (1978, 2001).
- City of Quito (1978).
- Sangay National Park (1983).
- Historic Centre of Santa Ana de los Ríos de Cuenca (1999).

Egypt

- Abu Mena (1979).
- Ancient Thebes with its Necropolis (1979).
- Historic Cairo (1979).
- Memphis and its Necropolis—the Pyramid Fields from Giza to Dahshur (1979).
- Nubian Monuments from Abu Simbel to Philae (1979).
- Saint Catherine Area (2002).
- Wadi Al-Hitan (Whale Valley) (2005).

El Salvador

- Joya de Cerén Archaeological Site (1993).

Estonia

- Historic Centre (Old Town) of Tallinn (1997).
- Struve Geodetic Arc (2005).

Ethiopia

- Simien National Park (1978).
- Rock-Hewn Churches, Lalibela (1978).
- Fasil Ghebbi, Gondar Region (1979).
- Aksum (1980).
- Lower Valley of the Awash (1980).
- Lower Valley of the Omo (1980).
- Tiya (1980).
- Harar Jugol, the Fortified Historic Town (2006).

Finland

- Fortress of Suomenlinna (1991).
- Old Rauma (1991).
- Petäjävesi Old Church (1994).
- Verla Groundwood and Board Mill (1996).
- Bronze Age Burial Site of Sammallahdenmäki (1999).
- Kvarken Archipelago/High Coast (2000, 2006).
- Struve Geodetic Arc (2005).

France

- Chartres Cathedral (1979).
- Mont-Saint-Michel and its Bay (1979, 2007).
- Palace and Park of Versailles (1979, 2007).
- Prehistoric Sites and Decorated Caves of the Vézère Valley (1979).
- Vézelay, Church and Hill (1979, 2007).
- Amiens Cathedral (1981).
- Arles, Roman and Romanesque Monuments (1981).
- Cistercian Abbey of Fontenay (1981, 2007).
- Palace and Park of Fontainebleau (1981).
- Roman Theatre and its Surroundings and the "Triumphal Arch" of Orange (1981, 2007).

- Royal Saltworks of Arc-et-Senans (1982).
- Abbey Church of Saint-Savin sur Gartempe (1983, 2007).
- Gulf of Porto: Calanche of Piana, Gulf of Girolata, Scandola Reserve (1983).
- Place Stanislas, Place de la Carrière and Place d'Alliance in Nancy (1983).
- Pont du Gard (Roman Aqueduct) (1985, 2007).
- Strasbourg—Grande île (1988).
- Cathedral of Notre-Dame, Former Abbey of Saint-Remi and Palace of Tau, Reims (1991).
- Paris, Banks of the Seine (1991).
- Bourges Cathedral (1992).
- Historic Centre of Avignon: Papal Palace, Episcopal Ensemble and Avignon Bridge (1995).
- Canal du Midi (1996).
- Historic Fortified City of Carcassonne (1997).
- Pyrénées—Mont Perdu (1997, 1999).
- Historic Site of Lyons (1998).
- Routes of Santiago de Compostela in France (1998).
- Belfries of Belgium and France (1999, 2005).
- Jurisdiction of Saint-Emilion (1999).
- The Loire Valley between Sully-sur-Loire and Chalonnes (2000).
- Provins, Town of Medieval Fairs (2001).
- Le Havre, the City Rebuilt by Auguste Perret (2005).
- Bordeaux, Port of the Moon (2007).

Gabon

- Ecosystem and Relict Cultural Landscape of Lopé-Okanda (2007).

Gambia

- James Island and Related Sites (2003).
- Stone Circles of Senegambia (2006).

Georgia

- Bagrati Cathedral and Gelati Monastery (1994).

- Historical Monuments of Mtskheta (1994).
- Upper Svaneti (1996).

Germany

- Aachen Cathedral (1978).
- Speyer Cathedral (1981).
- Würzburg Residence with the Court Gardens and Residence Square (1981).
- Pilgrimage Church of Wies (1983).
- Castles of Augustusburg and Falkenlust at Brühl (1984).
- St. Mary's Cathedral and St. Michael's Church at Hildesheim (1985).
- Roman Monuments, Cathedral of St. Peter and Church of Our Lady in Trier (1986).
- Frontiers of the Roman Empire (1987, 2005).
- Hanseatic City of Lübeck (1987).
- Palaces and Parks of Potsdam and Berlin (1990, 1992, 1999).
- Abbey and Altenmünster of Lorsch (1991).
- Mines of Rammelsberg and Historic Town of Goslar (1992).
- Maulbronn Monastery Complex (1993).
- Town of Bamberg (1993).
- Collegiate Church, Castle, and Old Town of Quedlinburg (1994).
- Völklingen Ironworks (1994).
- Messel Pit Fossil Site (1995).
- Bauhaus and its Sites in Weimar and Dessau (1996).
- Cologne Cathedral (1996).
- Luther Memorials in Eisleben and Wittenberg (1996).
- Classical Weimar (1998).
- Museumsinsel (Museum Island), Berlin (1999).
- Wartburg Castle (1999).
- Garden Kingdom of Dessau-Wörlitz (2000).
- Monastic Island of Reichenau (2000).
- Zollverein Coal Mine Industrial Complex in Essen (2001).
- Historic Centres of Stralsund and Wismar (2002).
- Upper Middle Rhine Valley (2002).

- Dresden Elbe Valley (2004).
- Muskauer Park/Park Muzakowski (2004) .
- Town Hall and Roland on the Marketplace of Bremen (2004).
- Old town of Regensburg with Stadtamhof (2006).

Ghana

- Forts and Castles, Volta, Greater Accra, Central and Western Regions (1979).
- Asante Traditional Buildings (1980).

Greece

- Temple of Apollo Epicurius at Bassae (1986).
- Acropolis, Athens (1987).
- Archaeological Site of Delphi (1987).
- Medieval City of Rhodes (1988).
- Meteora (1988).
- Mount Athos (1988).
- Paleochristian and Byzantine Monuments of Thessalonika (1988).
- Sanctuary of Asklepios at Epidaurus (1988).
- Archaeological Site of Mystras (1989).
- Archaeological Site of Olympia (1989).
- Delos (1990).
- Monasteries of Daphni, Hosios Loukas and Nea Moni of Chios (1990).
- Pythagoreion and Heraion of Samos (1992).
- Archaeological Site of Aigai (modern name Vergina) (1996).
- Archaeological Sites of Mycenae and Tiryns (1999).
- Historic Centre (Chorá) with the Monastery of Saint John "the Theologian" and the Cave of the Apocalypse on the Island of Pátmos (1999).
- Old Town of Corfu (2007).

Guatemala

- Antigua Guatemala (1979).

- Tikal National Park (1979).
- Archaeological Park and Ruins of Quirigua (1981).

Guinea

- Mount Nimba Strict Nature Reserve (1981, 1982).

Haiti

- National History Park—Citadel, Sans Souci, Ramiers (1982).

Holy See

- Historic Centre of Rome, the Properties of the Holy See in that City Enjoying Extraterritorial Rights and San Paolo Fuori le Mura (1980, 1990).
- Vatican City (1984).

Honduras

- Maya Site of Copan (1980).
- Río Plátano Biosphere Reserve (1982).

Hungary

- Budapest, including the Banks of the Danube, the Buda Castle Quarter and Andrássy Avenue (1987, 2002).
- Old Village of Hollókö and its Surroundings (1987).
- Caves of Aggtelek Karst and Slovak Karst (1995, 2000).
- Millenary Benedictine Abbey of Pannonhalma and its Natural Environment (1996).
- Hortobágy National Park—the *Puszta* (1999).
- Early Christian Necropolis of Pécs (Sopianae) (2000).
- Fertö/Neusiedlersee Cultural Landscape (2001).
- Tokaj Wine Region Historic Cultural Landscape (2002).

Iceland

- Pingvellir National Park (2004).

India

- Agra Fort (1983).
- Ajanta Caves (1983).
- Ellora Caves (1983).
- Taj Mahal (1983).
- Group of Monuments at Mahabalipuram (1984).
- Sun Temple, Konârak (1984).
- Manas Wildlife Sanctuary (1985).
- Kaziranga National Park (1985).
- Keoladeo National Park (1985).
- Churches and Convents of Goa (1986).
- Fatehpur Sikri (1986).
- Group of Monuments at Hampi (1986).
- Khajuraho Group of Monuments (1986).
- Elephanta Caves (1987).
- Great Living Chola Temples (1987, 2004).
- Group of Monuments at Pattadakal (1987).
- Sundarbans National Park (1987).
- Nanda Devi and Valley of Flowers National Parks (1988, 2005).
- Buddhist Monuments at Sanchi (1989).
- Humayun's Tomb, Delhi (1993).
- Qutb Minar and its Monuments, Delhi (1993).
- Mountain Railways of India (1999, 2005).
- Mahabodhi Temple Complex at Bodh Gaya (2002).
- Rock Shelters of Bhimbetka (2003).
- Champaner-Pavagadh Archaeological Park (2004).
- Chhatrapati Shivaji Terminus (formerly Victoria Terminus) (2004).
- Red Fort Complex (2007).

Indonesia

- Borobudur Temple Compounds (1991).
- Komodo National Park (1991).
- Prambanan Temple Compounds (1991).
- Ujung Kulon National Park (1991).
- Sangiran Early Man Site (1996).
- Lorentz National Park (1999).

- Tropical Rainforest Heritage of Sumatra (2004).

Iran (Islamic Republic of)

- Meidan Emam, Esfahan (1979).
- Persepolis (1979).
- Tchogha Zanbil (1979).
- Takht-e-Soleyman (2003).
- Bam and its Cultural Landscape (2004, 2007).
- Pasargadae (2004).
- Soltaniyeh (2005).
- Bisotun (2006).

Iraq

- Hatra (1985).
- Ashur (Qal'at Sherqat) (2003).
- Samarra Archaeological City (2007).

Ireland

- Archaeological Ensemble of the Bend of the Boyne (1993).
- Skellig Michael (1996).

Israel

- Masada (2001).
- Old City of Acre (2001).
- White City of Tel-Aviv—the Modern Movement (2003).
- Biblical Tels—Megiddo, Hazor, Beer Sheba (2005).
- Incense Route—Desert Cities in the Negev (2005).

Italy

- Rock Drawings in Valcamonica (1979).
- Church and Dominican Convent of Santa Maria delle Grazie with "The Last Supper" by Leonardo da Vinci (1980).
- Historic Centre of Rome, the Properties of the Holy See in that City Enjoying Extraterritorial Rights and San Paolo Fuori le Mura (1980, 1990).

- Historic Centre of Florence (1982).
- Piazza del Duomo, Pisa (1987, 2007).
- Venice and its Lagoon (1987).
- Historic Centre of San Gimignano (1990).
- The Sassi and the Park of the Rupestrian Churches of Matera (1993).
- City of Vicenza and the Palladian Villas of the Veneto (1994, 1996).
- Crespi d'Adda (1995).
- Ferrara, City of the Renaissance, and its Po Delta (1995, 1999).
- Historic Centre of Naples (1995).
- Historic Centre of Siena (1995).
- Castel del Monte (1996).
- Early Christian Monuments of Ravenna (1996).
- Historic Centre of the City of Pienza (1996).
- The *Trulli* of Alberobello (1996).
- 18th-Century Royal Palace at Caserta with the Park, the Aqueduct of Vanvitelli, and the San Leucio Complex (1997).
- Archaeological Area of Agrigento (1997).
- Archaeological Areas of Pompei, Herculaneum and Torre Annunziata (1997).
- Botanical Garden (Orto Botanico), Padua (1997).
- Cathedral, Torre Civica and Piazza Grande, Modena (1997).
- Costiera Amalfitana (1997).
- Portovenere, Cinque Terre, and the Islands (Palmaria, Tino and Tinetto) (1997).
- Residences of the Royal House of Savoy (1997).
- Su Nuraxi di Barumini (1997).
- Villa Romana del Casale (1997).
- Archaeological Area and the Patriarchal Basilica of Aquileia (1998).
- Cilento and Vallo di Diano National Park with the Archeological sites of Paestum and Velia, and the Certosa di Padula (1998).
- Historic Centre of Urbino (1998).
- Villa Adriana (Tivoli) (1999).
- Assisi, the Basilica of San Francesco and Other Franciscan Sites (2000).

- City of Verona (2000).
- Isole Eolie (Aeolian Islands) (2000).
- Villa d'Este, Tivoli (2001).
- Late Baroque Towns of the Val di Noto (South-Eastern Sicily) (2002).
- *Sacri Monti* of Piedmont and Lombardy (2003).
- Etruscan Necropolises of Cerveteri and Tarquinia (2004).
- Val d'Orcia (2004).
- Syracuse and the Rocky Necropolis of Pantalica (2005).
- Genoa: *Le Strade Nuove* and the system of the *Palazzi dei Rolli* (2006).

Japan

- Buddhist Monuments in the Horyu-ji Area (1993).
- Himeji-jo (1993).
- Shirakami-Sanchi (1993).
- Yakushima (1993).
- Historic Monuments of Ancient Kyoto (Kyoto, Uji and Otsu Cities) (1994).
- Historic Villages of Shirakawa-go and Gokayama (1995).
- Hiroshima Peace Memorial (Genbaku Dome) (1996).
- Itsukushima Shinto Shrine (1996).
- Historic Monuments of Ancient Nara (1998).
- Shrines and Temples of Nikko (1999).
- Gusuku Sites and Related Properties of the Kingdom of Ryukyu (2000).
- Sacred Sites and Pilgrimage Routes in the Kii Mountain Range (2004).
- Shiretoko (2005).
- Iwami Ginzan Silver Mine and its Cultural Landscape (2007).

Jerusalem (Site Proposed by Jordan)

- Old City of Jerusalem and its Walls (1981).

Jordan

- Petra (1985).

- Quseir Amra (1985).
- Um er-Rasas (Kastrom Mefa'a) (2004).

Kazakhstan

- Mausoleum of Khoja Ahmed Yasawi (2003).
- Petroglyphs within the Archaeological Landscape of Tamgaly (2004).

Kenya

- Lake Turkana National Parks (1997, 2001).
- Mount Kenya National Park/Natural Forest (1997).
- Lamu Old Town (2001).

Lao People's Democratic Republic

- Town of Luang Prabang (1995).
- Vat Phou and Associated Ancient Settlements within the Champasak Cultural Landscape (2001).

Latvia

- Historic Centre of Riga (1997).
- Struve Geodetic Arc (2005).

Lebanon

- Anjar (1984).
- Baalbek (1984).
- Byblos (1984).
- Tyre (1984).
- Ouadi Qadisha (the Holy Valley) and the Forest of the Cedars of God (Horsh Arz el-Rab) (1998).

Libyan Arab Jamahiriya

- Archaeological Site of Cyrene (1982).
- Archaeological Site of Leptis Magna (1982).

- Archaeological Site of Sabratha (1982).
- Rock-Art Sites of Tadrart Acacus (1985).
- Old Town of Ghadamès (1986).

Lithuania

- Vilnius Historic Centre (1994).
- Curonian Spit (2000) .
- Kernavë Archaeological Site (Cultural Reserve of Kernavë) (2004).
- Struve Geodetic Arc (2005) .

Luxembourg

- City of Luxembourg: its Old Quarters and Fortifications (1994).

Madagascar

- Tsingy de Bemaraha Strict Nature Reserve (1990).
- Royal Hill of Ambohimanga (2001).
- Rainforests of the Atsinanana (2007).

Malawi

- Lake Malawi National Park (1984).
- Chongoni Rock-Art Area (2006).

Malaysia

- Gunung Mulu National Park (2000).
- Kinabalu Park (2000).

Mali

- Old Towns of Djenné (1988).
- Timbuktu (1988).
- Cliff of Bandiagara (Land of the Dogons) (1989).
- Tomb of Askia (2004).

Malta

- City of Valletta (1980).
- Hal Saflieni Hypogeum (1980).
- Megalithic Temples of Malta (1980, 1992).

Mauritania

- Banc d'Arguin National Park (1989).
- Ancient *Ksour* of Ouadane, Chinguetti, Tichitt and Oualata (1996).

Mauritius

- Aapravasi Ghat (2006).

Mexico

- Historic Centre of Mexico City and Xochimilco (1987).
- Historic Centre of Oaxaca and Archaeological Site of Monte Albán (1987).
- Historic Centre of Puebla (1987).
- Pre-Hispanic City and National Park of Palenque (1987).
- Pre-Hispanic City of Teotihuacan (1987).
- Sian Ka'an (1987).
- Historic Town of Guanajuato and Adjacent Mines (1988).
- Pre-Hispanic City of Chichen-Itza (1988).
- Historic Centre of Morelia (1991).
- El Tajin, Pre-Hispanic City (1992).
- Historic Centre of Zacatecas (1993).
- Rock Paintings of the Sierra de San Francisco (1993).
- Whale Sanctuary of El Vizcaino (1993).
- Earliest 16th-Century Monasteries on the Slopes of Popocatepetl (1994).
- Historic Monuments Zone of Querétaro (1996).
- Pre-Hispanic Town of Uxmal (1996).
- Hospicio Cabañas, Guadalajara (1997).
- Archeological Zone of Paquimé, Casas Grandes (1998).
- Historic Monuments Zone of Tlacotalpan (1998).

- Archaeological Monuments Zone of Xochicalco (1999).
- Historic Fortified Town of Campeche (1999).
- Ancient Maya City of Calakmul, Campeche (2002).
- Franciscan Missions in the Sierra Gorda of Querétaro (2003).
- Luis Barragán House and Studio (2004).
- Islands and Protected Areas of the Gulf of California (2005, 2007).
- Agave Landscape and Ancient Industrial Facilities of Tequila (2006).
- Central University City Campus of the *Universidad Nacional Autónoma de México* (UNAM) (2007).

Mongolia

- Uvs Nuur Basin (2003).
- Orkhon Valley Cultural Landscape (2004).

Montenegro

- Natural and Culturo-Historical Region of Kotor (1979).
- Durmitor National Park (1980, 2005).

Morocco

- Medina of Fez (1981).
- Medina of Marrakesh (1985).
- Ksar of Ait-Ben-Haddou (1987).
- Historic City of Meknes (1996).
- Archaeological Site of Volubilis (1997).
- Medina of Tétouan (formerly known as Titawin) (1997).
- Medina of Essaouira (formerly Mogador) (2001).
- Portuguese City of Mazagan (El Jadida) (2004).

Mozambique

- Island of Mozambique (1991).

Namibia

- Twyfelfontein or/Ui-//aes (2007).

Nepal

- Kathmandu Valley (1979, 2006).
- Sagarmatha National Park (1979).
- Royal Chitwan National Park (1984).
- Lumbini, the Birthplace of the Lord Buddha (1997).

Netherlands

- Schokland and Surroundings (1995).
- Defence Line of Amsterdam (1996).
- Historic Area of Willemstad, Inner City and Harbour, Netherlands Antilles (1997).
- Mill Network at Kinderdijk-Elshout (1997).
- Ir. D.F. Woudagemaal (D.F. Wouda Steam Pumping Station) (1998).
- Droogmakerij de Beemster (Beemster Polder) (1999).
- Rietveld Schröderhuis (Rietveld Schröder House) (2000).

New Zealand

- Te Wahipounamu—South West New Zealand (1990).
- Tongariro National Park (1990, 1993).
- New Zealand Sub-Antarctic Islands (1998).

Nicaragua

- Ruins of León Viejo (2000).

Niger

- Air and Ténéré Natural Reserves (1991).
- W. National Park of Niger (1996).

Nigeria

- Sukur Cultural Landscape (1999).
- Osun-Osogbo Sacred Grove (2005).

Norway

- Bryggen (1979).

- Urnes Stave Church (1979).
- Røros Mining Town (1980).
- Rock Art of Alta (1985).
- Vegaøyan—The Vega Archipelago (2004).
- Struve Geodetic Arc (2005).
- West Norwegian Fjords—Geirangerfjord and Nærøyfjord (2005).

Oman

- Bahla Fort (1987).
- Archaeological Sites of Bat, Al-Khutm and Al-Ayn (1988).
- Arabian Oryx Sanctuary (1994) Delisted 2007.
- Land of Frankincense (2000).
- *Aflaj* Irrigation Systems of Oman (2006).

Pakistan

- Archaeological Ruins at Moenjodaro (1980).
- Buddhist Ruins of Takht-i-Bahi and Neighbouring City Remains at Sahr-i-Bahlol (1980).
- Taxila (1980).
- Fort and Shalamar Gardens in Lahore (1981).
- Historical Monuments of Thatta (1981).
- Rohtas Fort (1997).

Panama

- Fortifications on the Caribbean Side of Panama: Portobelo-San Lorenzo (1980).
- Darien National Park (1981).
- Talamanca Range-La Amistad Reserves/La Amistad National Park (1983, 1990).
- Archaeological Site of Panamá Viejo and Historic District of Panamá (1997, 2003).
- Coiba National Park and its Special Zone of Marine Protection (2005).

Paraguay

- Jesuit Missions of La Santísima Trinidad de Paraná and Jesús de Tavarangue (1993).

Peru

- City of Cuzco (1983).
- Historic Sanctuary of Machu Picchu (1983).
- Chavin (Archaeological Site) (1985).
- Huascarán National Park (1985).
- Chan Chan Archaeological Zone (1986).
- Manú National Park (1987).
- Historic Centre of Lima (1988, 1991).
- Río Abiseo National Park (1990, 1992).
- Lines and Geoglyphs of Nasca and Pampas de Jumana (1994).
- Historical Centre of the City of Arequipa (2000).

Philippines

- Baroque Churches of the Philippines (1993).
- Tubbataha Reef Marine Park (1993).
- Rice Terraces of the Philippine Cordilleras (1995).
- Historic Town of Vigan (1999).
- Puerto-Princesa Subterranean River National Park (1999).

Poland

- Cracow's Historic Centre (1978).
- Wieliczka Salt Mine (1978).
- Auschwitz Birkenau German Nazi Concentration and Extermination Camp (1940-1945) (1979).
- Belovezhskaya Pushcha/BialowiezaForest (1979, 1992).
- Historic Centre of Warsaw (1980).
- Old City of Zamość (1992).
- Castle of the Teutonic Order in Malbork (1997).
- Medieval Town of Toruń (1997).
- Kalwaria Zebrzydowska: the Mannerist Architectural and Park Landscape Complex and Pilgrimage Park (1999).
- Churches of Peace in Jawor and Swidnica (2001).
- Wooden Churches of Southern Little Poland (2003).
- Muskauer Park/Park Muzakowski (2004).

- Centennial Hall in Wroclaw (2006).

Portugal

- Central Zone of the Town of Angra do Heroismo in the Azores (1983).
- Convent of Christ in Tomar (1983).
- Monastery of Batalha (1983).
- Monastery of the Hieronymites and Tower of Belém in Lisbon (1983).
- Historic Centre of Évora (1986).
- Monastery of Alcobaça (1989).
- Cultural Landscape of Sintra (1995).
- Historic Centre of Oporto (1996).
- Prehistoric Rock-Art Sites in the Côa Valley (1998).
- Laurisilva of Madeira (1999).
- Alto Douro Wine Region (2001).
- Historic Centre of Guimarães (2001).
- Landscape of the Pico Island Vineyard Culture (2004).

Republic of Korea

- Haeinsa Temple Janggyeong Panjeon, the Depositories for the *Tripitaka Koreana* Woodblocks (1995).
- Jongmyo Shrine (1995).
- Seokguram Grotto and Bulguksa Temple (1995).
- Changdeokgung Palace Complex (1997).
- Hwaseong Fortress (1997).
- Gochang, Hwasun and Ganghwa Dolmen Sites (2000).
- Gyeongju Historic Areas (2000).
- Jeju Volcanic Island and Lava Tubes (2007).

Republic of Moldova

- Struve Geodetic Arc (2005) .

Romania

- Danube Delta (1991).

- Churches of Moldavia (1993).
- Monastery of Horezu (1993).
- Villages with Fortified Churches in Transylvania (1993, 1999).
- Dacian Fortresses of the Orastie Mountains (1999).
- Historic Centre of Sighişoara (1999).
- Wooden Churches of Maramureş (1999).

Russian Federation

- Historic Centre of Saint Petersburg and Related Groups of Monuments (1990).
- Kizhi Pogost (1990).
- Kremlin and Red Square, Moscow (1990).
- Cultural and Historic Ensemble of the Solovetsky Islands (1992).
- Historic Monuments of Novgorod and Surroundings (1992).
- White Monuments of Vladimir and Suzdal (1992).
- Architectural Ensemble of the Trinity Sergius Lavra in Sergiev Posad (1993).
- Church of the Ascension, Kolomenskoye (1994).
- Virgin Komi Forests (1995).
- Lake Baikal (1996).
- Volcanoes of Kamchatka (1996, 2001).
- Golden Mountains of Altai (1998).
- Western Caucasus (1999).
- Curonian Spit (2000).
- Ensemble of the Ferrapontov Monastery (2000).
- Historic and Architectural Complex of the Kazan Kremlin (2000).
- Central Sikhote-Alin (2001).
- Citadel, Ancient City and Fortress Buildings of Derbent (2003).
- Uvs Nuur Basin (2003).
- Ensemble of the Novodevichy Convent (2004).
- Natural System of Wrangel Island Reserve (2004).
- Historical Centre of the City of Yaroslavl (2005).
- Struve Geodetic Arc (2005).

Saint Kitts and Nevis

- Brimstone Hill Fortress National Park (1999).

Saint Lucia

- Pitons Management Area (2004).

Senegal

- Island of Gorée (1978).
- Niokolo-Koba National Park (1981).
- Djoudj National Bird Sanctuary (1981).
- Island of Saint-Louis (2000, 2007).
- Stone Circles of Senegambia (2006).

Serbia

- Stari Ras and Sopoćani (1979).
- Studenica Monastery (1986).
- Medieval Monuments in Kosovo (2004, 2006).
- Gamzigrad-Romuliana, Palace of Galerius (2007).

Seychelles

- Aldabra Atoll (1982).
- Vallée de Mai Nature Reserve (1983).

Slovakia

- Historic Town of Banská Štiavnica and the Technical Monuments in its Vicinity (1993).
- Spišský Hrad and its Associated Cultural Monuments (1993).
- Vlkolínec (1993).
- Caves of Aggtelek Karst and Slovak Karst (1995, 2000) .
- Bardejov Town Conservation Reserve (2000).
- Primeval Beech Forests of the Carpathians (2007) .

Slovenia

- Škocjan Caves (1986).

Solomon Islands

- East Rennell (1998).

South Africa

- Fossil Hominid Sites of Sterkfontein, Swartkrans, Kromdraai and Environs (1999, 2005).
- Greater St. Lucia Wetland Park (1999).
- Robben Island (1999).
- uKhahlamba/Drakensberg Park (2000).
- Mapungubwe Cultural Landscape (2003).
- Cape Floral Region Protected Areas (2004).
- Vredefort Dome (2005).
- Richtersveld Cultural and Botanical Landscape (2007).

Spain

- Alhambra, Generalife and Albayzín, Granada (1984, 1994).
- Burgos Cathedral (1984).
- Historic Centre of Cordoba (1984, 1994).
- Monastery and Site of the Escurial, Madrid (1984).
- Works of Antoni Gaudí (1984, 2005).
- Altamira Cave (1985).
- Monuments of Oviedo and the Kingdom of the Asturias (1985, 1998).
- Old Town of Ávila with its Extra-Muros Churches (1985, 2007).
- Old Town of Segovia and its Aqueduct (1985).
- Santiago de Compostela (Old Town) (1985).
- Garajonay National Park (1986).
- Historic City of Toledo (1986).
- Mudejar Architecture of Aragon (1986, 2001).
- Old Town of Cáceres (1986).
- Cathedral, Alcázar and Archivo de Indias in Seville (1987).
- Old City of Salamanca (1988).
- Poblet Monastery (1991).
- Archaeological Ensemble of Mérida (1993).
- Route of Santiago de Compostela (1993).
- Royal Monastery of Santa María de Guadalupe (1993).

- Doñana National Park (1994, 2005).
- Historic Walled Town of Cuenca (1996).
- La Lonja de la Seda de Valencia (1996).
- Las Médulas (1997).
- Palau de la Música Catalana and Hospital de Sant Pau, Barcelona (1997).
- Pyrénées—Mont Perdu (1997, 1999) .
- San Millán Yuso and Suso Monasteries (1997).
- Rock Art of the Mediterranean Basin on the Iberian Peninsula (1998).
- University and Historic Precinct of Alcalá de Henares (1998).
- Ibiza, Biodiversity and Culture (1999).
- San Cristóbal de La Laguna (1999).
- Archaeological Ensemble of Tárraco (2000).
- Archaeological Site of Atapuerca (2000).
- Catalan Romanesque Churches of the Vall de Boí (2000).
- Palmeral of Elche (2000).
- Roman Walls of Lugo (2000).
- Aranjuez Cultural Landscape (2001).
- Renaissance Monumental Ensembles of Úbeda and Baeza (2003).
- Vizcaya Bridge (2006).
- Teide National Park (2007).

Sri Lanka

- Ancient City of Polonnaruwa (1982).
- Ancient City of Sigiriya (1982).
- Sacred City of Anuradhapura (1982).
- Old Town of Galle and its Fortifications (1988).
- Sacred City of Kandy (1988).
- Sinharaja Forest Reserve (1988).
- Golden Temple of Dambulla (1991).

Sudan

- Gebel Barkal and the Sites of the Napatan Region (2003).

Suriname

- Central Suriname Nature Reserve (2000).

- Historic Inner City of Paramaribo (2002).

Sweden

- Royal Domain of Drottningholm (1991).
- Birka and Hovgården (1993).
- Engelsberg Ironworks (1993).
- Rock Carvings in Tanum (1994).
- Skogskyrkogården (1994).
- Hanseatic Town of Visby (1995).
- Church Village of Gammelstad, Luleå (1996).
- Laponian Area (1996).
- Naval Port of Karlskrona (1998).
- Agricultural Landscape of Southern Öland (2000).
- Kvarken Archipelago/High Coast (2000, 2006).
- Mining Area of the Great Copper Mountain in Falun (2001).
- Varberg Radio Station (2004).
- Struve Geodetic Arc (2005) .

Switzerland

- Benedictine Convent of St. John at Müstair (1983).
- Convent of St. Gall (1983).
- Old City of Berne (1983).
- Three Castles, Defensive Wall and Ramparts of the Market-Town of Bellinzone (2000).
- Jungfrau-Aletsch-Bietschhorn (2001, 2007).
- Monte San Giorgio (2003).
- Lavaux, Vineyard Terraces (2007).

Syrian Arab Republic

- Ancient City of Damascus (1979).
- Ancient City of Bosra (1980).
- Site of Palmyra (1980).
- Ancient City of Aleppo (1986).
- Crac des Chevaliers and Qal'at Salah El-Din (2006).

Thailand

- Historic City of Ayutthaya (1991).

- Historic Town of Sukhothai and Associated Historic Towns (1991).
- Thungyai-Huai Kha Khaeng Wildlife Sanctuaries (1991).
- Ban Chiang Archaeological Site (1992).
- Dong Phayayen-Khao Yai Forest Complex (2005).

The Former Yugoslav Republic of Macedonia

- Natural and Cultural Heritage of the Ohrid region (1979, 1980).

Togo

- Koutammakou, the Land of the Batammariba (2004).

Tunisia

- Amphitheatre of El Jem (1979).
- Medina of Tunis (1979).
- Site of Carthage (1979).
- Ichkeul National Park (1980).
- Punic Town of Kerkuane and its Necropolis (1985, 1986).
- Kairouan (1988).
- Medina of Sousse (1988).
- Dougga/Thugga (1997).

Turkey

- Göreme National Park and the Rock Sites of Cappadocia (1985).
- Great Mosque and Hospital of Divriği (1985).
- Historic Areas of Istanbul (1985).
- Hattusha: the Hittite Capital (1986).
- Nemrut Dağ (1987).
- Hierapolis-Pamukkale (1988).
- Xanthos-Letoon (1988).
- City of Safranbolu (1994).
- Archaeological Site of Troy (1998).

Turkmenistan

- State Historical and Cultural Park "Ancient Merv" (1999).
- Kunya-Urgench (2005).
- Parthian Fortresses of Nisa (2007).

Uganda

- Bwindi Impenetrable National Park (1994).
- Rwenzori Mountains National Park (1994).
- Tombs of Buganda Kings at Kasubi (2001).

Ukraine

- Kiev: Saint-Sophia Cathedral and Related Monastic Buildings, Kiev-Pechersk Lavra (1990, 2005).
- L'viv—the Ensemble of the Historic Centre (1998).
- Struve Geodetic Arc (2005).
- Primeval Beech Forests of the Carpathians (2007).

United Kingdom of Great Britain and Northern Ireland

- Castles and Town Walls of King Edward in Gwynedd (1986).
- Durham Castle and Cathedral (1986).
- Giant's Causeway and Causeway Coast (1986).
- Ironbridge Gorge (1986).
- St. Kilda (1986, 2004, 2005).
- Stonehenge, Avebury and Associated Sites (1986).
- Studley Royal Park including the Ruins of Fountains Abbey (1986).
- Blenheim Palace (1987).
- City of Bath (1987).
- Frontiers of the Roman Empire (1987, 2005).
- Westminster Palace, Westminster Abbey and Saint Margaret's Church (1987).
- Canterbury Cathedral, St. Augustine's Abbey, and St. Martin's Church (1988).
- Henderson Island (1988).
- Tower of London (1988).

- Gough and Inaccessible Islands (1995, 2004).
- Old and New Towns of Edinburgh (1995).
- Maritime Greenwich (1997).
- Heart of Neolithic Orkney (1999).
- Blaenavon Industrial Landscape (2000).
- Historic Town of St. George and Related Fortifications, Bermuda (2000).
- Derwent Valley Mills (2001).
- Dorset and East Devon Coast (2001).
- New Lanark (2001).
- Saltaire (2001).
- Royal Botanic Gardens, Kew (2003).
- Liverpool—Maritime Mercantile City (2004).
- Cornwall and West Devon Mining Landscape (2006).

United Republic of Tanzania

- Ngorongoro Conservation Area (1979).
- Ruins of Kilwa Kisiwani and Ruins of Songo Mnara (1981).
- Serengeti National Park (1981).
- Selous Game Reserve (1982).
- Kilimanjaro National Park (1987).
- Stone Town of Zanzibar (2000).
- Kondoa Rock-Art Sites (2006).

United States of America

- Mesa Verde National Park (1978).
- Yellowstone National Park (1978).
- Everglades National Park (1979).
- Grand Canyon National Park (1979).
- Independence Hall (1979).
- Kluane/Wrangell-St. Elias/Glacier Bay/Tatshenshini-Alsek (1979, 1992, 1994).
- Redwood National and State Parks (1980).
- Mammoth Cave National Park (1981).
- Olympic National Park (1981).
- Cahokia Mounds State Historic Site (1982).

- La Fortaleza and San Juan National Historic Site in Puerto Rico (1983).
- Great Smoky Mountains National Park (1983).
- Statue of Liberty (1984).
- Yosemite National Park (1984).
- Chaco Culture (1987).
- Hawaii Volcanoes National Park (1987).
- Monticello and the University of Virginia in Charlottesville (1987).
- Pueblo de Taos (1992).
- Carlsbad Caverns National Park (1995).
- Waterton Glacier International Peace Park (1995).

Uruguay

- Historic Quarter of the City of Colonia del Sacramento (1995).

Uzbekistan

- Itchan Kala (1990).
- Historic Centre of Bukhara (1993).
- Historic Centre of Shakhrisyabz (2000).
- Samarkand—Crossroads of Cultures (2001).

Venezuela (Bolivarian Republic of)

- Coro and its Port (1993).
- Canaima National Park (1994).
- Ciudad Universitaria de Caracas (2000).

Vietnam

- Complex of Hué Monuments (1993).
- Ha Long Bay (1994, 2000).
- Hoi an Ancient Town (1999).
- My Son Sanctuary (1999).
- Phong Nha-Ke Bang National Park (2003).

Yemen

- Old Walled City of Shibam (1982).
- Old City of Sana'a (1986).
- Historic Town of Zabid (1993).

Zambia

- Mosi-oa-Tunya/Victoria Falls (1989).

Zimbabwe

- Mana Pools National Park, Sapi and Chewore Safari Areas (1984).
- Great Zimbabwe National Monument (1986).
- Khami Ruins National Monument (1986).
- Mosi-oa-Tunya/Victoria Falls (1989).
- Matobo Hills (2003).

THE WORLD HERITAGE CONVENTION

The most significant feature of the 1972 World Heritage Convention is that it links together in a single document the concepts of nature conservation and the preservation of cultural properties. The Convention recognizes the way in which people interact with nature, and the fundamental need to preserve the balance between the two. The Convention defines the kind of natural or cultural sites which can be considered for inscription on the **World Heritage List.** The Convention sets out the duties of **States Parties** in identifying potential sites and their role in protecting and preserving them. By signing the Convention, each country pledges to conserve not only the World Heritage sites situated on its territory, but also to protect its national heritage. The States Parties are encouraged to integrate the protection of the cultural and natural heritage into regional planning programmes, set up staff and services at their sites, undertake scientific and technical conservation research and adopt measures which give this heritage a function in the day-to-day life of the community. It explains how the **World Heritage Fund** is to be used and managed and under what conditions international financial assistance may be provided. The Convention stipulates the obligation of States Parties to report regularly to the World Heritage Committee on the state of conservation of their World Heritage properties. These reports are crucial to the work of the Committee as they enable it to assess the conditions of the sites, decide on specific programme needs and resolve recurrent problems. It also encourages States Parties to strengthen the appreciation of the public for World Heritage properties and to enhance their protection through educational and information programmes.

The idea of creating an international movement for protecting heritage emerged after World War I. The 1972, **Convention concerning the Protection of the World Cultural and Natural Heritage** developed from the merging of two separate movements: the first focusing on the preservation of cultural sites, and the other dealing with the conservation of nature.

Preserving Cultural Heritage

The event that aroused particular international concern was the decision to build the Aswan High Dam in Egypt, which would have flooded the valley containing the **Abu Simbel temples** (pictured here), a treasure of ancient Egyptian civilization. In 1959, after an appeal from the governments of Egypt and Sudan, UNESCO launched an international safeguarding campaign. Archaeological research in the areas to be flooded was accelerated. Above all, the Abu Simbel and Philae temples were dismantled, moved to dry ground and reassembled. The campaign cost about US$80 million, half of which was donated by some 50 countries, showing the importance of solidarity and nations' shared responsibility in conserving outstanding cultural sites. Its success led to other safeguarding campaigns, such as saving **Venice and its Lagoon (Italy)** and the **Archaeological Ruins at Moenjodaro (Pakistan)**, and restoring the **Borobodur Temple Compounds (Indonesia).** Consequently, UNESCO initiated, with the help of the International Council on Monuments and Sites (ICOMOS), the preparation of a draft convention on the protection of cultural heritage.

Linking the Protection of Cultural and Natural Heritage

The idea of combining conservation of cultural sites with those of nature comes from the United States of America. A White House Conference in Washington, D.C., in 1965 called for a 'World Heritage Trust' that would stimulate international cooperation to protect 'the world's superb natural and scenic areas and historic sites for the present and the future of the entire world citizenry.' In 1968, the International Union for Conservation of Nature (IUCN) developed similar proposals for its members. These proposals were presented to the 1972 United Nations conference on Human Environment in Stockholm. Eventually, a single text was agreed upon by all parties concerned. The Convention concerning the Protection of World Cultural and Natural Heritage was adopted by the General Conference of UNESCO on 16 November, 1972. By regarding heritage as both cultural and natural, the Convention reminds us of the ways in which people interact with nature, and of the fundamental need to preserve the balance between the two.

TEXT OF CONVENTION CONCERNING THE PROTECTION OF THE WORLD CULTURAL AND NATURAL HERITAGE

Adopted by the General Conference at its Seventeenth Session
Paris, 16 November, 1972
Implimented by
United Nations Educational, Scientific and Cultural Organization (UNESCO)

Convention Concerning the Protection of the World Cultural and Natural Heritage

The General Conference of the United Nations Educational, Scientific and Cultural Organization meeting in Paris from 17 October to 21 November, 1972, at its seventeenth session.

Noting that the cultural heritage and the natural heritage are increasingly threatened with destruction not only by the traditional causes of decay, but also by changing social and economic conditions which aggravate the situation with even more formidable phenomena of damage or destruction,

Considering that deterioration or disappearance of any item of the cultural or natural heritage constitutes a harmful impoverishment of the heritage of all the nations of the world,

Considering that protection of this heritage at the national level often remains incomplete because of the scale of the resources which it requires and of the insufficient economic, scientific, and technological resources of the country where the property to be protected is situated,

Recalling that the Constitution of the Organization provides that it will maintain, increase, and diffuse knowledge by assuring the conservation and protection of the world's heritage, and recommending to the nations concerned the necessary international conventions,

Considering that the existing international conventions, recommendations and resolutions concerning cultural and natural property demonstrate the importance, for all the peoples of the world, of safeguarding this unique and irreplaceable property, to whatever people it may belong,

Considering that parts of the cultural or natural heritage are of outstanding interest and therefore need to be preserved as part of the world heritage of mankind as a whole,

Considering that, in view of the magnitude and gravity of the new dangers threatening them, it is incumbent on the international community as a whole to participate in the protection of the cultural and natural heritage of outstanding universal value, by the granting of collective assistance which, although not taking the place of action by the State concerned, will serve as an efficient complement thereto,

Considering that it is essential for this purpose to adopt new provisions in the form of a convention establishing an effective system of collective protection of the cultural and natural heritage of outstanding universal value, organized on a permanent basis and in accordance with modern scientific methods,

Having decided, at its sixteenth session, that this question should be made the subject of an international convention,

Adopts this sixteenth day of November 1972 this Convention.

I. Definition of the Cultural and Natural Heritage

Article 1

For the purpose of this Convention, the following shall be considered as "cultural heritage":

Monuments: Architectural works, works of monumental sculpture and painting, elements or structures of an archaeological nature, inscriptions, cave dwellings and combinations of features, which are of outstanding universal value from the point of view of history, art or science;

Groups of buildings: Groups of separate or connected buildings which, because of their architecture, their homogeneity or their place in the landscape, are of outstanding universal value from the point of view of history, art or science;

Sites: Works of man or the combined works of nature and man, and areas including archaeological sites which are of outstanding universal value from the historical, aesthetic, ethnological or anthropological point of view.

Article 2

For the purposes of this Convention, the following shall be considered as "natural heritage":

Natural features consisting of physical and biological formations or groups of such formations, which are of outstanding universal value from the aesthetic or scientific point of view;

Geological and physiographical formations and precisely delineated areas which constitute the habitat of threatened species of animals and plants of outstanding universal value from the point of view of science or conservation;

Natural sites or precisely delineated natural areas of outstanding universal value from the point of view of science, conservation or natural beauty.

Article 3

It is for each State Party to this Convention to identify and delineate the different properties situated on its territory mentioned in Articles 1 and 2.

II. National Protection and International Protection of the Cultural and Natural Heritage

Article 4

Each State Party to this Convention recognizes that the duty of ensuring the identification, protection, conservation, presentation and transmission to future generations of the cultural and natural heritage referred to in Articles 1 and 2 and situated on its territory, belongs primarily to that State. It will do all it can to this end, to the utmost of its own resources and, where appropriate, with any international assistance and co-operation, in particular, financial, artistic, scientific and technical, which it may be able to obtain.

Article 5

To ensure that effective and active measures are taken for the protection, conservation and presentation of the cultural and natural heritage situated on its territory, each State Party to this Convention shall endeavour, insofar as possible, and as appropriate for each country:

(*a*) to adopt a general policy which aims to give the cultural and natural heritage a function in the life of the community and to integrate the protection of that heritage into comprehensive planning programmes;
(*b*) to set up within its territories, where such services do not exist, one or more services for the protection, conservation and presentation of the cultural and natural heritage with an appropriate staff and possessing the means to discharge their functions;
(*c*) to develop scientific and technical studies and research and to work out such operating methods as will make the State capable of counteracting the dangers that threaten its cultural or natural heritage;
(*d*) to take the appropriate legal, scientific, technical, administrative and financial measures necessary for the identification, protection, conservation, presentation and rehabilitation of this heritage; and

(*e*) to foster the establishment or development of national or regional centres for training in the protection, conservation and presentation of the cultural and natural heritage and to encourage scientific research in this field:

Article 6

1. Whilst fully respecting the sovereignty of the States on whose territory the cultural and natural heritage mentioned in Articles 1 and 2 is situated, and without prejudice to property right provided by national legislation, the States Parties to this Convention recognize that such heritage constitutes a world heritage for whose protection it is the duty of the international community as a whole to co-operate.
2. The States Parties undertake, in accordance with the provisions of this Convention, to give their help in the identification, protection, conservation and presentation of the cultural and natural heritage referred to in paragraphs 2 and 4 of Article 11 if the States on whose territory it is situated so request.
3. Each State Party to this Convention undertakes not to take any deliberate measures which might damage directly or indirectly the cultural and natural heritage referred to in Articles 1 and 2 situated on the territory of other States Parties to this Convention.

Article 7

For the purpose of this Convention, international protection of the world cultural and natural heritage shall be understood to mean the establishment of a system of international cooperation and assistance designed to support States Parties to the Convention in their efforts to conserve and identify that heritage.

III. Intergovernmental Committee for the Protection of the World Cultural and Natural Heritage

Article 8

1. An Intergovernmental Committee for the Protection of the

Cultural and Natural Heritage of Outstanding Universal Value, called "the World Heritage Committee", is hereby established within the United Nations Educational, Scientific and Cultural Organization. It shall be composed of 15 States Parties to the Convention, elected by States Parties to the Convention meeting in general assembly during the ordinary session of the General Conference of the United Nations Educational, Scientific and Cultural Organization. The number of States members of the Committee shall be increased to 21 as from the date of the ordinary session of the General Conference following the entry into force of this Convention for at least 40 States.

2. Election of members of the Committee shall ensure an equitable representation of the different regions and cultures of the world.
3. A representative of the International Centre for the Study of the Preservation and Restoration of Cultural Property (Rome Centre), a representative of the International Council of Monuments and Sites (ICOMOS) and a representative of the International Union for Conservation of Nature and Natural Resources (IUCN), to whom may be added, at the request of States Parties to the Convention meeting in general assembly during the ordinary sessions of the General Conference of the United Nations Educational, Scientific and Cultural Organization, representatives of other intergovernmental or non-governmental organizations, with similar objectives, may attend the meetings of the Committee in an advisory capacity.

Article 9

1. The term of office of States members of the World Heritage Committee shall extend from the end of the ordinary session of the General Conference during which they are elected until the end of its third subsequent ordinary session.
2. The term of office of one-third of the members designated at the time of the first election shall, however, cease at the end of the first ordinary session of the General Conference following that at which they were elected; and the term of

office of a further third of the members designated at the same time shall cease at the end of the second ordinary session of the General Conference following that at which they were elected. The names of these members shall be chosen by lot by the President of the General Conference of the United Nations Educational, Scientific and Cultural Organization after the first election.

3. States members of the Committee shall choose as their representatives persons qualified in the field of the cultural or natural heritage.

Article 10

1. The World Heritage Committee shall adopt its Rules of Procedure.
2. The Committee may at any time invite public or private organizations or individuals to participate in its meetings for consultation on particular problems.
3. The Committee may create such consultative bodies as it deems necessary for the performance of its functions.

Article 11

1. Every State Party to this Convention shall, insofar as possible, submit to the World Heritage Committee an inventory of property forming part of the cultural and natural heritage, situated in its territory and suitable for inclusion in the list provided for in paragraph 2 of this article. This inventory, which shall not be considered exhaustive, shall include documentation about the location of the property in question and its significance.
2. On the basis of the inventories submitted by States in accordance with paragraph 1, the Committee shall establish, keep up to date and publish, under the title of "World Heritage List," a list of properties forming part of the cultural heritage and natural heritage, as defined in Articles 1 and 2 of this Convention, which it considers as having outstanding universal value in terms of such criteria as it shall have established. An updated list shall be distributed at least every two years.

3. The inclusion of a property in the World Heritage List requires the consent of the State concerned. The inclusion of a property situated in a territory, sovereignty or jurisdiction over which is claimed by more than one State shall in no way prejudice the rights of the parties to the dispute.
4. The Committee shall establish, keep up to date and publish, whenever circumstances shall so require, under the title of "list of World Heritage in Danger", a list of the property appearing in the World Heritage List for the conservation of which major operations are necessary and for which assistance has been requested under this Convention. This list shall contain an estimate of the cost of such operations. The list may include only such property forming part of the cultural and natural heritage as is threatened by serious and specific dangers, such as the threat of disappearance caused by accelerated deterioration, large-scale public or private projects or rapid urban or tourist development projects; destruction caused by changes in the use or ownership of the land; major alterations due to unknown causes; abandonment for any reason whatsoever; the outbreak or the threat of an armed conflict; calamities and cataclysms; serious fires, earthquakes, landslides; volcanic eruptions; changes in water level, floods and tidal waves. The Committee may at any time, in case of urgent need, make a new entry in the List of World Heritage in Danger and publicize such entry immediately.
5. The Committee shall define the criteria on the basis of which a property belonging to the cultural or natural heritage may be included in either of the lists mentioned in paragraphs 2 and 4 of this article.
6. Before refusing a request for inclusion in one of the two lists mentioned in paragraphs 2 and 4 of this article, the Committee shall consult the State Party in whose territory the cultural or natural property in question is situated.
7. The Committee shall, with the agreement of the States concerned, co-ordinate and encourage the studies and research needed for the drawing up of the lists referred to in paragraphs 2 and 4 of this article.

Article 12

The fact that a property belonging to the cultural or natural heritage has not been included in either of the two lists mentioned in paragraphs 2 and 4 of Article 11 shall in no way be construed to mean that it does not have an outstanding universal value for purposes other than those resulting from inclusion in these lists.

Article 13

1. The World Heritage Committee shall receive and study requests for international assistance formulated by States Parties to this Convention with respect to property forming part of the cultural or natural heritage, situated in their territories, and included or potentially suitable for inclusion in the lists mentioned referred to in paragraphs 2 and 4 of Article 11. The purpose of such requests may be to secure the protection, conservation, presentation or rehabilitation of such property.
2. Requests for international assistance under paragraph 1 of this article may also be concerned with identification of cultural or natural property defined in Articles 1 and 2, when preliminary investigations have shown that further inquiries would be justified.
3. The Committee shall decide on the action to be taken with regard to these requests, determine where appropriate, the nature and extent of its assistance, and authorize the conclusion, on its behalf, of the necessary arrangements with the government concerned.
4. The Committee shall determine an order of priorities for its operations. It shall in so doing bear in mind the respective importance for the world cultural and natural heritage of the property requiring protection, the need to give international assistance to the property most representative of a natural environment or of the genius and the history of the peoples of the world, the urgency of the work to be done, the resources available to the States on whose territory the threatened property is situated and in particular the extent to which they are able to safeguard such property by their own means.

5. The Committee shall draw up, keep up to date and publicize a list of property for which international assistance has been granted.
6. The Committee shall decide on the use of the resources of the Fund established under Article 15 of this Convention. It shall seek ways of increasing these resources and shall take all useful steps to this end.
7. The Committee shall co-operate with international and national governmental and non-governmental organizations having objectives similar to those of this Convention. For the implementation of its programmes and projects, the Committee may call on such organizations, particularly the International Centre for the Study of the Preservation and Restoration of Cultural Property (the Rome Centre), the International Council of Monuments and Sites (ICOMOS) and the International Union for Conservation of Nature and Natural Resources (IUCN), as well as on public and private bodies and individuals.
8. Decisions of the Committee shall be taken by a majority of two-thirds of its members present and voting. A majority of the members of the Committee shall constitute a quorum.

Article 14

1. The World Heritage Committee shall be assisted by a Secretariat appointed by the Director-General of the United Nations Educational, Scientific and Cultural Organization.
2. The Director-General of the United Nations Educational, Scientific and Cultural Organization, utilizing to the fullest extent possible the services of the International Centre for the Study of the Preservation and the Restoration of Cultural Property (the Rome Centre), the International Council of Monuments and Sites (ICOMOS) and the International Union for Conservation of Nature and Natural Resources (IUCN) in their respective areas of competence and capability, shall prepare the Committee's documentation and the agenda of its meetings and shall

have the responsibility for the implementation of its decisions.

IV. Fund for the Protection of the World Cultural and Natural Heritage

Article 15

1. A Fund for the Protection of the World Cultural and Natural Heritage of Outstanding Universal Value, called "the World Heritage Fund", is hereby established.
2. The Fund shall constitute a trust fund, in conformity with the provisions of the Financial Regulations of the United Nations Educational, Scientific and Cultural Organization.
3. The resources of the Fund shall consist of:
   (*a*) compulsory and voluntary contributions made by States Parties to this Convention,
   (*b*) Contributions, gifts or bequests which may be made by:
      (*i*) other States;
      (*ii*) the United Nations Educational, Scientific and Cultural Organization, other organizations of the United Nations system, particularly the United Nations Development Programme or other intergovernmental organizations;
      (*iii*) public or private bodies or individuals;
   (*c*) any interest due on the resources of the Fund;
   (*d*) funds raised by collections and receipts from events organized for the benefit of the fund; and
   (*e*) all other resources authorized by the Fund's regulations, as drawn up by the World Heritage Committee.
4. Contributions to the Fund and other forms of assistance made available to the Committee may be used only for such purposes as the Committee shall define. The Committee may accept contributions to be used only for a certain programme or project, provided that the Committee shall have decided on the implementation of such programme or project. No political conditions may be attached to contributions made to the Fund.

Article 16

1. Without prejudice to any supplementary voluntary contribution, the States Parties to this Convention undertake to pay regularly, every two years, to the World Heritage Fund, contributions, the amount of which, in the form of a uniform percentage applicable to all States, shall be determined by the General Assembly of States Parties to the Convention, meeting during the sessions of the General Conference of the United Nations Educational, Scientific and Cultural Organization. This decision of the General Assembly requires the majority of the States Parties present and voting, which have not made the declaration referred to in paragraph 2 of this Article. In no case shall the compulsory contribution of States Parties to the Convention exceed 1 per cent of the contribution to the regular budget of the United Nations Educational, Scientific and Cultural Organization.
2. However, each State referred to in Article 31 or in Article 32 of this Convention may declare, at the time of the deposit of its instrument of ratification, acceptance or accession, that it shall not be bound by the provisions of paragraph 1 of this Article.
3. A State Party to the Convention which has made the declaration referred to in paragraph 2 of this Article may at any time withdraw the said declaration by notifying the Director-General of the United Nations Educational, Scientific and Cultural Organization. However, the withdrawal of the declaration shall not take effect in regard to the compulsory contribution due by the State until the date of the subsequent General Assembly of States parties to the Convention.
4. In order that the Committee may be able to plan its operations effectively, the contributions of States Parties to this Convention which have made the declaration referred to in paragraph 2 of this article, shall be paid on a regular basis, at least every two years, and should not be less than the contributions which they should have paid if they had been bound by the provisions of paragraph 1 of this article.

5. Any State Party to the Convention which is in arrears with the payment of its compulsory or voluntary contribution for the current year and the calendar year immediately preceding it shall not be eligible as a Member of the World Heritage Committee, although this provision shall not apply to the first election.

The terms of office of any such State which is already a member of the Committee shall terminate at the time of the elections provided for in Article 8, paragraph 1 of this Convention.

Article 17

The States Parties to this Convention shall consider or encourage the establishment of national public and private foundations or associations whose purpose is to invite donations for the protection of the cultural and natural heritage as defined in Articles 1 and 2 of this Convention.

Article 18

The States Parties to this Convention shall give their assistance to international fund-raising campaigns organized for the World Heritage Fund under the auspices of the United Nations Educational, Scientific and Cultural Organization. They shall facilitate collections made by the bodies mentioned in paragraph 3 of Article 15 for this purpose.

V. Conditions and Arrangements for International Assistance

Article 19

Any State Party to this Convention may request international assistance for property forming part of the cultural or natural heritage of outstanding universal value situated within its territory. It shall submit with its request such information and documentation provided for in Article 21 as it has in its possession and as will enable the Committee to come to a decision.

Article 20

Subject to the provisions of paragraph 2 of Article 13, sub-paragraph (c) of Articles 22 and 23, international assistance provided for by this Convention may be granted only to property forming part of the cultural and natural heritage which the World Heritage Committee has decided, or may decide, to enter in one of the lists mentioned in paragraphs 2 and 4 of Article 11.

Article 21

1. The World Heritage Committee shall define the procedure by which requests to it for international assistance shall be considered and shall specify the content of the request, which should define the operation contemplated, the work that is necessary, the expected cost thereof, the degree of urgency and the reasons why the resources of the State requesting assistance do not allow it to meet all the expenses. Such requests must be supported by experts' reports whenever possible.
2. Requests based upon disasters or natural calamities should, by reasons of the urgent work which they may involve, be given immediate, priority consideration by the Committee, which should have a reserve fund at its disposal against such contingencies.
3. Before coming to a decision, the Committee shall carry out such studies and consultations as it deems necessary.

Article 22

Assistance granted by the World Heritage Fund may take the following forms:

(*a*) studies concerning the artistic, scientific and technical problems raised by the protection, conservation, presentation and rehabilitation of the cultural and natural heritage, as defined in paragraphs 2 and 4 of Article 11 of this Convention;

(*b*) provisions of experts, technicians and skilled labour to ensure that the approved work is correctly carried out;

(*c*) training of staff and specialists at all levels in the field of identification, protection, conservation, presentation and rehabilitation of the cultural and natural heritage;
(*d*) supply of equipment which the State concerned does not possess or is not in a position to acquire;
(*e*) low-interest or interest-free loans which might be repayable on a long-term basis;
(*f*) the granting, in exceptional cases and for special reasons, of non-repayable subsidies.

Article 23

The World Heritage Committee may also provide international assistance to national or regional centres for the training of staff and specialists at all levels in the field of identification, protection, conservation, presentation and rehabilitation of the cultural and natural heritage.

Article 24

International assistance on a large scale shall be preceded by detailed scientific, economic and technical studies. These studies shall draw upon the most advanced techniques for the protection, conservation, presentation and rehabilitation of the natural and cultural heritage and shall be consistent with the objectives of this Convention. The studies shall also seek means of making rational use of the resources available in the State concerned.

Article 25

As a general rule, only part of the cost of work necessary shall be borne by the international community. The contribution of the State benefitting from international assistance shall constitute a substantial share of the resources devoted to each programme or project, unless its resources do not permit this.

Article 26

The World Heritage Committee and the recipient State shall define in the agreement they conclude the conditions in which a programme or project for which international assistance under the terms of this Convention is provided, shall be carried out. It shall be the responsibility of the State receiving such international assistance to continue to protect, conserve and present the property so safeguarded, in observance of the conditions laid down by the agreement.

VI. Educational Programmes

Article 27

1. The States Parties to this Convention shall endeavour by all appropriate means, and in particular by educational and information programmes, to strengthen appreciation and respect by their peoples of the cultural and natural heritage defined in Articles 1 and 2 of the Convention.
2. They shall undertake to keep the public broadly informed of the dangers threatening this heritage and of the activities carried on in pursuance of this Convention.

Article 28

States Parties to this Convention which receive international assistance under the Convention shall take appropriate measures to make known the importance of the property for which assistance has been received and the role played by such assistance.

VII. Reports

Article 29

1. The States Parties to this Convention shall, in the reports which they submit to the General Conference of the United Nations Educational, Scientific and Cultural Organization on dates and in a manner to be determined by it, give information on the legislative and administrative provisions which they have adopted and other action which they have taken for the application of this Convention, together with details of the experience acquired in this field.

2. These reports shall be brought to the attention of the World Heritage Committee.
3. The Committee shall submit a report on its activities at each of the ordinary sessions of the General Conference of the United Nations Educational, Scientific and Cultural Organization.

VIII. Final Clauses

Article 30

This Convention is drawn up in Arabic, English, French, Russian and Spanish, the five texts being equally authoritative.

Article 31

1. This Convention shall be subject to ratification or acceptance by States members of the United Nations Educational, Scientific and Cultural Organization in accordance with their respective constitutional procedures.
2. The instruments of ratification or acceptance shall be deposited with the Director-General of the United Nations Educational, Scientific and Cultural Organization.

Article 32

1. This Convention shall be open to accession by all States not members of the United Nations Educational, Scientific and Cultural Organization which are invited by the General Conference of the Organization to accede to it.
2. Accession shall be effected by the deposit of an instrument of accession with the Director-General of the United Nations Educational, Scientific and Cultural Organization.

Article 33

This Convention shall enter into force three months after the date of the deposit of the twentieth instrument of ratification, acceptance or accession, but only with respect to those States which have deposited their respective instruments of ratification, acceptance or accession on or before that date. It shall enter into force with respect to any other State three months after the deposit of its instrument of ratification, acceptance or accession.

Article 34

The following provisions shall apply to those States Parties to this Convention which have a federal or non-unitary constitutional system:

(*a*) With regard to the provisions of this Convention, the implementation of which comes under the legal jurisdiction of the federal or central legislative power, the obligations of the federal or central government shall be the same as for those States parties which are not federal States;

(*b*) With regard to the provisions of this Convention, the implementation of which comes under the legal jurisdiction of individual constituent States, countries, provinces or cantons that are not obliged by the constitutional system of the federation to take legislative measures, the federal government shall inform the competent authorities of such States, countries, provinces or cantons of the said provisions, with its recommendation for their adoption.

Article 35

1. Each State Party to this Convention may denounce the Convention.
2. The denunciation shall be notified by an instrument in writing, deposited with the Director-General of the United Nations Educational, Scientific and Cultural Organization.
3. The denunciation shall take effect twelve months after the receipt of the instrument of denunciation. It shall not affect the financial obligations of the denouncing State until the date on which the withdrawal takes effect.

Article 36

The Director-General of the United Nations Educational, Scientific and Cultural Organization shall inform the States members of the

Organization, the States not members of the Organization which are referred to in Article 32, as well as the United Nations, of the deposit of all the instruments of ratification, acceptance, or accession provided for in Articles 31 and 32, and of the denunciations provided for in Article 35.

Article 37

1. This Convention may be revised by the General Conference of the United Nations Educational, Scientific and Cultural Organization. Any such revision shall, however, bind only the States which shall become Parties to the revising convention.
2. If the General Conference should adopt a new convention revising this Convention in whole or in part, then, unless the new convention otherwise provides, this Convention shall cease to be open to ratification, acceptance or accession, as from the date on which the new revising convention enters into force.

Article 38

In conformity with Article 102 of the Charter of the United Nations, this Convention shall be registered with the Secretariat of the United Nations at the request of the Director-General of the United Nations Educational, Scientific and Cultural Organization.

Done in Paris, this twenty-third day of November 1972, in two authentic copies bearing the signature of the President of the seventeenth session of the General Conference and of the Director-General of the United Nations Educational, Scientific and Cultural Organization, which shall be deposited in the archives of the United Nations Educational, Scientific and Cultural Organization, and certified true copies of which shall be delivered to all the States referred to in Articles 31 and 32 as well as to the United Nations.

Benefits of Ratification

The overarching benefit of ratifying the **World Heritage Convention** is that of belonging to an international community of appreciation and concern for universally significant properties that embody a world of outstanding examples of cultural diversity and natural wealth. The **States Parties to the Convention**, by joining hands to protect and cherish the world's natural and cultural heritage, express a shared commitment to preserving our legacy for future generations. The prestige that comes from being a State Party to the Convention and having sites inscribed on the **World Heritage List** often serves as a catalyst to raising awareness for heritage preservation. A key benefit of ratification, particularly for developing countries, is access to the **World Heritage Fund**. Annually, about US$4 million is made available to assist States Parties in identifying, preserving and promoting World Heritage sites. Emergency assistance may also be made available for urgent action to repair damage caused by human-made or natural disasters. In the case of sites included on the **List of World Heritage in Danger**, the attention and the funds of both the national and the international community are focused on the conservation needs of these particularly threatened sites. Today, the World Heritage concept is so well understood that sites on the List are a magnet for international coöperation and may thus receive financial assistance for heritage conservation projects from a variety of sources. Sites inscribed on the World Heritage List also benefit from the elaboration and implementation of a comprehensive management plan that sets out adequate preservation measures and monitoring mechanisms. In support of these, experts offer technical training to the local site management team. Finally, the inscription of a site on the World Heritage List brings an increase in public awareness of the site and of its outstanding values, thus also increasing the tourist activities at the site. When these are well planned for and organized respecting sustainable tourism principles, they can bring important funds to the site and to the local economy.

Acronym and Glossary of Terms

AA: Automobile Association.

ABA: American Bus Association; comprised of bus companies, operators and owners.

Aboriginal Tourism: Aboriginal Tourism describes all tourism businesses that are owned or operated by First Nation, Métis and Inuit people. *(Definition used by Aboriginal Tourism Team Canada).*

ABTA: Association of British Travel Agents. Represents the interests of the larger UK tour operators and travel agents (with around 670 members as of 2000), and operates a bonding scheme whereby customers booking with ABTA members have their holidays protected should the operator/agent in question collapse.

Accommodation Capacity: The measure of accommodation stock at a defined destination. May be given by various different measures: e.g. number of establishments; number of main units within an establishment (e.g. rooms, caravan stances); capacity in terms of residents (e.g. bedspaces).

Accounting Period: Normally one year, the period for which accounts are drawn up.

Accreditation Manual: The collection of documents and procedures gathered by a business during the process of obtaining accreditation. This becomes a very useful resource and some quality systems require that the accreditation folder is kept as a reference.

Accreditation: A procedure to establish if a tourism business meets certain standards of management and operation.

Advanced Ecotourism: A level of accreditation consisting of all core criteria as well as some of the advanced certification criteria.

Adventure Tourism: A form of tourism in natural areas that incorporates an element of risk, higher levels of physical exertion, and the need for specialised skills.

AITO: Association of Independent Tour Operators. Performs a similar function to ABTA, although its membership (and therefore its agenda) differs in comprising some 160 of the smaller UK tour operators.

All-inclusive Hotels: Resort facilities that offer all meals, activities and entertainments on site. All holiday expenses at these hotels are covered by one pre-paid price. Caribbean destinations are noted for their high profile brands of all-inclusive hotels which offer unlimited alcoholic drinks, snacks between meals and motorised sports all included in one price.

All-inclusive: A form of package holiday where the majority of services offered at the destination are included in the price paid prior to departure (e.g. refreshments, excursions, amenities, gratuities, etc).

Allocentric: Of a minority of tourists—adventurous, outgoing, self-confident, independent, needing little tourist infrastructure. Enjoys high contact with locals.

Alternative Tourism: In essence, tourism activities or development that are viewed as non-traditional. It is often defined in opposition to large-scale mass tourism to represent small-scale sustainable tourism developments. AT is also presented as an 'ideal type', that is, an improved model of tourism development that redresses the ills of traditional, mass tourism.

Antifoul: Applied to ship's hull to prevent encrusting of barnacles, seaweed, and other marine organisms.

APEC: Asia Pacific Economic Community.

Around Texas: Complete calendar of events, fairs, festivals, sports, shows, concerts, exhibits and other events across Texas. Endorsed by the Texas Festivals and Events Association (TFEA).

Artefact: An object; an item of material culture.

Assets: Something of value that will provide future benefit or utility, can be used to generate revenue. Usually owned, so simply described as 'things we own'.

ATOL: Air Travel Organiser's License. A requirement of the Civil Aviation Authority for all UK tour operators wishing to sell air seats on chartered or scheduled services. Necessitates a financial 'health check' and the putting up of a bond to cover the expense of reimbursing/repatriating tourists in the event of operator failure.

Attendance Building: Marketing and promotional programmes designed to increase attendance at conventions, trade shows, meetings and events.

Attraction: Any visitor service or product which tourists would enjoy visiting or using. An attraction may not be an 'attractor' but can still be an attraction. To be considered an attraction, a product must be: (*a*) Findable (clearly located on maps and street addresses, and directions provided). If tourists can't find the facility, it is not a tourist attraction. (*b*) Hours of operation clearly denoted in any and all promotional materials (if a tourist arrives only to find the attraction closed, it is not an attraction). Examples of attractions include everything from a theme park that attracts over a million visitors a year, to a produce stand by the side of the road.

Attractions: General all-inclusive term travel industry marketers use to refer to products that have visitor appeal, like museums, historic sites, performing arts institutions, preservation districts, theme parks, entertainment and national sites.

Attractor: A significant tourist attraction, which compels visitation. The primary 'must sees' in an area. The top reasons a tourist would choose to visit this area.

Auditing: A process to measure and verify the practices of a business.

Average Room Rate Achieved: The average of the room rates resulting in room sales which a hotel has experienced for a given time period.

Background Sound Pressure Level: A weighted sound pressure level, including impulse noise, which is equalled or exceeded for 90 per cent of the time. See Australian Standards AS1055-1997 and AS 2659.1 for further information.

Backpacker: A visitor in NZ for the purpose of a holiday or special event who stays in a backpackers lodge/hostel.

Balance of Payments: Record of one country's financial transactions with the rest of the world.

Baseline Practice Level: Green Globe 21 level of an Earth Check™ indicator that if exceeded demonstrates a Community is achieving sound environmental and social performance.

Bed Tax (Hotel Occupancy Tax HOT): City or county tax added to the price of a hotel room.

Benchmarking: Measuring your performance against that of best in class companies, determining how the best-in-class achieve those performance levels and using this information as a basis for your own company's targets, strategies and implementation (Pryor, 1989).

Benchmarking: The process of comparing performance and processes within an industry to assess relative position against either a set industry standard or against those who are 'best in class' (Synergy, 2000).

Benchmarks: Points of reference or comparison, which may include standards, critical success factors, indicators, metrics.

Best Practice Level: Green Globe 21 level of an Earth Check™ indicator that demonstrates the community is achieving exemplary performance.

Best Practice(s): A term used to designate highest quality, excellence, or superior practices in a particular field by a tourism operator.

Best Practice: Operational standards considered the most effective and efficient means of achieving desired outcomes.

Biological Diversity (Biodiversity): The variety of life forms and genes they contain, and the ecosystems they form. Biodiversity is usually considered at four levels; genetic diversity, species diversity, community diversity, and ecosystem diversity.

Blocked: Hotel rooms held without deposit.

Booked: Hotel rooms, airline tickets or other travel services held for a specific client.

Booking: Term used to refer to a completed sale by a destination, convention centre, facility, hotel or supplier (i.e. convention, meeting, trade show or group business booking).

Built Heritage: Built heritage is the most common manifestation of cultural tangible heritage. It consists of buildings or structures of architectural, engineering or historical significance, notably archaeological sites and objects, open spaces, gardens and parks, archival materials, industrial objects and machines; transportation vehicles and other man-made elements with cultural, social or historical significance.

Bureaucracy: An organisation typified by formal processes, standardisation, hierarchic procedures, and written communication.

Business Travel: (1) Travel for a purpose and to a destination determined by a business, and where all costs are met by that business.

Business Travel: (2) Travel for commercial, governmental or educational purposes with leisure as a secondary motivation.

Business Travel: (3) Travel for commercial, governmental or educational purposes with leisure as a secondary motivation.

Business Travel: (4) Travel of 1-365 days duration for the purpose of attending a convention or training, conducting official/ government or private business.

Buyer: A member of the travel trade who reserves room blocks from accommodations or coordinates the development of a travel product.

C of C: Chamber of Commerce.

CAM: Commercial Accommodation Monitor.

Camp: The programme and activities that take place at a campsite.

Campsite Operator: The owner, lessee or committee of management, or their agents.

Campsite: Premises from which the business is conducted and the various offsite locations used to deliver the service. Includes land, buildings, facilities and activity equipment, or any combination of these.

Capacity Management: A process that seeks to ensure that their organisations operate at optimum capacity whilst maintaining customer satisfaction levels.

Capital Expenditure: The cost of long-term assets; such as computer equipment, vehicles and premises. Importantly these are bought to use over several years and not to resell.

Carrier: Any provider of mass transportation, usually used in reference to an airline.

Carrying Capacity: The amount of visitor activity that a site or destination can sustain.

Carrying-capacity Analysis: Originally a term applied in ecology referring to the maximum number of animals of a given species that a particular habitat could support. In the context of tourism, it refers to the maximum number of tourists a destination can support.

Case: A case describes a dispute taken to court, and specific cases set legal precedents—a legal principle, created by a court decision, which provides an example or authority for judges deciding similar issues later.

Chain of Distribution: The means by which products (package holidays in this instance) are distributed from producers (principals) to consumers (tourists), often via wholesalers and retailers (tour operators and travel agents).

Chambers of Commerce: Typically, a Chamber of Commerce will specialize in local economic development that can include tourism promotion.

Chaos Theory: Views organisations/businesses as complex, dynamic, non-linear, co-creative and far-from-equilibrium systems the future performance of which cannot be decided alone by past and present events and actions. In a state of chaos, organisations behave in ways which are simultaneously both unpredictable (chaotic) and patterned (orderly).

Charter Group: Group travel in which a previously organized group travels together, usually on a custom itinerary.

Charter: A legal contract between an owner and an organisation for the hire of a means of transport for a particular purpose. An individual traveller will use an intermediary to arrange to be carried on the transport. Often applied to a flight which is the result of a charter.

CIPA (International Committee for Architectural Photogrammetry): One of the international committees of ICOMOS. Its main purpose is the improvement of all methods for surveying of cultural monuments and sites, specially by synergy effects gained by the combination of methods under special consideration of photogrammetry with all its aspects, as an important contribution to recording and perceptual monitoring of cultural heritage, to preservation and restoration of any valuable architectural or other cultural monument, object or site, as a support to architectural, archaeological and other art-historical research.

City Marketing: In Germany City Management or City Marketing (Statmarketing) is often understood as a strategy for cooperative city development, the improvement of the city and its achievements for citizens and visitors, and the improvement of communication and to establish long-term partnerships between various participants within the city.

CIVVIH: International Committee on Historic Towns and Villages from ICOMOS.

Class Action: A lawsuit filed by a number of people in a similar situation, e.g. participants in a particular package holiday might file a class action against the tour operator rather than take action individually.

Coach Tour: A guided bus tour for a group of holiday makers that follows a scheduled itinerary. Visitors purchase all arrangements from the Inbound Tour Operator prior to arrival in NZ.

Code of Conduct: Guidelines advising a tourism stakeholder, including tourists, on how to behave in an environmentally responsible manner.

Code of Ethics / Conduct / Practice: Recommended practices based on a system of self-regulation intended to promote environmentally and/or socio-culturally sustainable behaviour.

Collaboration: The process of working together in pursuit of common objectives.

Collateral: Promotional materials distributed to travel trade partners, for the purpose of educating sellers about and/or assisting in the sale of suppliers' products.

Commissions: A percent of the total product cost paid to travel agents and other travel product distributors for selling the product to the consumer.

Competitive Strategies: Offensive or defensive strategies that aim at providing strategic competitive advantage and at increasing the competitiveness of an organisation.

Computer Reservation Systems (CRS): Computerised Reservation Systems used for inventory management by airlines, hotels and other facilities. CRSs can allow direct access through terminals for intermediaries to check availability, make reservations and print tickets.

Conservation: Can be broadly interpreted as action taken to protect and preserve the natural world from harmful features of tourism, including pollution and overexploitation of resources.

Conservation: The protection and maintenance of nature while allowing for its ecologically sustainable use.

Consolidators: Based in some offshore markets, consolidators buy air fares in bulk from airlines and sell these to retail agents for on-sale to consumers.

Consumer Show: A product showcase for the general public. Differs from a 'Trade Show' as a trade show generally targets industry professionals. Consumer Shows target the consumer. Often there is a charge to get into the show.

Contract: A legal agreement entered into by two or more parties.

Control: Monitoring and if necessary adjusting the performance of the organisation and its members.

Convention and Visitors Bureau (CVB): These organizations are local tourism marketing organizations specializing in developing conventions, meetings, conferences and visitations to a city, county or region.

Convention and Visitors Bureau: These organizations are local tourism marketing organizations specializing in developing conventions, meetings, conferences and visitations to a city, county or region.

Convention Concerning the Protection of World Cultural and Natural Heritage (World Heritage Convention): Convention, saying that all state parties (that have ratified it) are now together responsible for the safeguarding of cultural and natural sites of outstanding universal value.

Conventions and Trade Shows: Major segment of travel industry business. Trade shows differ from conventions in that they have exhibit space that provides product exhibition and sales opportunities for suppliers, as well as information gathering and buying opportunities for customers.

Conversion Study: Research study to analyze whether advertising respondents actually were converted to travellers as a result of advertising and follow-up material.

Co-op Advertising: Advertising funded by two or more destinations and/or suppliers.

Cooperative Marketing: Marketing programmes involving two or more participating companies, institutions or organizations.

Cooperative Partner: An independent firm or organization that works with a tourism office by providing cash or in-kind contributions to expand the marketing impact of the tourism office's programme.

Cost-benefit Analysis: Full analysis of public and private costs and benefits of project.

Cost-plus Pricing: A method of pricing where an amount, to cover profit, is added to costs to establish the selling price, this is an internally orientated pricing method.

Country of Residence: Consists of the country where she/he has lived for most of the past year (12 months), or for a shorter period if she/he intends to return within 12 months to live there.

Cover: Each diner at a restaurant.

Critical Incident Point (CIP): A critical incident point or 'moment of truth' is any event which occurs when the customer has (or even perceives that he has) contact with a service organisation.

CRM: Customer Relationship Management.

CRS: Computerised Reservation System.

CTRLA: Car and Truck Rental and Leasing Association.

Cultural Authenticity: Ensuring the appropriate dreaming stories, spiritual beliefs, history, ceremony and art is attributed to the relevant area.

Cultural Heritage: Cultural heritage has both tangible and intangible components. Tangible heritage refers to built heritage, cultural landscapes and all man-made elements with cultural significance. Intangible heritage refers to the practices, representations, expressions, memories, attachments, as well as the knowledge and skills that communities, groups and, in some cases, individuals, recognise as part of their cultural heritage. It is sometimes called living cultural heritage, and is manifested inter alias in the following domains: oral traditions and expressions, including language as a vehicle of the intangible cultural heritage; performing arts; social practices, rituals and festive events; knowledge and practices concerning nature and the universe; traditional craftsmanship.

Cultural Tourism: Cultural Tourism is a form of tourism that focuses on the culture, the cultural environment (including the landscapes of the destination), values and lifestyles, local heritage, visual and performing arts, industries, traditions and leisure assets of the host community. It can include attendance to cultural events, visits to museums and heritage places and mixing with the locals. It should not only be regarded as a definable economic niche within the broad range of tourism activities, but rather as encompassing all experiences absorbed by the visitors to a place that is beyond their own living environment for more than one night and less than one year in private or public accommodation in the destination.

Cultural Tourism: Travel for the purpose of learning about cultures or aspects of cultures (NEAP, 2000).

Cultural Tourism: Travel for the purpose of learning about cultures or aspects of cultures.

Cultural: See 'culture'.

Culture: A set of shared norms and values which establish a sense of identity for those who share them. Typically applied at the level of nation and/or race.

Culture: The sum total of ways of living by a group of human beings that is transmitted from one generation to another.

Customer: "An organization or a person that receives a product" (ISO, 2000a:10).

CVB: Convention and Visitors Bureau.

Day Visitors: Visitors who arrive and leave the same day for leisure, recreation and holidays, visiting friends and relatives, and business and professional.

Decision-Making Unit (DMU): The combination of inputs to a purchasing decision.

Degradation: Any decline in the quality of natural or cultural resources, or the viability of ecosystems, that is caused directly or indirectly by humans.

Delegation: The assignment to others of the authority for particular functions, tasks and decisions.

Demographic Profile: Characteristics used in research such as age, gender, occupation, income, marital status, place of residence, etc.

Dependency Theory: This theory maintains that developing countries are kept in a position of dependency and underdevelopment due to existing economic and institutional power structures sustained by leading Western nations. Dependency theorists argue that the policies and activities of multinational corporations, national bilateral and multinational aid agencies such as the World Bank and the International Monetary Fund (IMF) tend to widen the gap between rich and poor countries and perpetuate the dependency of developing nations.

Deregulation: Removal or relaxing of barriers to travel such as restrictions on the nature of outbound travel, amount of money taken out of the country, visa requirements and costs, air service agreements.

Designation: The act of conferring a legal status on a building which requires compliance with specific legislation on conservation and preservation.

Desktop Review: A review conducted by the quality system operator of all submitted documentation to ensure requirements have been satisfied.

Destination Marketing Organization (DMO): A company or other entity involved in the business of increasing tourism to a destination or improving its public image.

Destination Marketing Organization: Local tourism marketing organizations, such as convention and visitors bureaus or chambers of commerce.

Destination Marketing: Marketing a city, state, country, area or region to consumers and trade.

Destination Marketing: Marketing a city, state, country, area or region to consumers and trade.

Destination: A hotel, resort, attraction, city, region, or state.

Discounted Fare: Negotiated airfare for convention, trade show, meeting, group and corporate travel.

Discretionary Income: Money received from employment or other sources which can be freely spent on leisure pursuits (such as travel and tourism) after general living costs, taxation etc. are taken into consideration.

Discrimination: Unequal treatment of persons on grounds which are not justifiable in law, e.g. in the UK, discrimination on the grounds of sex or race.

Disintermediation: A process by which the consumer 'bypasses' the services of an intermediary or intermediaries in the chain of distribution, in order to purchase products direct from those who supply them. In the travel industry, examples of disintermediation include airlines selling tickets direct to the public over the internet, thus cutting out the travel agent in the selling process.

Distribution: The process employed to provide customers access to the product. For travel products distribution focuses largely on the ways in which the customer can reserve or purchase the product.

Disturbance: Accelerated change caused by human activity or extreme natural events.

Diversification: The process of developing new products for new markets, in order to achieve business growth.

DOC/DoC: Department of Conservation.

Domestic Supply of Tourism Commodities: Domestic supply of tourism commodities is defined as the total production in

Canada of the tourism commodities which are mainly produced by tourism industries. Not all of domestic supply is purchased by visitors, so that supply exceeds tourism demand for the National Tourism Indicators (NTI). For example, visitors purchase only a small proportion of food and beverage services, with most going to local consumption. Also, supply does not include imports. For example, the sale of a ticket on a non-Canadian airline is excluded from supply.

Domestic Tourism: Travel within the country of residence.

Dominant Scenic Alteration: An alteration in the scenic landscape that is visually obtrusive.

Door Rate: Retail price for accommodation/activity.

DTS: Domestic Travel Study.

Due Diligence: Taking what is considered in law to be reasonable care.

Earth Check™ Indicators: Proprietary system belonging to Green Globe 21, which uses carefully selected indicators to measure and benchmark key environmental and social impacts, as well as operational efficiency.

ECAT: E-Commerce Action Team.

Ecological Integrity: Means, with respect to a park, "a condition that is determined to be characteristic of its natural region and likely to persist, including abiotic components (physical elements) and the composition and abundance of native species and biological communities, rates of change and supporting processes." *(Definition set forth in the Canada National Parks Act).*

Ecologically Sustainable: Using, conserving and enhancing the community's resources so that ecological development is maintained, and the total quality of life can be sustained now and in the future.

eCommerce: Internet facilitated commerce, using electronic means for promoting, selling, distributing and servicing products.

Economic Growth: An increase in real output per capita.

Ecosystem: A dynamic system of plant, animal, fungal and micro-organism communities, and the associated non-living physical and chemical factors.

Ecotourism: "Responsible travel to natural areas that conserves the environment and improves the welfare of local people," according to *The International Ecotourism Society*.

Ecotourism: Ecologically sustainable tourism with a primary focus on experiencing natural areas that foster environmental and cultural understanding, appreciation and conservation.

Ecotourism: It is a segment of sustainable tourism that offers experiences that enable visitors to discover natural areas while preserving their integrity, and to understand, through interpretation and education, the natural and cultural sense of place. It fosters respect towards the environment, reflects sustainable business practices, creates socio-economic benefits for communities/regions, and recognizes and respects local and indigenous cultures, traditions and values. *(Definition developed by the Tourism Industry Association of Canada).*

e-mediaries: Electronic booking systems (usually web-based) which combine commerce and the traditional intermediary role of travel agents. Products and services are usually sourced from a range of other product providers allowing customers to book a range of different tourism and travel services from one website, and may enable price/product comparisons between competing suppliers.

Employee Relations: Covers communications, employee participation in management decisions, conflict and grievance resolution, trade unions and collective bargaining.

Energy Conservation: Positive initiatives to reduce the consumption of energy to the minimum level required.

Environmental Auditing: Inspection of a tourism organisation to assess the environmental impact of its activities.

Environmental Education: Formal and informal learning processes that are designed to raise awareness and teach new values, knowledge and skills, in order to encourage more sustainable behaviour.

Environmental Impact Assessment: A study undertaken to assess the effect of an action upon a specific environment or the social or cultural integrity of a community.

Environmental Impact Statement: The report resulting from an environmental impact assessment.

Environmental Impact: The effects that a community has on the environment as a consequence of its activities.

Environmental Management Systems: Systems established by tourism organisations with the aim of mitigating negative environmental impacts.

Environmental Scanning: The process of collecting information to carry out a systematic analysis of the forces effecting the organisation and identifying potential threats and opportunities with view to generating future strategies.

Evolutionary Theories: Theories of tourism which see destinations evolving, in the sense that the types of tourists change, or evolve, over time.

Exclusion Clause: This is a term in a contract that tries to exclude or limit the liability of one of the parties if there is a breach. Such clauses often take the form of "small print" in the standard terms and conditions of the dominant partner in the contract e.g. tour operators.

Exotic Plants: Plants whose genetic stock comes from beyond the area in which they are found.

Externalities: Those costs or benefits arising from production or consumption of goods and services which are not reflected in market prices.

Eyeshine: The reflected light that bounces off a mirror-like layer near the back of an animal's eye.

Fam Tours: Organized trips for travel agents, tour operators, tour wholesalers or other members of the travel trade for the purpose of educating and "familiarizing" them with tourism destinations. By seeing the destinations where they are sending travellers, the travel trade is better prepared to answer customer questions and promote travel to the location. Also called "fams" or "familiarization tours."

Familiarisation Trips: (Fam trips) Visits to tourism destinations made in order to experience and learn more about the destination. Such trips are usually organised either by tour operators or by destination managers to improve knowledge of the destination. When travel agents are taken on such trips it is expected that their increased knowledge will lead to greater level of sales of holidays to that destination.

Familiarization Trip: A complimentary or reduced-rate travel programme for travel agents, airline or rail employees or other travel buyers, designed to acquaint participants with specific destinations or suppliers and to stimulate the sale of travel. Familiarization tours, also called fam tours, are sometimes offered to journalists as research trips for the purpose of cultivating media coverage of specific travel products.

Feeder Airport/City: An outlying city that feeds travellers to hubs or gateway cities.

FIT (Free Independent Travel): Individual travel in which a tour operator has previously arranged blocks of rooms at various destinations in advance for use by individual travellers. These travellers travel independently, not in a group, usually by rental car or public transportation.

FIT: Free Independent Travellers—visitors coming to NZ on holiday who do not purchase pre-packaged travel or pay for anything other than international airfares prior to arriving in NZ. Whilst in NZ, they organise their own travel as they go, do not travel as part of a tour group or on a coach tour.

Force Majeure: This is an unforeseeable or uncontrollable situation or train of events that would excuse a breach of contract.

Foreign Independent Travel or Foreign Individual Travel (FIT): An international pre-paid unescorted tour that includes several travel elements such as accommodations, rental cars and sightseeing. A FIT operator specialises in preparing FITs documents at the request of retail travel agents. FITs usually receive travel vouchers to present to on-site services as verification of pre-payment.

FOREX: Foreign Exchange Earnings.

FoRST: Foundation of Research, Science and Technology.

Frequency: The number of times an advertisement appears during a given campaign.

FTE: Full Time Equivalent employee.

Fulfillment: Servicing consumers and trade who request information as a result of advertising or promotional programmes. Service often includes an 800 number, sales staff and distribution of materials.

Gate Rate: Retail price for accommodation/activity.

Gateway or Gateway City: A major airport, seaport, rail or bus centre through which tourists and travellers enter from outside the region.

GBA: General Booking Agreement.

GDP (Per Cap): Gross Domestic Product (earned per capita).

Geotourism (1998): Tourism that sustains or enhances the geographic character of the place being visited—its environment, culture, aesthetics, heritage, and the well-being of its residents.

German Foundation for Monument Protection: Private Foundation (Deutsche Stiftung Denkmalschutz) that is raising awareness for monument preservation and funding preservation work.

GIT (Groups Independent Travel): Group travel in which individuals purchase a group package in which they will travel with others along a pre-set itinerary.

Global Distribution System (GDS): The reservation network which links bookers such as travel agencies to travel suppliers' booking systems.

Globalisation: Generally defined as the network of connections of organisations and peoples are across national, geographic and cultural borders and boundaries. These global networks are creating a shrinking world where local differences and national boundaries are being subsumed into global identities. Within the field of tourism, globalisation is also viewed in terms of the revolutions in telecommunications, finance and transport that are key factors currently influencing the nature and pace of growth of tourism in developing nations.

Greenhouse Effect: The trapping of the sun's thermal radiation by gases and water vapour, keeping the surface of the earth warmer than it would be otherwise.

Greenhouse Gases: Gases that contribute to the greenhouse affect. These include carbon dioxide, methane and water vapour. One source of greenhouse gases is the burning of fossil fuels, such as oil, gas and coal.

Gross Lettings: This refers to all room lettings, i.e. both paid and complimentary listings are included.

Group Norms: Informal standards of behaviour and performance that develop from the interaction of the group.

Group Rate: Negotiated hotel rate for convention, trade show, meeting, tour or incentive group.

Group Tour and Group Leader: *Group Tour*—a travel agent type company which plans motor coach trips. *Group Leader*: A small, informal group, such as a church group, scout troop, or social group. Usually one person plans the activities for the group. Some travel shows target these planners such as GLAMER.

Group Travel: Often used to mean coach tour travellers, but can also refer to holiday-makers who travel with a group of two or more couples, a family group, a school or special interest group, etc.

GSA: General Sales Agreement.

HANZ: Hospitality Association of New Zealand.

Heads in Beds: Industry slang referring to the primary marketing objective of accommodations and most destinations—increasing the number of overnight stays.

Heritage: Things of value that are inherited which people want to keep. Heritage can be natural, cultural, tangible, intangible, personal or collective. Natural heritage is often conserved in places such as reserves and national parks. Cultural heritage practices are often conserved through ongoing traditions and practices.

Heritage: Today's perception of a pattern of events in the past.

High Conservation Value: Recognition of the great significance of a natural or cultural site.

HIS: Hospitality and Service Industry Training Organisation.

History: A pattern of events in the past.

Holiday Travel: Travel of 1—365 days duration, for the purpose of a holiday, a honeymoon, skiing/snowboarding, or as an incentive/reward for good work.

Hospitality Industry: Another term for the travel industry.

Hospitality: A general term used in travel & tourism describing the 'hospitality industry'; refers to the general greeting, welcoming, food service, etc.

HOT (Hotel Occupancy Tax)**:** City or county tax added to the price of a hotel room. Local dollars are often designated to support cultural tourism within the community.

Hotel Package: A package offered by a hotel, sometimes consisting of no more than a room and breakfast; sometimes, especially at resort hotels, consisting of (ground) transportation, rooms, meals, sports facilities and other components.

HRM (Human Resource Management): Concerned with the strategic management of human resources to achieve a competitive advantage.

Hub and Spoke: Air carriers use of selected cities as "hubs" or connected points for service on their systems to regional destinations.

Hub: An airport or city which serves as a central connecting point for aircraft, trains or buses from outlying feeder airports or cities.

IATA: International Air Transport Association.

ICCROM: International Centre for the Study of the Preservation and Restoration of Cultural Property.

ICOMOS: International Council of Monuments and Sites.

ICOMOS: International Council of Monuments and Sites; ICOMOS is an international, non-governmental organization dedicated to the conservation of the world's historic monuments and sites. The organization was founded in 1965, as a result of the international adoption of the Charter for the Conservation and Restoration of Monuments and Sites in Venice the year before. Today the organization has National Committees in over 107 countries.

Icon: A facility or landmark that is visually synonymous with a destination.

IMP: International Media Programme—A Tourism New Zealand programme to attract quality media to cover New Zealand.

Impacts: Effects, which may be either positive or negative, felt as a result of tourism-associated activity. Tourists have at least three kinds of impacts on a destination: economic, socio-cultural and environmental. Tourism also has effects on tourists, in terms of possible attitude and behaviour changes.

Impromptu Travel: No arrangements booked in country of destination prior to travel. (Another name for FIT travel).

Inbound Tour Operator: NZ based tourism operators who put together itineraries and process reservations (including accommodation, transport, activities and attractions) on behalf of offshore tour wholesalers and retail agents.

Inbound Travel/Tourism: Short-term arrivals into a country by nationals/residents of other countries.

Incentive Tour: A trip offered as a prize, usually by a company to stimulate employee sales or productivity.

Incentive Travel: Travel offered as a reward for top performance and the business that develops, markets and operates these programmes.

Inclusive Tour: A tour programme that includes a variety of feature for a single rate (airfare, accommodations, sightseeing, performances, etc.)

Independent Travel: Travellers who make their own arrangements and devise their own itineraries, i.e. both FIT and SIT travellers but not group or coach tour travellers.

Indigenous People: Australia's indigenous peoples are those who are descendants of the Aboriginal and Torres Straight Islander people, who identify as Aboriginal and/or Torres Straight Islander and are accepted by the Aboriginal and Torres Straight Islander communities in which they live or come from.

Indigenous Species: A species that occurs at a place within its historically known natural range, and forms part of the natural biological diversity of a place.

Industry Structure: An explanation of the functions, form and inter-relationships of individual elements, organisations and activities within a defined industrial sector (such as tourism).

Info-mediaries: Organisations which provide websites/electronic guides as an information resource, sharing other resources such as web links to organisations that sell tourism/travel. The infomediary may be an organisation or company in its own right, or may form part of an individual company's or organisation's customer service.

Information Systems: Systems that use information technology to capture, transmit, store, retrieve, manipulate, or display information.

Infrastructure: Construction needed to support economic development.

Innovative Best Practice: A practice that is considered to be of the highest quality, excellence, or standing – A leader in the field.

Inquiry: A request for more information about an attraction or destination.

Inseparability: The characteristic of service consumption being inseparable from its production, meaning that any errors made in production are seen by the consumer.

Institutions: Institutions are "an established law, custom, usage, practice, organisation, or other element in the political or social life of a people; a regulative principle or convention subservient to the needs of an organized community or the general needs of civilization" (Scrutton 1982:225, in Hall and Jenkins 1995).

Intangibility: The characteristic of not being touchable—A good is tangible whereas a service is intangible.

Intangible Heritage: Good examples of intangible heritage in the different domains mentioned in Article 2 of the Convention are Masterpieces of the Oral and Intangible Heritage of Humanity that UNESCO proclaimed in 2001 and 2003, such as the oral traditions and expressions of the Aka Pygmies of

Central Africa, and the Hudhud Chants of the Ifugao in the Philippines; performing arts like the Royal Ballet of Cambodia; social practices, rituals and festive events like the carnival of Binche in Belgium, the Indigenous Festivity Dedicated to the Dead in Mexico, or the Vanuatu Sand Drawings; knowledge and practices concerning nature and the universe such as the Andean Cosmovision of the Kallawaya in Bolivia; traditional craftsmanship like Woodcrafting of the Zafimaniry in Madagascar, or cultural spaces such as the Jemaa-el-Fnâ Square in Morocco or the Boyson District in Uzbekistan.

Integration: The linking (through changes of ownership such as mergers, acquisitions and takeovers) of different stages of the chain of distribution to form larger, more powerful organisations. Integration can be vertical (where links are developed with suppliers and distributors) or horizontal (where links are at the same stage of the distribution chain).

Intermediary: An organisation within the chain of distribution whose function is to facilitate the supply of a given product from producers to consumers. In the travel industry examples are travel agencies and tourism information offices.

International Marketing: Marketing a destination, product or service to consumers and the trade outside of the United States.

Interpretation: An educational process that is intended to stimulate and facilitate people's understanding of place, so that empathy towards, conservation, heritage, culture and landscape is developed.

Interpretation: Revealing the significance and meanings of natural and cultural phenomena to visitors, usually with the intent of providing a satisfying learning experience and encouraging more sustainable behaviour.

Interpretive Message: The essence of what is to be communicated. The use of messages ensures that the interpretation has meaning, and helps to put definition and focus into a theme.

Interpretive Theme: A central idea, story or message that you wish to convey. Themes focus and follow a specific thread of the tapestry that makes up the heritage of the place in order to present effective interpretation.

Introduced Species: A Translocated or alien species found at a place outside its historically known natural range, as a result of the intentional or accidental dispersal by human activities. Includes genetically modified organisms.

Invisible Trade: Trade in services.

Itinerary: A travel schedule provided by a travel agent for his/her customer. A proposed or preliminary itinerary may be rather vague or specific. A final itinerary however provides all details (flight numbers, departure times, reservation confirmation numbers) and describes planned activities.

ITOC: Inbound Tour Operators Council.

ITOs: Industry Training Organisations or Inbound Tour Operator.

IUCN: International Union for Conservation of Nature and Natural Resources: founded 1948 as the International Union for the Protection of Nature. For natural sites in UNESCO's World Heritage List or those who wants to be included it is the most important advisory body.

IVA: International Visitor Arrivals—Research on the number of international arrivals to NZ.

IVS: International Visitor Survey—Research on the behaviour of international visitors to NZ.

Joint Venture: A form of strategic alliance or co-operative arrangement where ownership is shared and a separate enterprise formed. This may strengthen existing businesses through shared expertise, capital, removal of competition and creation of economies of scale. International tourism joint ventures between foreign organisations and local partners facilitate introduction of foreign products into local markets.

Jungle Tourism: Jungle tours have become a major component of green tourism in tropical destinations. A jungle is a subclimax tropical forest consisting of a tangled growth of lianas, trees and scrub which may form an almost impenetrable barrier to the tourist. Jungle tours are a relatively recent phenomenon of Western international tourism.

Key-informant Survey: This involves interviewing people who are likely to have some insight into a problem: operating managers; sales staff; managers; suppliers; and consultants.

Keying: A social convention by which social 'reality' is transformed and seen as something else, such as the presentation of a fight as mere horseplay. In tourism, a peculiar, inverted variety of keying is frequently employed: the 'as if' situation in which participants are induced to playfully make believe that presented settings, activities or events are 'real', when as tourists they may be well-aware that such occurrences are contrived.

Labour Market: The pool of employees from which an employer can fill vacancies.

Leadership: Influencing and directing the performance of group members towards the achievement of organisational goals.

Learning and Enrichment Travel: It refers to vacations with authentic, hands-on or interactive learning experiences featuring themes such as adventure, agriculture, anthropology, archeology, arts, culture, cuisine, education, forestry, gardening, language, maritime, mining, nature, science, spirituality, sports, wine, and wildlife to name a few! These are the travel experiences that broaden the mind and enrich the soul. (Definition used by the *Learning and Enrichment Travel Alliance*)

Leisure Tourist: Leisure tourists, in contrast with business travellers, travel for pleasure and thus are not under any obligations to frequent specific destinations or facilities. They tend to be price and fashion conscious, concentrate their touristic activities to specific (vacation) times, and are influenced by marketing and publicity. Leisure tourism is heavily influenced by living standards, discretionary income levels and vacation entitlements.

Leisure Travel: Travel for recreational, educational, sightseeing, relaxing and other experiential purposes.

Leisure Travel: Travel undertaken for pleasure and unrelated to paid work time.

Length of Stay: This refers to the period of time which people spend in a destination. Many definitions require that visitors to a destination stay at least 24 hours or overnight, and less than one year, to be considered a tourist. Destination areas often look for means to extend tourists' length of stay in order to increase positive economic impacts.

LGNZ: Local Government New Zealand.

Liabilities: An obligation to pay money or provide service in the future. Simply described as 'things we owe'.

Lifecycle: The particular pattern through which a destination evolves.

Limits of Acceptable Change: Environmental indicators that can monitor changes over time as a consequence of tourism.

Litigation: Legal action to resolve an issue before a court.

Long-haul Travel: Air travel of 8 or more hours duration.

LOS/LoS: Length of Stay—the amount of time a tourist spends in a particular place.

Luxury Sports Tourism: Active or passive sports tourism serviced by high quality facilities and luxuriant accommodation and attendant services.

Macro Region: Grouping of Regional Tourism Organisations into a larger regional marketing entity.

Marginal or Contribution Pricing: A method of cost plus pricing which focuses on the variable or marginal cost only and thus establishes the lowest possible selling price.

Market Orientated Pricing: A method of pricing that benchmarks prices against competitors when deciding on price.

Market Segmentation: Market segmentation is a marketing approach that encompasses the identification of different groups of customers with different needs or responses to marketing activity. The market segmentation process also considers which of these segments to target.

Market Share: The percentage of business within a market category.

Market Volume: The total number of travellers within a market category.

Mass Tourism: Traditional, large scale tourism commonly, but loosely used to refer to popular forms of leisure tourism pioneered in Southern Europe, the Caribbean, and North America in the 1960s and 1970s.

Mature Market: A market in which a wide range of substitutable products or services are available to consumers who exhibit a sophisticated approach to consumer decision-making.

MAVERICS: Characterisation of tourists of the future as multi-holidaying, autonomous, variegated, energised, restless, irresponsible, constrained and segmented.

Maximum Room Nights: This is calculated based on the total room inventory for all gazetted hotels.

Mediation: An attempt to settle a dispute using a neutral third party.

Medium-haul Travel: Air travel of between 4 and 8 hours duration.

Merit Good: One with public as well as private benefits.

MFE: Ministry for the Environment.

MICE: Meetings, Incentives, Conventions and Events.

Midcentric: Of the majority of tourists—displaying a mix of allocentric and psychcentric characteristics. Prefers to be cushioned from contact with locals.

Minimal Impact Practices: Deliberate human behaviour that reduces the negative impact of people or objects on the environment to a minimum.

Mission (Sales): A promotional and sales trip coordinated by a state travel office, conventional and visitors bureau or key industry member to increase product awareness, sales and to enhance image. Target audiences may include tour operators, wholesales, incentive travel planners, travel agents, meeting planners, convention and trade show managers and media. Missions often cover several international or domestic destinations and include private and public sector participants. Mission components can include receptions, entertainment representatives of the destination, presentations and pre-scheduled sales and media calls.

Mode of Travel: The type of transport used to make a journey between an origin and a destination, and can include walking and cycling as well as all forms of mechanical transport.

Modernisation Theory: The socio-economic development and process that evolves from a traditional society to modern economies such as the United States and Western Europe. Harrison (1992) argues that modernisation is a process of westernisation where developing countries emulate Western development patterns.

Monitoring: The ongoing review and assessment of the natural or cultural integrity of a place in order to detect changes in its condition with reference to a baseline condition.

Motivation: Internal and external forces and influences that drive an individual to achieving certain goals.

Motorcoach: Deluxe equipment used by most tour operators for group tour programmes. Amenities include reclining seats, bathrooms, air conditioning, good lighting and refreshment availability.

Mystery Shoppers: These researchers investigate companies through using their services, whilst pretending to be customers (or potential customers). They usually monitor such areas as the level of customer service and product knowledge.

National Estate: The places that have been formally recognised for their aesthetic, historic, scientific or social significance or other special value, and have been placed on the Register of the National Estate.

National Income: A measure of the total level of economic activity which takes place in an economy over a year.

Native Title: Recognition in Australian law of Indigenous Australians' rights and interests in land and waters according to their traditional laws and customs.

Nature Tourism: Travel to unspoiled places to experience and enjoy nature.

Negligence: Failing to exercise what is legally considered to be reasonable care.

Net Rate: The rate provided to wholesalers and tour operators that can be marked up to sell to the customer.

Net Worth/Total Net Assets: The net value of all operational assets and liabilities, shows the amount of money invested in operational capacity of the business. Calculated by deducting current and long-term liabilities from the value of Fixed assets and Current assets.

NewRTOs: Proposed 'new generation' RTOs.

Niche Tourism: Small specialised sector of tourism which appeals to a correspondingly tightly-defined market segment.

No Show: A customer with a reservation at a restaurant, hotel, etc., who fails to show up and does not cancel.

No-frills: A low-cost scheduled travel package based on minimising operator service and costs, which are passed to the consumer as a low price.

Non-profit: Non-profit organisations are those which are driven by non-financial organisational objectives, i.e. other than for profit or shareholder return.

NTA: National Tour Association, comprised of domestic tour operators.

NTO: National Tourism Organisation—the body responsible for marketing the nation to tourists.

NZTB: New Zealand Tourist Board, trading as Tourism New Zealand.

NZTE: New Zealand Trade and Enterprise.

Occupancies: A percentage indicating the number of bed nights sold (compared to number available) in a hotel, resort, motel or destination.

Occupancy Rate: A tourism business occupancy rate refers to the number of airline seats or the units of hotel room space sold. This demand is usually measured as a percentage of available seats or space occupied for a given period of time. It is calculated by dividing the number of occupied rooms/seats by the total number available for sale during the same period.

Occupancy Rate: The measure of capacity utilised within an accommodation unit for a given time period (e.g. day, week, month or year).

OECD: Organisation for Economic Co-operation and Development.

Office of the Governor, Economic Development and Tourism: Texas agency charged with marketing Texas to audiences out of Texas and the international tourism audience.

Online Agency: Travel agencies who operate using the World Wide Web to provide information to potential customers as well as allowing the customer to book travel and related products without the necessity of speaking to a salesperson.

Operational Guidelines: The Operational Guidelines for the Implementation of the World Heritage Convention aim to facilitate the implementation of the Convention concerning the Protection of the World Cultural and Natural Heritage, by setting forth the procedure for:

(*a*) the inscription of properties on the World Heritage List and the List of World Heritage in Danger;

(*b*) the protection and conservation of World Heritage properties;

(*c*) the granting of International Assistance under the World Heritage Fund; and

(*d*) the mobilization of national and international support in favour of the Convention.

Operations Management: "The ongoing activities of designing, reviewing and using the operating system, to achieve service outputs as determined by the organization for customers" (Wright, 1999).

OPODO: A web based booking site linking the reservation systems of co-operating airlines, allowing bookers to compare times and prices for particular journeys.

Organisation: A deliberate arrangement of people to achieve a particular purpose.

Other Recruitment Difficulties: Includes poor recruitment/retention practices, poor image, low remuneration, poor employment conditions which arise despite sufficient skilled individuals.

OTSP/OTSp: Office of Tourism and Sport—now know as the Ministry of Tourism, te Manatu Tapoi (TMT).

Outbound Travel: Short term departures by nationals/residents of a country.

Outbound: Outbound tourism is defined as tourism involving residents of a country travelling to another country. Outbound tour operators offer package tours abroad. They either operate the tours themselves, or they commission the services of an inbound operator to handle local arrangements at the destination. The country from which the tourists originate is known as the generating market or country.

Owners' Equity: Combines the original investment and any retained profit to show the total value of the owners' interest in the business.

Package Holiday: Also known as an inclusive tour. Defined in law as 'the pre-arranged combination of at least two of the following components when sold or offered for sale at an inclusive price and when the service covers a period of more than 24 hours or includes overnight accommodation: (*a*) transport; (*b*) accommodation; and (*c*) other tourist services not ancillary to transport or accommodation', as set out in Section 2(1) of the European Union's Package Travel Regulations, 1992 (cited in Sharpley 2002:72-3).

Package Tour: A saleable travel product offering an inclusive price with several travel elements that would otherwise be purchased separately. Usually has a predetermined price, length of time and features but can also offer options for separate purchase.

Package Traveller: Travellers who buy pre-packaged travel arrangements such as international airfares, accommodation, transport, activities/attractions prior to arriving in NZ for a holiday.

Package: A fixed price salable travel product that makes it easy for a traveller to buy and enjoy a destination or several destinations. Packages offer a mix of elements like transportation, accommodations, restaurants, entertainment, cultural activities, sightseeing and car rental.

Paid Lettings: This refers to room lettings that are paid for by hotel guests.

PATA: Pacific Asia Travel Association.

Peaks and Valleys: The high and low end of the travel season. Travel industry marketers plan programmes to build consistent year-round business and event out the "peaks and valleys."

Perishability: The characteristic of being perishable. In tourism the term is used to describe, for example, a particular hotel room on a specific night or a particular seat on a specific flight—they cannot be 'stored' and sold later, so they are perishable.

Person Trip Visit: Every time a person travels more than 100 miles (round-trip) in a day or stays overnight away from their primary domicile, whether for business or leisure purposes, they make one "person trip visit."

Personal Disposable Income: The amount an individual has left over for personal expenditure on goods and services, after payment of personal direct taxes, national insurance and pension contributions.

Personal Travel: Includes Visiting Friends and Relatives (VFR)

Personnel: Concerned with the practical management and administration of people at work.

Person-trip: A person-trip for non-residents begins each time a non-resident traveller enters Canada. The person-trip concludes when the traveller leaves Canada. For residents, each time a person departs from Canada a person-trip begins. It ends when the traveller returns to Canada.

PESTEL Analysis: Examines the political, economic, socio-cultural, technological, (physical) environmental and legal forces within which businesses operate and which act on them.

Physical Evidence: The tangible evidence of a service, including everything which can be seen, touched, smelt and heard.

Politics: Politics has been defined in many ways. According to Heywood, politics is 'The activity through which people make, preserve and amend the general rules under which they live' (Heywood 1997:410). According to Davis *et al.*, 'Politics is the process by which the structure, process and institutions are brought to a decision [including non-decisions] or outcome. It is an endless activity; while politics operates, all decisions [and non-decisions and actions] are provisional' (Davis *et al.*, 1988:61). So politics means no decision or action is final. All decisions and actions of a government or institution of the state is open to question and is up for debate and argument and is, ultimately, subject to change.

Pollution: Harmful effects on the environment as a by-product of tourism activity. Types include: air; noise; water; and aesthetic.

Population Ageing: The effect of slowing birth rates and longer life expectancy on the median age of the population.

Porter's Forces: A model which suggests that the profit potential for companies is influenced by the interaction of five competitive forces: rivalry in the market place; the threat of substitutes; buyer power; supplier power; and barriers to entry into the market for new players.

Positioning: The process of ensuring potential customers have a desired perception of a product or service, relative to the competition. Price elasticity of demand: A relationship between the changes in prices charged for a good or service (here taken as hotel rooms) and the change in the amount demanded. Price elasticity of demand: A measure of the variability that can be expected in sales when prices are changed. Unity elasticity would see equal increase in sales to in reaction to a decrease in price. Inelastic demand would not change when prices went down or up.

Pow Wow: The largest international travel marketplace held in the United States, sponsored by the Travel Industry Association of America.

Pre-booked Travel: Domestic airfares, accommodation, activities/ attractions or transport paid for prior to arrival in NZ.

Press Trips: Organized trips for travel writers and broadcasters for the purpose of assisting them in developing stories about tourism destinations. Often, journalists travel independently, though with the assistance of a state's office of tourism of a destination marketing organization.

Press/Publicity Release: A news article or feature story written by the subject of the story for delivery and potential placement in the media.

Principal: A term that encompasses accommodation providers, carriers, ground handlers and any other provider of services to tourists, except for those whose primary function is to package and distribute tourism products (i.e., tour operators and travel agents).

Process Control: A systematic use of tools to identify significant variations in operational performance and output quality, determine root causes, make corrections and verify results (Evans and Lindsay, 1999:345).

Process Design: Involves specifying all practices needed, flowcharting, rationalisation and error prevention (Rao *et al.*, 1996:540-541).

Process Improvement: A proactive task of management aimed at continual monitoring of a process and its outcome and developing ways to enhance its future performance (James, 1996:359).

Process Management: Planning and administering the activities necessary to achieve a high level of performance in a process and identifying opportunities for improving quality, operational performance and ultimately customer satisfaction. It involves design, control and improvement of key business processes (Evans and Lindsay, 1999:340).

Process: "A set of interrelated or interacting activities which transforms inputs into outputs" (ISO, 2000a:7). Product: "The result of a process" (i.e. output), which may be either a service, or a good (hardware or processed materials) or software (e.g. information) or their combination (ISO, 2000a:7).

Profit: The excess of revenue over expenses, if expenses exceed revenues in a given period the organisation will make a loss.

Property: A hotel, motel, inn, lodge or other accommodation facility.

Psychocentric: Of a minority of tourists—preferring 'away' to be like 'home'; requiring appropriate tourism infrastructure.

Public Policy: Is whatever governments choose to do or not to do (Thomas Dye, 1992:2). Such a definition covers government action, inaction, decisions and non-decisions as it implies a very deliberate choice between alternatives (see Hall and Jenkins, 1995).

Quality: In tourism, the product is often intangible and quality is not apparent until after it is consumed. Quality has been defined as zero defects or defections, but still may be defined by the customer. The International Organisation for Standardization defines quality as 'the totality of features and characteristics of a product or service that bear on its ability to satisfy stated or implied needs'. Others believe that quality is a combination of outcome and processes, including internal and external conditions, and is obtained when the expectations and needs of customers are met.

Quality: The degree to which a set of inherent characteristics of a product fulfils customer requirements (ISO, 2000a).

Qualmark: Classification and grading system for the New Zealand tourism industry, using 5 star system.

Rack Card: The typical tourism brochure sized 4" x 9" and used primarily in tourism racks. Also known as a "teaser."

Rack Rate: Retail price of accommodation, airfares, activities/ attractions.

Rack Rate: The official cost posted by a hotel, attraction or rental car, but not used by tour operators.

Rack Rate: The rate accommodations quote to the public. Group rates, convention, trade show, meeting and incentive travel rates are negotiated by the hotel and programme organizers.

Reach: The percentage of people within a specific target audience reached by an advertising campaign.

Receptive Operator: Specialists in handling arrangements for incoming visitors at a destination including airport transfers, local sightseeing, restaurants, accommodations, etc. Receptive operators can be a travel agent or tour operator.

Regulation: Control through formalised processes.

Relationship Marketing: Relationship marketing is a business philosophy which aims to develop strong relationships with a range of stakeholders, such as suppliers, media, intermediaries and public organisations, as well as with customers.

Repeat Business: Business that continues to return, thereby generating increased profits.

Requirements: Stated, generally implied (as a custom or common practice for the organisation, its customers and other interested parties) or obligatory needs (ISO, 2000a).

Reservation Systems (Automation Vendors): Computerized systems leased to travel agencies offering airline, hotel, car rental and selected tour availability and bookings. Systems are affiliated with major carriers, including American (Sabre), United (Apollo), Eastern (System One), TWA (PARS), and Delta (DATAS II) and feature flight schedules of the sponsoring and other carriers, plus additional travel products.

Resident: A person living in a given country, whether he is a national or not.

Responsible Tourism: Type of tourism which is practised by tourists who make responsible choices when choosing their holidays. These choices reflect reponsible attitudes to the limiting of the extent of the sociological and environmental impacts their holiday may cause.

Retail Agent: A travel agent.

Retailer: Another term for travel agents who sell travel products directly to consumers.

Retailer: Firms such as travel agents and airlines, that promote and sell travel to consumers.

Retained Profit: The profit left in the business at the end of the accounting period after all deductions and appropriations have been made.

Revenue Expenditure: The cost of resources consumed or used up in the process of generating revenue, generally referred to as expenses.

Revenue Management: Revenue management is a management approach to optimising revenue, often based on managing revenues around capacity and timing (yield management), for different market segments or from different sources of funding.

RMA: Resource Management Act.

Room Blocks: Several rooms held for a group.

Room: Double: No guarantee of two beds; Double Double: Two double beds (or two queens or kings); Twin: Two twin beds (or two doubles or queens).

RTO: Regional Tourism Organisation—the entity responsible for marketing a region to tourists.

Sales Mission: Where suppliers from one DMO travel together to another state of country for the purpose of collectively promoting travel to their area. Sales missions may include educational seminars for travel agents and tour operators.

Sales Seminar: An educational session in which travel agents, tour operators, tour wholesales or other members of the travel trade congregate to receive briefings about tourism destinations.

Sales: Revenue from ordinary activities—not necessarily cash.

Seasonality: A phenomenon created by either tourism supply or demand (or both) changing according to the time of the year.

Seasonality: The influence of the time of the year on patterns in travel. The volume of travel to NZ is far greater during our summer and lower over winter.

Service Encounter: The moments of interface between customer and supplier.

Service Marketing Mix: The addition of People, Physical Evidence and Process to the four areas of activity more usually associated with marketing products—Price, Place, Promotion and Product.

Servicescape: The location in which the service encounter takes place.

SFRITO: Sports, Fitness, Recreation Industry Training Organisation

Shells: A marketing and sales promotional piece that depicts a destination, accommodation or attraction on the cover and provides space for copy to be added at a later date. Usually shells fit a #10 envelope.

Short-haul Travel: Air travel of less than 4 hours duration.

SIT: Semi-Independent Travellers—Visitors coming to NZ on holiday who do not purchase a fully pre-planned travel package. They may organise their own travel arrangements prior to or after arriving in NZ.

Site Inspection: An assessment tour of a destination or facility by a meeting planner, convention or trade show manager, site selection committee, tour operator, wholesaler or incentive travel manager to see if it meets their needs and requirements prior to selecting a specific site for an event. After site selection, a site inspection may be utilized to make arrangements.

Skills Gaps: Employers perceive existing employees have lower skill levels than needed to achieve business objectives, or where new, apparently trained and qualified for specific occupations, entrants still lack requisite skills.

Skills Shortages: Lack of adequately skilled individuals in the labour market due to low unemployment, sufficiently skilled people in the labour market but not easily geographically accessible or insufficient appropriately-skilled individuals.

Small Business: A small business is one which has a small number of employees, profit and/or revenue. Often these are owner-managed, with few specialist managers. Some definitions of small businesses distinguish between businesses with under 10 employees, which are micro-businesses, and those with 10-49 employees, which are classified as small businesses.

SME(s): Small and Medium Enterprises.

Social: Relating to human society and interaction between its members.

Sports Event Tourism: Tourism where the prime purpose of the trip is to take part in sports events as either a participant or spectator.

Sports Participation Tourism: Active participation in sports that is the prime purpose of the tourism trip.

Sports Tourism: A social, cultural and economic phenomenon arising from the unique interaction of activity, people and place.

Sports Training Tourism: Sports tourism trips where the prime purpose is sports instruction or training.

Sport-tourism Link: Not just sports holidays, but all areas in which a link between sport and tourism might be of mutual benefit (e.g. joint facility development, marketing and information provision).

Spouse Programme: Special activities planned for those who accompany an attendee to a convention, trade show or meeting. Note that programmes today are not simply for women, but rather for men and women, spouses and friends. Programmes must be creatively designed to interest intelligent and curious audiences.

STA: Student Travel Association.

Stakeholder: Any person, group or organisation with an interest in, or who may be affected by, the activities of another organisation.

State: 'The state' is a set of officials with their own preferences and capacities to effect public policy, or in more structural terms a relatively permanent set of political institutions operating in relation to civil society (Nordlinger 1981, in Hall and Jenkins 1995). The state includes elected politicians, interest or pressure groups, law enforcement agencies, the bureaucracy, and a plethora of rules, regulations, laws, conventions and policies.

Statute: The law as made by parliament, e.g. in the UK, the Disability Discrimination Act (1995). A statute is made up of many parts called 'sections' or 'provisions'.

Statutory Instrument: The vast majority of delegated legislation in the UK is in the form of statutory instruments governed by the Statutory Instruments Act, 1946.

Step on Guide: A representative from a community, attraction, or

DMO that can "step on" the bus and provide guide services for tour groups.

Strategic Information Systems: Systems designed to support the strategic management decision processes and implementation.

Strategy Pyramid: A visual way of representing the different levels of the strategy conceptualisation and implementation process. The most general assumptions are shown at the apex and the practical, implementation actions are at the base.

Supplier: New Zealand based tourism companies, includes accommodation providers, activities/attractions, event organisers, retail shops, tour and transport operators.

Supplier: Those businesses that provide industry products like accommodations, transportation, car rentals, restaurants and attractions.

Suppliers: Individuals, companies or other organisations which provide goods or services to a recognizable customer or consumer.

Sustainable Tourism: It is envisaged as leading to management of all resources in such a way that economic, social and aesthetic needs can be fulfilled while maintaining cultural integrity, essential ecological processes, biological diversity and life support systems.

Sustainable Tourism: It is "tourism which actively fosters appreciation and stewardship of the natural, cultural and historic resources and special places by local residents, the tourism industry, governments and visitors. It is tourism which can be sustained over the long term because it results in a net benefit for the social, economic, natural and cultural environments of the area in which it takes place." *(Definition used by Parks Canada)* Three general types of travel have been identified, according to the motivation, purpose or reason for the trip, along with various sub-categories:

Pleasure/Leisure Travel: Includes Group Travel and Fully Independent Travel (FIT).

Business Travel: Includes Conventions and Meetings; Incentive Travel.

Personal Travel: Includes Visiting Friends and Relatives (VFR).

Sustainable Tourism: This is, according to the World Tourism Organisation, "envisaged as leading to management of all resources in such a way that economic, social and aesthetic needs can be fulfilled with maintaining cultural integrity, essential ecological processes, biological diversity, and life support systems."

Sustainable Tourism: Tourism that is economically, socio-culturally and environmentally sustainable. With sustainable tourism, socio-cultural and environmental impacts are neither permanent nor irreversible.

SWOT Analysis: Brings together the internal and external environmental scanning to identify the business's internal strengths and weaknesses and external opportunities and threats.

TAANZ: Travel Agents Association of New Zealand—Association for NZ based travel agents.

TACVB: Texas Association of Convention and Visitors Bureaus.

TAM: Texas Association of Museums.

Target Audience/Market: A specific demographic, sociographic target at which marketing communications are directed.

Target Rating Points: TRP's are a statistical measurement that allows one to evaluate the relative impact of differing advertising campaigns.

Tariff: Rate of fare quoted and published by a travel industry supplier (i.e. hotels, tour operators, etc.). Usually an annual tariff is produced in booklet form for use in sales calls at trade shows.

TCA: Texas Commission on the Arts.

Tentative Lists: A Tentative List is an inventory of those properties which each State Party intends to consider for nomination during the following years.

TFEA: Texas Festivals and Events Association.

THC: Texas Historical Commission.

TIA/TIANZ: Tourism Industry Association of New Zealand—Association that represents members in the tourism industry, mainly small and medium sized businesses.

TIA: Travel Industry Association of America.

TIC: Travel Information Centres that are owned and operated by the Texas Department of Transportation.

TLAs: Territorial Local Authorities.

TMT: The Ministry of Tourism, te Manatu Tapoi (also known as OTSp).

TNZ: Tourism New Zealand (also known as NZTB).

Tort: A civil wrong.

Tour Operator: An individual or organisation in the business of (bulk) buying, and subsequently bundling, the various components that make up a package holiday (see above), for sale via a travel agent or direct to the consumer.

Tour Operator: Develops, markets and operates group travel programmes that provide a complete travel experience for one price and includes transportation (airline, rail, motorcoach, and/ or ship), accommodations, sightseeing, selected meals and an escort. Tour operators market directly to the consumer, through travel agents and are beginning to be listed on computerized reservation systems.

Tour Wholesaler: An individual or company that sells tour packages and tour product to travel agents. Tour wholesalers usually receive a 20 per cent discount from accommodations, transportation companies and attractions and pass on a 10 to 15 per cent discount to the retail agent.

Tourism Commodity: Tourism Commodity is one for which a significant part of its total demand in Canada comes from visitors.

Tourism Demand: Tourism Demand is defined as the spending of Canadian and non-resident visitors on domestically produced commodities. It is the sum of tourism domestic demand and tourism exports.

Tourism Domestic Demand: Tourism Domestic Demand is the spending in Canada by Canadian visitors on domestically produced commodities.

Tourism Employment: Tourism Employment is a measure of employment in tourism and non-tourism industries. It is based on an estimate of jobs rather than "hours of work". Thus, someone who works 10 hours a week counts for as much, by this measure, as someone who works 50 hours a week.

Tourism Exports: Tourism Exports is spending by foreign visitors on Canadian-produced goods and services. It includes spending that may take place outside of Canada, for instance, the purchase of an airline ticket from a Canadian international carrier, to travel to Canada.

Tourism Flows: The major movements of tourists from specific home areas to destinations.

Tourism Income Multiplier (TIM): Exaggerated effect of a change in tourism expenditure on an area's income.

Tourism Industry: Tourism Industry is an industry that would cease to exist or would continue to exist only at significantly reduced levels of activity in the absence of tourism.

Tourism Marketing: In order to be considered *export ready*, an organization should:

- Have been in business for at least one year, with a proven track record of safe and professional operation;
- Provide contracted wholesale net rates to tour operators, travel wholesalers and retail travel agents. As a general guideline, requirements are 15 per cent off retail for activities and transportation and 20-30 per cent off retail for accommodation;
- Provide detailed pricing and programme information to tour operators, travel wholesalers and retail travel agents at least one year in advance of selling season, e.g. May 2004 for the summer/fall 2005 season;
- Communicate and accept reservations by telephone, fax or email. Provide same-day confirmation of booking arrangements;
- Set up billing arrangements with the operator, agency or receptive tour operator. Accept client vouchers as confirmation of booking arrangements;
- Carry adequate business liability insurance;
- Provide support (free or at reduced rates) for international media and FAM tours; and
- Hold all appropriate operating licenses *(Definition used by Rendez-vous Canada).*

Tourism Receipts: Tourism Receipts (TR) measures the total revenue received by Singapore from tourism activity. It includes all payments and prepayments for goods and services made by visitors, transit passengers, air and sea crew and foreign students (staying for one year or less) during their stay in Singapore. Visitors' payments to our national carriers (SIA and Silk Air) for international transport are also included.

Tourism Satellite Account: System of accounting at national or regional level which reveals the total direct impact of tourism on the economy.

Tourism System: A framework that identifies tourism as being made up of a number of components, often taken to include the tourist, the tourist generating region, the transit route region, the tourist destination and the tourism industry (Leiper, 1990).

Tourism with Sports Content: Tourism products that include participation in sport that is not the prime purpose of the trip.

Tourism: Leisure travel.

Tourism: The activity of persons travelling to and staying in places outside their usual environment for not more than one consecutive year for leisure, business or any other purpose. (United Nations approved definition).

Tourism: The business of providing and marketing services and facilities for pleasure travellers. Thus, the concept or tourism is of direct concern to governments, carriers, and the lodging, restaurant and entertainment industries and of indirect concern to virtually every industry and business in the world.

Tourism: The definition of tourism used in the National Tourism indicators (NTI) is that adopted by the World Tourism Organization and the United Nations Statistical Commission: "the activities of persons travelling to and staying in places outside their usual environment for not more than one consecutive year for leisure, business and other purposes."

Tourism: Itself has been defined by the World Tourism Organization as "the activities of persons travelling to and staying in places outside their usual environment for not more than one consecutive year for leisure, business or other purposes."

Tourist Attractions: Tourist attractions are defined as being destinations for visitors' excursions which are routinely accessible to visitors during opening hours. Visitors can include local residents, day-trippers or people who are travelling for business or leisure purposes. Formal definitions exclude shops, sports stadia, theatres and cinemas, as these meet a wider purpose, although in practice tourists may consider the excluded categories to be tourist attractions.

Tourist/Visitor/Traveller: Any person who travels either for leisure or business purposes more than 100 miles (round-trip) in a day or who stays overnight away from his/her primary domicile.

Tourist: Anyone who spends at least one night away from home, no matter what the purpose.

Tourist: Temporary visitor staying at least twenty-four hours in the country visited for a purpose classified as either holiday (recreation, leisure, sport and visit to family, friends or relatives), business, official mission, convention, or health reasons.

TOWS Matrix: Uses a SWOT analysis to develop strategies by matching strengths with opportunities, using opportunities to reduce weaknesses, using strengths to overcome threats, and reducing weaknesses and avoiding threats.

TPW: Texas Parks and Wildlife.

Tracking Research: Ongoing research conducted at regular intervals to track changes in specific factors, for example, potential customers' intention to travel to NZ.

Trade Show: A product showcase for a specific industry. Generally it is not open to the public. Differs from a 'Consumer Show' in that a trade show targets the professional industry, while a consumer show targets consumers.

Transient Occupancy Tax: TOT or bed tax is a locally set tax on the cost of commercial accommodations and campgrounds.

Travel Agent: An individual who arranges travel for individuals or groups. Travel agents may be generalists or specialists (cruises, adventure travel, conventions and meetings.) The agents receive a 10 to 15 per cent commission from accommodations, transportation companies and attractions for coordinating the booking of travel. They typically coordinate travel for their customers at the same or lower cost than if the customer booked the travel on his/her own.

Travel Agent: The individual who sells travel services, issues tickets and provides other travel services to the travel services to the traveller sat the retail level.

Travel Agent: The retailer of travel and related products. Whilst this refers to the sales person employed to sell travel products, the term is often applied in reference to the business that is established to sell travel products (the travel agency).

Travel Product: Refers to any product or service that is bought by or sold to consumers of trade including accommodations, attractions, events, restaurants, transportation, etc.

Travel Seasons: Travel industry business cycles including:

- Peak: Primary travel season.
- Off Peak: Period when business is slowest.
- Shoulder: Period between peak and off peak periods when business is stronger, but has room for growth.

Travel Tex: The Official Site of Texas Tourism presented by Office of the Governor, Economic Development and Tourism.

Travel Trade: The collective term for tour operators, wholesalers and travel agents.

Travel: Leisure and other travel including travel for business, medical care, education, etc. All tourism is travel, but not all travel is tourism.

Traveller: Definitions very, but in general a traveller is someone who leaves their own economic trade area, (usually going a distance of a minimum of fifty to one hundred miles) and stays overnight.

TRCNZ: Tourism Research Council New Zealand.

TRENZ: Tourism Rendezvous New Zealand—Annual exhibition at which tourism operators to market their products and services to wholesalers.

TRM: Trade Relations Management.

TSA: Tourism Satellite Account—Official calculation of the contribution of tourism to the New Zealand economy.

TTIA: Texas Travel Industry Association.

TxDOT: Texas Department of Transportation.

Underdevelopment: Within development theory, the concept of underdevelopment suggests that wealthy capitalist countries have held back the development of so-called Third World countries. Tourism in Third World destinations is controlled for the economic benefit of foreign owners, reinforces dependency, lacks involvement of local decision makers, leads to negative socio-cultural impacts, and results in the promotion of staged attractions to capture an international tourism market.

UNESCO: United Nations Educational, Scientific and Cultural Organization.

Uniquely Texas: A video project highlighting cultural and heritage tourism in Texas with a supporting Website.

Urban Cultural Tourism: Urban cultural tourism is a multidimensional phenomenon. First, it refers to cultural tourism in a built environment, which in this context, consists of a complex network of built heritage elements (monuments, museums, sites, open spaces and accompanying buildings) and urban intangible elements (local habits and customs, traditions and legends), in various activities (shopping, eating, entertainment), as well as in the overall dynamic ambience and experiences of the tourists that confer unique identity upon a given city. Second, it refers to the development of cultural tourism in a complex network of relationship between various economic, political and social urban actors.

Urban Governance: The concept of urban governance refers to the collaborative process which allows the mobilization and cooperation of a great number of urban actors in order to mould the necessary political and operational consensus to affect directly the every day life of all members of an urban community.

Urban Recreation: The concept of urban recreation covers recreational activity that takes place in an urban environment in contrast to a rural setting. Participants in such activities are either urban residents themselves, day visitors from rural areas, or tourists. The major activities are shopping, visits to heritage sites, museums, movie theatres, operas, sport and music events, and indoor sports activities.

USP: Unique Selling Proposition—Your point of difference, the thing that makes your product/service uniquely marketable to customers.

Variability: Because the production and the consumption of a tourism experience are inseparable and because differing circumstances and people will affect each experience, those experiences are prone to variance and create a challenge for tourism managers to achieve consistency of standards.

VFR: A trip for the purpose of Visiting Friends or Relatives for 1-365 days.

VFR: Visiting friends and relatives.

VIN: Visitor Information Network—Officially recognised network of information centres.

Virtual Organisation: Organisation in which major processes are outsourced to partners.

Visitor Arrivals: Includes all who go through immigration clearance regardless of length of stay. This excludes the following:

(*a*) All Malaysian citizens arriving by land.
(*b*) Returning Singapore citizens residing abroad.
(*c*) Non-resident air and sea crew (except for sea crew flying in to join ship).
(*d*) All visitors arriving and leaving Singapore on the same

ship/vessel and stayed in Singapore for less than 24 hours are not required to complete Disembarkation/ Embarkation (D/E) cards, if passenger manifest is submitted.

(*e*) All organised tour groups leaving Singapore for Johor Bahru, Batam and Bintan, returning on the same day are not required to complete Disembarkation/Embarkation (D/E) cards, if passenger manifest is submitted.

(*f*) Air transit passengers VISITOR DAYS = Number of Visitor Arrivals x Average Length of Stay.

Visitor Expenditure: Includes expenditure incurred during a visitor's stay in Singapore, or prepayment by non-package tour visitors (this took effect from 1995). This excludes: *International Air and Sea Fare*—It is made up of the following components:

(*i*) Shopping,
(*ii*) Accommodation,
(*iii*) Entertainment,
(*iv*) Sightseeing,
(*v*) Food & beverage,
(*vi*) Local transportation,
(*vii*) Medical/dental treatment,
(*viii*) Miscellaneous.

Visitor: Any person visiting a country other than that in which he has his usual place of residence for any reason other than following an occupation remunerated from within the country visited.

Visitors Centre: Travel information centre located at a destination to make it easier for visitors to plan their stay; often operated by a convention and visitors bureau, chamber of commerce or tourism promotion organization.

Visitors Centre: Travel information centre located at a destination to make it easier for visitors to plan their stay; often operated by a convention and visitors bureau, chamber of commerce or tourism promotion organisation.

Visitors: A broader category than 'tourist', includes tourists and same-day visitors.

Visitors: Visitors are persons who undertake tourism as defined above. They are referred to as either tourists (those who stay overnight or longer in the place visited), or same-day visitors.

Vouchers: Forms or coupons provided to a traveller who purchases a tour that indicate that certain tour components have been prepaid. Vouchers are then exchanged for tour components like accommodations, meals, sightseeing, theatre tickets, etc. during the actual trip.

Wellness Tourism: It is the sum of all the relationships and phenomena resulting from a journey and residence by people whose main motivation is to preserve or promote their health. They stay in a specialized hotel which provides the appropriate professional know how and individual care. They require a comprehensive service package comprising physical fitness/ beauty care, healthy nutrition/diet, relaxation/meditation and mental activity/education. *(Definition developed by the Research Institute for Leisure and Tourism, University of Berne, Switzerland).*

Wholesaler: Develop and markets inclusive tours and individual travel programmes to the consumer through travel agents. Wholesalers do not sell directly to the public.

Wholesaler: Firms that purchase products or ground arrangements from New Zealand suppliers or inbound operators, and package products for sale. Wholesalers deal primarily with retailers, but sometimes also sell directly to the public.

Wine/Culinary Tourism: It is tourism in which the opportunity for wine and/or culinary related experiences contributes significantly to the reason for travel to the destination or to itinerary planning while at the destination. *(Definition used by the Ontario Ministry of Tourism, Culture and Recreation and the Wine Council of Ontario).*

WOM/WoM: Word of Mouth—What customers say to others about your product/service.

Working Capital: Operational assets and liabilities needed for everyday operation, e.g. cash or bank overdraft, stock and trade creditors, known as net current assets/liabilities.

World Heritage Committee: The World Heritage Committee meets once a year, and consists of representatives from 21 of the States Parties to the Convention elected by their General Assembly for terms up to six years.

World Heritage Day: ICOMOS declared the International Day for Monuments and Sites, the 18th of April as World Heritage Day.

World Heritage in Young Hands: World Heritage Educational Resource Kit published by UNESCO.

World Heritage-List: List of all UNESCO World Heritage Sites worldwide.

World Monuments Fund: The World Monuments Fund is the only private, non-profit organization devoted to onsite conservation of monuments and sites worldwide.

World Tourism Organisation (WTO): The World Tourism Organisation, a UN-related institution based in Madrid that collects data on tourism and lobbies on behalf of the industry.

World Travel and Tourism Council (WTTC): The WTTC is made up of chief executives from all sectors of the tourism industry, including accommodation, catering, cruises, entertainment, recreation, transportation and travel-related services. Its central goal is to work with governments to realise the full economic impact of tourism. Its millennium vision is to make tourism a strategic economic and employment priority, to move towards open and competitive markets, to pursue sustainable development, and to eliminate barriers to growth.

WTO: World Tourism Organization.

WTTC: World Travel & Tourism Council.

Xenophobia: Xenophobia is an irrational fear or contempt of strangers or foreigners. This ancient cultural and political phenomenon is also present in contemporary tourism, mainly manifesting itself in the hostile attitudes of residents towards tourists. Xenophobia should be considered in domestic and international tourism in terms of economic, social and cultural distance, which is accentuated by the type and the number of tourists and the rate of tourism development.

YHA: Youth Hostels Association.

Yield Management: "A revenue maximization technique which aims to increase net yield through the predicted allocation of available ... capacity to predetermined market segments at optimal price" (Donaghy *et al.*, 1997a).

Yield Management: The concept of maximising the revenue by raising or lowering prices in respect to demand is known as yield management. The necessary conditions for a successful application of yield management include a fairly fixed capacity, high fixed costs, low variable costs, fluctuations in demand and similarity of inventory capacity. Yield management was popularised with the deregulation of the US airline industry and it is extensively used by this and other tourism sectors.

Yield Percentage: To demonstrate the variable effect of both average price rates and occupancy rates, tourism managers develop a comparison focusing upon the yield rates during a given period of time. Managers can increase the yield rate (see yield management) by raising rates when demand is high.

Zoning: Different eco-systems may be zoned in terms of their robustness to pressures from tourism in an attempt to mitigate environmental damage.

Zoning: Zoning seeks to regulate land uses by separating them based on incompatibility, or allowing like/compatible uses to co-exist. A basic principle of tourism zoning is the conservation of specific environmental features such as wetlands, archaeological and historic sites, important stands of vegetation and unusual geological features. Related to this is the maintenance of visual diversity. Also important is the achievement of successful functional groupings of resort facilities and activities, such as accommodation, commercial and cultural facilities, and recreation facilities in suitable areas. Buffer zones containing mixtures of tourism facilities and less fragile environmental preservation requirements may also be designated.

Bibliography/Websites

A Comprehensive Approach to the Planning of the Tourism Industry; Jona Bargur and Avner Arbel; *Journal of Travel Research*; 1975; Vol. 14; pp. 10-15.

A Small Community Adopts Tourism as a Development Tool; Edgell, David, Sr.; Business America, Washington; April 20, 1992; Vol. 113, Issue 8; pp. 16-21.

A Taste of Local Life; Katherine Tanko; *Far Eastern Economic Review*, Hong Kong; February 6, 2003; Vol. 166, Issue 5; pp. 54-56.

Actors, Discourses and Interfaces of Rural Tourism Development at the Local Community Level in Slovenia: Social and Political Dimensions of the Rural Tourism Development Process; Alenka Verbole; *Journal of Sustainable Tourism*; 2000; Vol. 8, No. 6; pp. 479-90.

Adams, G. Donald. "Cultural Heritage Tourism," Paper presented at a Heritage Tourism Conference sponsored by the Museum Department, City of Ketchikan, Alaska, May 23, 1990.

Adams, G. Donald 1995. "Cultural Tourism," *Museum News*, November/December.

Adejuwon, F., "Cultural Heritage as Tourism Product", *Tourist Review*, No. 1, 1985.

Agricultural Diversification into Tourism: Evidence of a European Community Development Programme; Anne-Mette Hjalager; *Tourism Management*; March 1996; Vol. 17, Issue 2; pp. 103-11.

American Association of Museums (1994). *Museums count*. Washington, D.C.: American Association of Museums.

Americans for the Arts 2002. *Arts and Economic Prosperity*; The Economic Impact of Non-profit Arts Organizations and Their Audiences.

Anderson, Beverly 1989. "Rocky Mountain House: Cultural and Community Tourism: A Case Study." Paper presented at the

Planning for Cultural Tourism Symposium, The University of Calgary, Calgary Alberta.

Ashley, J.M. 1989, "The Visitor Activity Management Process and National Historic Parks and Sites Serving the Visitor", *Recreation Research Review*, Vol. 14, 4 Special Issue.

Asia/Pacific Cultural Centre for UNESCO (ACCU), 1993. Regional Training Seminar for Cultural Personnel in Asia and the Pacific, Cultural Heritage and Tourism: Preservation and Presentation of Cultural Heritage, Tokyo, September 28-October 7, 1993.

Assessing Community Support and Sustainability for Ecotourism Development; Vern C. Vincent; *Journal of Travel Research, Boulder*; Nov. 2002; Vol. 41, Issue 2; pp. 153-161.

Attitudes to a Non-viable Community-owned Heritage Tourist Attraction; Bob McKercher; *Journal of Sustainable Tourism; 2001*; Vol. 9, No. 1; pp. 29-43.

Barkin, D., 2002. *Ecotourism for Sustainable Regional Development*. Current Issues in Tourism, 5(3-4): 245-53.

Bartholomew Dean and Jerome Levi (eds.) 2003. *At the Risk of Being Heard: Indigenous Rights, Identity and Postcolonial States* University of Michigan Press.

Baumol, W.J. and W.E. Oates, 1977. *Economics, Environmental Policy, and Quality of Life*. Englewood Cliffs, New Jersey, USA: Prentice Hall.

Belland, Greg and Erin Boss, 1994. "Cultural and Historic Sites: Assessing the Tourism Potential," *ICOMOS Canada Bulletin*, MOMENTUM 1994, 3(3), 26.

Bellerose, Pierre, 1994. "Le Vieux-Montreal et le tourisme: a I'heure de la concertation," *ICOMOS Canada Bulletin*, MOMENTUM 1994, 3(3), 35.

Bellinger, Dave, 1994. "Managing the Rideau Canal: Issues of Conservation and Tourism," *ICOMOS Canada Bulletin*, MOMENTUM 1994, 3(3), 38.

Binney, "Preservation Pays", *Livability Digest*, Fall 1981.

Blust, R., 1999. "Subgrouping, Circularity and Extinction: Some Issues in Austronesian Comparative Linguistics" in E. Zeitoun & P.J.K Li, ed., *Selected Papers from the Eighth International Conference on Austronesian Linguistics*. Taipei: Academia Sinica.

Bowes, Bob, 1994. "Cultural Tourism: Are We on the Brink?," *ICOMOS Canada Bulletin*, Momentum 1994, 3(3), 23.

Bowes, R.G., 1989. "Tourism and Heritage—A New Approach to the Product", *Recreation Research Review*, 14(4).

Brazil sees traces of more isolated Amazon tribes.

Brazil urged to protect Indians.

Brown, "Historic Jim Thorpe", *Livability Digest*, Fall 1981.

Buckley, R., 1994. Research Note, A Framework for Ecotourism. *Annals of Tourism Research*, 21(3): 661-69.

Budowski, 1976. "Tourism and Environmental Conservation: Conflict, Coexistence or Symbiosis?," *Environmental Conservation*, 3(1), 17-31.

Building Tourism Excellence at the Community Level: Capacity Building for Community-Based Entrepreneurs in Uganda; Raymond Victurine; *Journal of Travel Research*, Boulder; February 2000; Vol. 38, Issue 3; pp. 221-230.

Butler, "Historical and Conceptual Context", *A Workshop on a Strategy for Tourism and Sustainable Development*, J.G. Nelson, (ed.).

Campbell, Bernard F., 1994. "Aboriginal Cultural Tourism; The Market," *ICOMOS Canada Bulletin*, Momentum 1994, 3(3), 41.

Canadian Heritage, 1995. *Heritage Tourism: Discover the Opportunity*. Hull, Quebec.

Cater, E., 1994. in Cater, E., and G. Lowman: *Ecotourism in the Third World—Problems and Prospects for Sustainability in: Ecotourism, a Sustainable Option?* United Kingdom: John Wiley and Sons.

Cattaneo, Claudia. "Tourism Cashing in on the Past," *The Calgary Herald*, (no date).

Caucasian Peoples.

Chapter of Cultural Tourism, ICOMOS Tourism Committee.

Clarion Associates, 2002. *Investing in Michigan's Future: The Economic Benefits of Historic Preservation*. Lansing, MI: Michigan Historic Preservation Network.

Colbert, *The State of Tourism, Culture and Multiculturalism in Canada*, pp. 14-37.

Collaboration Theory and Community Tourism Planning; Tazim, B. Jamal and Donald Getz; *Annals of Tourism Research*; 1995; Vol. 22, Issue 1; pp. 186-204.

Collins, Robertson E., 1991. *A Disorderly Excursion: Notes of a Conservationist in the Asia/Pacific Region*. Macau: Hong Heng.

Community Attachment and Attitudes Toward Tourism Development; McCool, Stephen F; Journal of Travel Research, Boulder; Winter 1994; Vol. 32, Issue 3; pp. 29-35.

Community Based Mountain Tourism: Practices for Linking Conservation with Enterprise—Synthesis of an Electronic Conference, April 13-May 18, 1998. The Mountain Institute, first printing, April 1999.

Community Based Tourism for Conservation and Development: A Resource Kit. ©The Mountain Institute, 2000.

Crinion, D., 1998. *South Australian Tourism Strategy and the Role of Ecotourism.* Adelaide, Australia: Down to Earth Planning for an Out-of-the-Ordinary Industry, Presented at the South Australian Ecotourism Forum.

Cultural Tourism and Industrial Cities, *Environmental Comment,* January 1981.

Cultural Tourism in Rural Communities: The Residents' Perspective; Bachleitner, Reinhard; Journal of Business Research, New York; Mar 1999; Vol. 44, Issue 3; pp. 199-210.

Cultural Tourism, *Canadian Heritage,* May 1982.

Cummings, Debra. 27 January, 1995. "The Road to Higher Learning," *Calgary Herald,* J1-J2.

Dalibard, "The Collaborative Management of Change", *A Workshop on a Strategy for Tourism and Sustainable Development,* J.G. Nelson, (ed.).

David L. Edgell, *Best Practices Guidebook for International Tourism and Attraction Development for Rural Communities,* Sr., Ph.D. (2002). Publisher: Brigham Young University; contact: Brian J. Hill, Ph.D. at Brigham Young University, 273 RB, P.O. Box 22019, Provo, Utah 84602-2019; Phone (801) 422-1287; E-mail: brian_hill@byu.edu.

Dewar, K., 1978. "Interpretation as Attraction", *Recreation Research Review,* 14(4).

Diamond, Jared M. *"Taiwan's Gift to the World" PDF (107 KiB).* Nature, Volume 403, February 2000, pp. 709-10.

Eadington, W.R. and V.L. Smith, 1992. *The Emergence of Alternative Forms of Tourism, in Tourism Alternatives: Potentials and Problems in the Development of Tourism.* Pennsylvania, USA: University of Pennsylvania Press.

Economist, The. "No Longer the Pits," November 6, 1993.

Edmunds, "Charlestons Tourism Management Committee", *Livability Digest*, Fall 1981.

Elper-Wood, M., 1998. *Ecotourism at a Crossroads: Charting the Way Forward*. Nairobi, Kenya: The Final Report from the Conference of Ecotourism at the Crossroads.

English Tourism Board. *Tourism and the Environment, Maintaining the Balance*, 01 January, 1991.

Factors for Success in Rural Tourism Development; Suzanne Wilson; *Journal of Travel Research, Boulder*; November 2001; Vol. 40, Issue 2; pp. 132-39.

Fox, James J., *"Current Developments in Comparative Austronesian Studies" PDF (105 KiB)*. Paper prepared for Symposium Austronesia Pascasarjana Linguististik dan Kajian Budaya. Universitas Udayana, Bali 19-20 August, 2004.

FRITZ Jean-Claude, *L'humanité face à la mondialisation. Droit des peuples et environnement* (en co-direction avec Charalambos Apostolidis et Gérard Fritz), Paris, L'Harmattan, 1997.

FRITZ Jean-Claude, *La nouvelle question indigène. Peuples autochthones et ordre mondial* (en co-direction avec Frédéric Déroche, Gérard Fritz et Raphaël Porteilla), Paris, L'Harmattan, 2006.

Gender and Community Tourism Dependence Level; M. Jeannie Harvey, John Hunt and Charles C. Harris Jr.; *Annals of Tourism Research*; 1995; Vol. 22, Issue 2; pp. 349-66.

Globe and Mail, The. "Nouveau riche in Old West," July 18, 1992.

Hardin, G., 1968. *The Tragedy of the Commons*. Science, 162: 1243-48.

Henriksen, John B. 2001. *"Implementation of the Right of Self-Determination of Indigenous Peoples", Indigenous Affairs (Copenhagen: International Work Group for Indigenous Affairs) 3/2001: pp. 6-21, ISSN 1024-3283, OCLC 30685615, <http://www.iwgia.org/graphics/Synkron-Library/Documents/publications/Downloadpublications/IndigenousAffairs/selfdetermination.pdf>. Retrieved on 2007-09-01.*

Heritage Canada Foundation, The. *Regional Heritage Tourism Strategy*, April 1988.

Heritage Canada, 1995. *New Life for Rural Regions: Taking a Heritage Approach*. Ottawa.

Hewison, J. 1987. *The Heritage Industry*. London: Methuen.

Hewison, R. *The Heritage Industry*, London: Metheun, 1987. pp. 83-105, 131-146.

Hollis, S.M., "The Arts and Centre City Revitalization", *Issues in Supporting the Arts*, C. Violette.

Howell, Benita J. "Weighing the Risks and Rewards of Involvement in Cultural Conservation and Heritage Tourism", *Journal of the Society for Human Organization*, Summer 1994, 53:2.

http://www.un.org/depts/dhl/indigenous/.

Huges, H.L., 1987. "Culture as a Tourist Resource—a Theoretical Consideration", *Tourism Management*, 8(3).

Hughes, George. "The Cultural Construction of Sustainable Tourism," *Tourism Management*, February 1995, 16:1.

Hurt, Les. 1994. "Heritage Tourism in Alberta: Toward a Complete Picture," *ICOMOS Canada Bulletin*, MOMENTUM 1994, 3(3), 15.

ICOMOS International Committee on Cultural Tourism, Newsletter, November 1991.

ICOMOS International Committee on Cultural Tourism, 1993. *Tourism at World Heritage Cultural Sites: The Site Manager's Handbook*. Washington, D.C.

Improving Access for the Informal Sector to Tourism in The Gambia; Adama Bah and Harold Goodwin; Lesson-Sharing on Pro-Poor Tourism; February 2003; Working Paper No.15.

Indigenous Issues. *International Work Group on Indigenous Affairs*. Retrieved on September 5, 2005.

Indigenous Peoples and Environmental Issues: An Encyclopedia, by Bruce E. Johansen. Westport, CT, Greenwood Press, 2003.

Indigenous. *Merriam Webster's Online Dictionary* (2006-07). Merriam Webster. Retrieved on 2007-04-05.

Influences on Tourism Development Decision Making: Coastal Local Government Areas in Eastern Australia; Harold Richins and Philip Pearce; *Journal of Sustainable Tourism; 2000*; Vol. 8, No. 3; pp. 207-231.

International Committee on Monuments and Sites (ICOMOS). 1976. *Charter on Cultural Tourism*. Paris: ICOMOS International.

Isaacs, J.C. 2000. *The Limited Potential of Ecotourism to Contribute to Wildlife Conservation*. The Ecologist, 28(1): 61-69.

Jacobson, S.K. and R. Robles 1998. *Ecotourism, Sustainable Development, and Conservation Education: Development of a Tour Guide Training Programme in Tortuguero, Costa Rica*. Environmental Management, 16(6): 701-713.

James, Bruce. "For Art's Sake, Stop the Car," *ABM, Australian Business Monthly*, March 1994, 14:5.

Jamieson, Walter. "Planning for Small Town Cultural Tourism," Paper presented at the International Scientific Symposium, Sri Lanka, 1993.

Jamieson, Walter. "Realizing the Benefits of Rural Cultural Tourism."

Jamieson, Walter, 1994. "The Challenge of Cultural Tourism," *ICOMOS Canada Bulletin*, Momentum 1994, 3(3), 2.

Jarvenpa, Robert 1994. "Commoditization Versus Cultural Integration: Tourism and Image Building in the Klondike," *Arctic Anthropology*, 31:1.

Jeffrey A. Finkle, *Heritage and Cultural Tourism White Paper—Identifying and Developing Authentic Experiences*, Council for Urban Economic Development, 1730 K Street, NW Suite 700; Washington.

Kamauro, O., 1996. *Ecotourism: Suicide or Development? Voices from Africa #6: Sustainable Development, UN Non-Governmental Liaison Service*. United Nations News Service.

Kelly, John F., 1988. "Cultural Tourism: A Contradiction in Terms?" Proceedings, *National Conference on Heritage Interpretation*, Ottawa, Ontario.

Kerr, Alastair, 1994. "Strange Bedfellows: An Uneasy Alliance Between Cultural Conservation and Tourism," *ICOMOS Canada Bulletin*, MOMENTUM 1994, 3(3), p. 47.

Key Features of Community Based Tourism Project Development; Katrinka Ebbe, Frank Penna, Kreszentia Duer; Community Based Tourism Project Preparation Note; December 2002.

Krippendorf, J. 1986. "Tourism in the System of Industrial Society," Annals of Tourism Research, 13(4), 517-532.

Krippendorf, J. 1986. *The Holiday People—Towards a New Understanding of Leisure and Travel*. Zurich: Orell Fussli.

Lane, A., 2001. The Michigan Arts and Culture Industry: A Demographic and Economic Profile. Detroit, MI: Centre for Arts and Public Policy, College of Fine, Performing and Communication Arts, Wayne State University. Little-known Indian tribe spotted in Peru's Amazon.

MacGregor, James, 1989. "The Cultural Tourism Planning Process." Paper Presented at the Planning for Cultural Tourism Symposium, The University of Calgary, Calgary Alberta.

McGillivray, Louise, 1989. "Alberta's Tourism Response to Cultural Tourism." Paper Presented at the Planning for Cultural Tourism Symposium, The University of Calgary, Calgary Alberta.

McLaren, D., 1998. *Rethinking Tourism and Ecotravel: the Paving of Paradise and what you can do to stop it.* West Hartford, Connecticut, USA: Kamarian Press.

McNulty, "Cultural Tourism: New Opportunities for Wedding Conservation to Economic Development."

McNulty, *The Economics of Amenity:*
"Amenity Assets and Urban Economics"
"Cultural Resources: What Are the Arts Worth?"
"Tourism: Marketing Hidden Assets"
"The Meaning and Value of Image".

McPherson, David. "Tourism as a Cultural Process: A Model," New Zealand Journal of Geography, October, 1995, No. 100.

McPherson, David. "Tourism as a Cultural Process: A Worked Example Waitomo Caves," *New Zealand Journal of Geography*, October 1995, No. 100.

Mellgren, Doug (2007-05-16). Travel Experts See Worrisome Downside to Ecotourism. Associated Press. Retrieved on 2007-05-21.

Michigan Museums Association, 1998. Museums and Cultural Sites in Michigan: A Basis for Heritage Tourism. Lansing, MI: Michigan Museum Association.

Millar, S. "Heritage management for Heritage Tourism", *Tourism Management*, March 1989.

Moss, Laurence A.G., 1989. "Failing to Integrate Cultural Tourism Planning into Regional Development: The Cases of Northern New Mexico and Eastern Indonesia." Paper presented at the Planning for Cultural Tourism Symposium, The University of Calgary, Calgary Alberta.

Moulin, C. "Cultural Tourism Theory", *Planning for Cultural Tourism*, Walter Jamieson (ed.), Calgary: University of Calgary, pp. 43-61.

Moulin, Claude. "Cultural Heritage and Tourism Evolution," *Historic Environment*, Vols. VII 3 and 4, 1990.

Moulin, Claude, 1980. "Plan for Ecological and Cultural Tourism Involving Participation of Local Populations and Associations." Article in *Tourism Planning and Development*

Issues. Washington, D.C.: Washington University Press, 199-211.

Moulin, Claude, 1985. "Touristic Leisure: An Element of Mixing and Cultural Development of Hopes Rediscovered," *Revue de Tourisme*, No. 2, 2-5.

Moulin, Claude, 1989. "Cultural Tourism Theory". Paper Presented at the Planning for Cultural Tourism Symposium, The University of Calgary, Calgary Alberta.

Moulin, Claude, 1990. "Cultural Heritage and Tourism Evolution," *Historic Environments*, Vols. 3 and 4.

Moulin, Claude, 1994. "Tourisme International et sites du patrimoine mondial: la quadurature du cercle?," *ICOMOS Canada Bulletin*, Momentum 1994, 3(3), 7.

Mountain of Tongues: The Languages of the Caucasus.

Muir, Clive A., 1991. "The Role of Tourism and Other Service Industries in Rural Economic Development," Paper presented at the 23rd Annual Conference, Community Development Society, July 22-25, 1991.

Murphy, P. 1983. *Tourism: A Community Approach*. London: Methuen.

National Endowment for the Arts, National Endowment for the Humanities, Institute of Museum Services, President's Committee on the Arts and Humanities. 1995. *Cultural Tourism in the United States*. A Position paper for the White House Conference on Travel and Tourism, Washington, D.C.

National Governors Association, 2001. The role of the arts in economic development. On-line at: http://www.nga.org/centre/divisions/1,1188,C_ISSUE_ BRIEF%5ED_2225,00.htm

National Trust for Historic Preservation. 1993. *Getting Started: How to Succeed in Heritage Tourism*. Washington, D.C.

Old World Contacts/Colonists/Canary Islands.

Organising Resources for Rural Tourism Development: The Importance of Leadership, Planning, and Technical Assistance; Long, Patrick, and Jonelle. Nuckolls; *Tourism Recreation Research*; 1994; Vol. 19, No. 2; pp. 19-34.

Parker, Barry, 1994. "Canadian Aboriginal Tourism Association Presentation." Paper presented to the International Symposium on Crossing Frontiers: Issues of Heritage Culture and Identity in a Comparative Context, Ottawa/Hull.

Perry, Michael, 1993. "Aborigines find being Different can Mean Cash from Tourism," *The Globe and Mail*, 13 October, 1993.

Planning Week. "Putting the Heart back into the Village," November 18, 1993.

Power Relations and Community-Based Tourism Planning; Maureen G. Reed; Annals of Tourism Research; July 1997; Vol. 24, Issue 3; pp. 566-91.

Preservation News, 1991. "Making History Your Key to Tourism," November 1991.

Randall, A., 1987. *Resource Economics, Second Edition*. New York, USA: John Wiley and Sons.

Reisinger, Yvette. "Tourist—Host Contact as a Part of Cultural Tourism," *World Leisure & Recreation*, Summer 1994, 36:2.

Report of the African Commission's Working Group of Experts on Indigenous Populations/Communities, November 2003.

Residents' Support for Legalized Gaming and Perceived Impacts of Riverboat Casinos: Changes in Five Years; Cathy H C Hsu; Journal of Travel Research, Boulder; May 2000; Vol. 38, Issue 4; p. 396.

Richardson Sarah L., *Colorado Community Tourism Action Guide*, The Colorado Centre for Community Development, University of Colorado at Denver and The Centre for Recreation and Tourism Development, University of Colorado at Boulder, June 1991.

Ritchie, B. and M. Zins. "Culture as Determinant of the Attractiveness of a Tourism Region", *Annals of Tourism Research*, Volume 5, 1978.

Romanowski, Ed. 1989. "Marketing Cultural Tourism," Paper presented at the Planning for Cultural Tourism Symposium, The University of Calgary, Calgary Alberta.

Rural Tourism Development: Shifting Basis of Community Solidarity; Huang, Yueh-Huang; Journal of Travel Research, Boulder; Spring 1996; Vol. 34, Issue 4; pp. 26-32.

Sheedy, Carol, 1994. "Le ministere du Patrimoine canadien: l'initiative du tourisme patrimonial," *ICOMOS Canada Bulletin*, Momentum 1994, 3(3), 19.

Silberberg, Ted. "Cultural Tourism and Business Opportunities for Museums and Heritage Sites," *Tourism Management*, Aug. 1995, 16:5.

Small and Medium Tourism Enterprises; Stephen Wanhill; *Annals of Tourism Research*; January 2000; Vol. 27, Issue 1; pp. 132-147

Small Towns Hang On; William Fulton; *Planning*, Chicago; April 2001; Vol. 67, Issue 4; p. 4.

Stevens, Greg, The Hon, 1989. "Alberta Culture and Multiculturalism's Response to Cultural Tourism." Paper presented at the Planning for Cultural Tourism Symposium, The University of Calgary, Calgary Alberta.

Stewart, *Heritage Attractions and Tourism: Myths and Issues.*

Strategies for Monitoring Tourism in Your Community's Economy; Julie Leones and Douglas Dunn; March 1999; Arizona Cooperative Extension University of Arizona.

Stronge, W., 2000. The Economic Impact of the Florida Arts and Cultural Industry, West Palm Beach, FL: Florida Cultural Alliance.

Stynes, D.J., 2000. Michigan Tourism Economic Impact Model, MITEIM Model Documentation. East Lansing, MI: Department of Park, Recreation and Tourism Resources, Michigan State University.

Sustainable Community Tourism Development Revisited; Marion Joppe; *Tourism Management*; November 1996; Vol. 17, Issue 7; pp. 475-79.

Sustainable Tourism Development and Transformation in Central and Eastern Europe; Derek Hall; *Journal of Sustainable Tourism*; 2000; Vol. 8, No. 6; pp. 441-57.

Textile, Tourism and Community Development; Jeffrey H. Cohen; *Annals of Tourism Research*; 2001; Vol. 28, Issue 2; pp. 378-98.

The Environmental Attitudes and Practices of Family Businesses in the Rural Tourism and Hospitality Sectors; Jack Carlsen, Donald Getz, and Jane Ali-Knight; *Journal of Sustainable Tourism*; 2001; Vol. 9, No. 4; pp. 281-297.

Tighe, 1985. "Cultural Tourism in the USA", *Tourism Management*, December 1985.

Tourism and Sustainable Community Development; Gordon Taylor; *Tourism Management*; June 1996; Vol. 17, Issue 4; pp. 309-10.

Tourism and Sustainable Development: Exploring the Theoretical Divide; Richard Sharpley; *Journal of Sustainable Development*; 2000; Vol. 8, No. 1; pp.1-19.

Tourism Development Network Bulletin, The. "No. 20 Cultural Tourism".

Tourism Development Works for Any Size Community; Howard Feiertag; *Hotel and Motel Management*, Duluth; Aug 1999; Vol. 214, Issue 14; p. 18.

Tourist and Resident Perceptions of the Physical Impacts of Tourism at Lake Balaton, Hungary: Issues for Sustainable Tourism Management; Laszlo Puczko and Tamara Ratz; *Journal of Sustainable Tourism*; 2000; Vol. 8, No. 6; pp. 458-478.

Travel Industry Association of America, 2001. The Historic/ Cultural Traveller, 2001 edition. Washington, D.C.: TIA.

Travel Industry Association of America, 2003. The Historic/ Cultural Traveller, 2003 edition. Washington, D.C.: TIA.

Tuohino, A. and A. Hynonen, 2001. *Ecotourism—Imagery and Reality. Reflections on Concepts and Practices in Finnish Rural Tourism.* Nordia Geographical Publications, 30(4): 21-34.

Tuteur, John. "Cultural Conservation by the Chesapeake Public Art in Buffalo, San Diego's Economics of Amenity awards, Tourism Management in the Napa Valley," *Place,* May 1985, 5(5).

United Nations Working Group on Indigenous Populations, from *Study of the Problem of Discrimination Against Indigenous Populations*, J. Martinez Cobo, United Nations Special Rapporteur (1987).

Urry, John. "Cultural Change and Contemporary Tourism," *Leisure Studies*, Oct. 1994.

Utah State University, *Community Tourism Assessment Handbook: A Nine-step Guide Designed to Facilitate the Process of Determining Whether Tourism Development is right for your Community,* Copyright @ 1997 WRDC/MSU Extension.

Vivanco, L., 2002. *Ecotourism, Paradise lost—A Thai case study.* The Ecologist, 32(2): 28-30.

Wall, Geoffrey, 1994. "Tourism and Heritage: A Comparative Perspective." Paper presented to the International Symposium on Crossing Frontiers: Issues of Heritage Culture and Identity in a Comparative Context, Ottawa/Hull.

Wall, Geoffrey, 1995. Preserving Nature and Cultural Heritage, *Annals of Tourism Research*, 22:3.

WGIP, 2001. *"Indigenous Peoples and the United Nations System"*. Office of the High Commissioner for Human Rights, United Nations Office at Geneva.

Wight, P.A., 1993. *Ecotourism: Ethics or Eco-sell.* Journal of Travel Research, 31(3): 3-9.

Wingenbach, Gerry, 1990. "Tourism Project Puts Emphasis on Rich Culture," *The Calgary Herald*, 03 March, 1990.

Wood, Wilma, 1989. "The Cowichan and Chemainus Valleys Ecomuseum: A Case Study." Paper presented at the Planning for Cultural Tourism Symposium, The University of Calgary, Calgary Alberta.

Wry, "Recycling History with Urban Cultural Parks", *Place*, March 1982.

WWF International, 2001. *Guidelines for Community-based Ecotourism Development*, Prepared by Dr. Richard Denman, The Tourism Company; 11a High Street, Ledbury HR8 1DS, UK; Tel: +44 1531 635451; Fax: +44 1531 635453; ttcled@aol.com Published on the ICRT library at: http://www.theinternational centreforresponsibletourism.org/

Ziffer, K., 1989. *Ecotourism: the Uneasy Alliance*. Conservation International/Ernst and Young.

Websites

www.HaroldGoodwin.info
www.responsibletravel.com
www.propoortourism.org.uk
www.responsibletourismpartnership.org
www.mercuryassociates.co.uk
www.theinternationalcentreforresponsibletourism.org
www.senevolu.mypage.org/
www.visituganda.com/domestic/ucota.htm
www.costaricanruraltourism.org/
www.community-tourism.org/
www.gov.sangudo.ab.ca/page6.html
www.namibian.org/travel/community/

Index